Kennikat 119/70 · 10 ~

THE HUMAN APPROACH TO
LITERATURE

By WILLIAM FREEMAN

THE HUMAN APPROACH TO LITERATURE

KENNIKAT PRESS
Port Washington, N. Y./London

THE HUMAN APPROACH TO LITERATURE

First published in 1933
Reissued in 1970 by Kennikat Press
Library of Congress Catalog Card No: 72-105788
ISBN 0-8046-0953-5

Manufactured by Taylor Publishing Company   Dallas, Texas

To
A CERTAIN
SUNNY ROOM,
wherein dwelt
the Books of my Childhood

FOREWORD

THIS BOOK HAS BEEN written in the hope that it may fill
a gap which experience has shown me exists in the
shelves of those who possess a genuine, though not
necessarily profound, interest in the literature of our
country.

That there exist already innumerable 'Lives of
Authors', individual and collective, I am, of course,
aware, as I am also aware of the plethora of antho-
logies of which Palgrave's *Golden Treasury* and the
Oxford Book of English Verse are such popular examples.

But here I am trying to present authorship *humanized*,
to group a few of our greatest writers and their friends
against backgrounds which shall exhibit them as men
and women, and not merely the stiff cardboard figures
of convention.

For the past—their past—is so near. Red-faced black-
satined Queen Anne is dead, and has been dead for
over two hundred years, but Dr. Johnson remembered

being touched by her for the Evil, and one of *his* closest friends died within the life of people living to-day. The 'Gentle Elia' took tea with Carlyle, and Carlyle lived long enough to have criticized the first printed efforts of Kipling. And a son of the author of the *Pickwick Papers* has but lately retired after a long and honourable legal career.

A word concerning the list of volumes furnished at the end of each chapter. Most bibliographies appear to have been compiled chiefly as self-bestowed testimonials to the author's industry. But in the present instance I have tried to be of real assistance to the inquiring reader by classifying, under the different chapters in which they have played their part, such authorities as I thought might be of service to him. To them, as well as to innumerable fugitive and periodical articles, to say nothing of those sturdy stand-bys of the sedulous biographer, the Dictionary of National Biography and the Encyclopedia Britannica, I desire to acknowledge my heavy indebtedness.

Finally, let me remind the expert critic or critical expert of the acute differences of opinion which exist with regard to certain dates and events in literary history, and the conclusions to be drawn therefrom. To

8

this day no one knows for certain when Shakespeare left Stratford, or why, or what happened to him when he reached London, or when he wrote his first play, or which one it was, or where it was produced.

Every word of the dialogue does not, of course, pretend to possess full historical authenticity. But much of it *is* authentic, and I hope I may claim that none of it is incompatible or improbable.

WILLIAM FREEMAN

Spring, 1933

CONTENTS

CONTENTS

CONTENTS

Chapter One

AT THE SIGN OF THE TABARD

[1373]

IT WAS THE EVENING of May Day, and the restlessness of a public holiday that has reached its end was upon the City.

A short, sturdily-built man stood outside the Old Gate. His forked yellow beard was already streaked with grey; his brow was broad; his eyes, which he had a trick of raising suddenly, as though from the contemplation of some private jest, gleamed with puckish humour. Soberly dressed, with a black hood, he was obviously one of the upper or professional class, though a friendly geniality suggested that he was also of that type which can meet all men as equals.

About his neck hung a red cord from which was suspended quill and ink.

He had strolled abroad in the cool of the evening, and halted here on the off-chance of meeting a friend. Above the gate was a house, a pleasant, covetable dwelling which a year later was to become his own. The gate itself was a massive affair of stone with projecting towers on either side. It formed one of the nine entrances of varied design which broke the line of London's protecting walls. Within those walls what was then a vast population of twenty-three thousand people worked and played and slept, and prided themselves on being firstly, citizens of London, and secondly,

15

subjects of Edward Plantagenet, third ruler of that name, by the Grace of God and the valour of his armies *Rex Angliæ et Franciæ et Dominus Hiberniæ*. A wearied veteran, now over sixty, but still terrible in warfare.

The London of those days was walled on three sides; its fourth and longest side had the protection of the river, a stream of shimmering blue, on which floated a colony of swans. The citizens were proud of the Thames, at once a highway and a rampart. Above the red roofs of the houses rose three landmarks—the Palace and Abbey of Westminster, the square tower of the Cathedral of St. Paul, and the grim Tower fortress built by William the Red. The Pool, even in the fourteenth century, was crowded with vessels, and the riverside streets busy markets for alien traders.

It was a London at once crude and cultured, vigorously and shrewdly governed, insanitary, haphazard, crooked, and noble; where wild birds still nested at Charing Cross, where a man who concealed a stray falcon went to prison for two years, where, by ordinance, a roast pig of the best quality sold for 8d., a hen for 4d., a pullet for $2\frac{1}{2}$d., three roast thrushes for 2d., ten roast finches for a penny, and eggs at the same rate. Where a dishonest wine-merchant received simple and adequate punishment by being compelled to drink a draught of his own bad liquor, and to have the rest poured over him, while a baker who added to the weight of his bread by inserting a bar of iron was condemned to spend an hour in the pillory with the iron dangling from his neck—Where tennis and all ball games were specifically forbidden within the precincts of colleges; where Cornwall and the Scilly Isles were regarded by the Church as not only the end of the world, but 'the ends of the very end', and the Cornishman himself as a foreigner.

Geoffrey Chaucer, the sturdily-built man with the friendly brown eyes, was not merely a widely-travelled Englishman who had passionately preserved his nationality, but a Londoner by birth and breeding. Thames Street had been his first home; from his window in childhood's days he had looked out upon the river that like a crooked silver ribbon, frayed at the edges by a hundred wharves and houses and widening and narrowing with the rise and fall of the tide, linked England's capital with the sea. Upstream his eyes had rested on London Bridge, down stream on the Tower. Now, as then, the streets about him were still crowded and noisy with the same types—fine gentlemen, tradesmen, monks and friars, apprentices and villeins. Stout, springless wagons rumbled and clattered their way over the cobbles in and out of the puddles, with now and again cumbrous, gaily-decorated carriages, drawn by five horses, in which none but great ladies of Royal or noble rank would have dreamed of riding.

A tall, ascetic figure wearing a shabby brown robe that reached to his feet approached. His head was shaven, priestly fashion; his gaze had the aggressive and challenging fierceness of the fanatic. Chaucer, encountering that gaze, smiled his tolerant smile—and suppressed a sigh.

'Greetings, Will.'

'Greetings.' The tall man edged free of the crowds he had been studying with sombre bitterness. 'There be many kinds of fool in the world, Geoffrey—and many ensamples of each in such a City of abomination as this.'

Chaucer's eyes twinkled.

'With but one wise man, Will Langland to wit, to reprove their folly and guide them into the paths of true learning?'

'Will Langland maketh claim to be as great a fool as any, enduring that which no man should endure, bandying words when he should be working with his hands, busy with a quill's point upon vellum when—'

'Peace, peace, with thy melancholy flagellations! According to a story which hath been brought from the West, the day is coming when all labours with the pen shall become needless.'

'When the knight goeth to warfare unpanoplied, and ships cross the ocean without sails!'

'Maybe. But if this report be true, there hath been devised in China or Tartary a manner of pressing upon paper with raised symbols, assembled in lines, by which the sense and meaning of words may be conveyed far more swiftly and cheaply. And if such device spread to civilized parts—'

'Then the occupation of every scrivener and clerk will

be gone. Whence will follow further grievances, further bitterness 'twixt master and man, further suffering——'

'Also, perchance, a mighty spread of knowledge.'

'But not of happiness, thou of narrow vision.'

A man with long curling hair had joined them. His dress was rich without extravagance, his bearing that of one of assured position and estate. Chaucer clapped an affectionate hand on his shoulder. This was John Gower, his senior by half a dozen years, and one of his closest friends. 'The Moral Gower' was worthy of friendship. Scholar who could write and speak in three languages, Latin, French and his own, he, too, was a Londoner, though, unlike Chaucer, country-born, his father being a squire of Kent. He and Chaucer saw life, if not from the same angle, at least with something of the same detachment and tolerance. The one, a man of patient and enduring talent whose powers were limited but who used those powers nobly; the other a genius whose advance ended only with his life. (To-day you may see John Gower in effigy in the church of St. Saviour, Southwark, his head resting upon the three volumes which give him his title to a place among authors. Chaucer is commemorated by a white marble bust in the Guildhall Library.)

The crowd about the three friends was becoming noisier and rougher. Youth at any period has ever been the same, and the apprentice and young workman of the fourteenth century, released from the thrall of shop and bench, had small patience with middle-aged, serious spectators who watched their revels but did not join

19

them. And a City gateway was at all times better as a meeting-place than a spot at which to linger gossiping. Chaucer, with cheerful farewells to Gower and the melancholy Langland, left them to endure the impatient thrusts and buffetings of returning holiday-makers, and went on his way.

Darkness had fallen, but the evening was still young, and the exquisite and elusive breath of Spring still stirred the reeds on the River bank. A stone's-throw distant was the house in which Philippa, his wife, awaited him. A notable housewife, skilled in needlecraft and cooking, if at times heavy in judgment upon husbands who lapsed too often into daydreams and had too great a liking for solitary wanderings. There, too, was his study, with its shelf of treasured volumes. (His Grace of Canterbury possessed no more than fourteen.) Nevertheless, he would not return just yet. The streets should entertain him for another hour or so.

Under a mild blue sky he threaded his way towards Southwark. The crowds grew yet denser. There were ugly rushes, shrill protests, threats. The trouble came abruptly to a head when a bag of money was snatched. No one seemed clear as to who was the owner and who the thief, but blows were struck. Somebody jostled Chaucer violently; he swung round to protest, was swept off his feet in a concerted rush of roughs, and fell headlong.

He opened his eyes to find himself lying on a bench in a small room lit with a guttering tallow dip. A pillow was under his head, and the tang of strong wine was in his mouth. A white-bearded man with a tankard in his hand was standing near. He had a face reddened with good living and country air, and at his waist was a dagger and a silk hawking-pouch.

'Thou'rt recovered?' he cried, and Chaucer, raising himself unsteadily on one elbow, nodded. 'Good! When I dragged thee free from the hooves of that drunken cattle, methought 'twas too late, and that the last breath had been trampled from thy body.'

Stiffly Chaucer sat up. His brain grew clearer; he stammered questions. The big man answered them cheerfully. The room was one in the Tabard Inn. 'Twas small and but rarely used; the good hostess had suggested that he should be carried there, remote from the crowd and clamour in the front.

'What injuries hath suffered?' asked the rescuer anxiously.

'Thanks to thy good offices, naught beyond a few trivial bruises and scratches. Natheless, I would be glad to rest here quietly for a space before I go upon my way.'

'I,' said the big man heartily, 'shall be glad of thy company, since I am a countryman having but little contact with the Court and City life, and am dependent for news upon pedlars, pilgrims and stray travellers. Though,' he added, 'my son hath won his spurs fighting under the banner of our liege lord, Edward, whom the Holy Virgin uphold and succour. Tell me, first, what dost call thyself?'

'I am Geoffrey Chaucer.'

'Of noble ancestry, perchance?'

Chaucer laughed his deep-throated jolly laugh. 'Perchance. But from mine own knowledge, I can best claim that the name cometh from "chausseur", a word of the French tongue, signifying a maker of shoon. As for my ancestors, my grandfather Richard was a vintner of Cordwainer Street. My father John followed in his trade, and did achieve no greater eminence than deputizing for the King's butler at Southampton and travelling abroad in the train of His Highness.'

'But concerning your good self?' The big man, conscious of tactlessness, changed the subject hurriedly. 'What may be thine own profession?'

'I am a clerk in the King's service.'

'So much, by thy very tone, should I have guessed! And dost set down His Highness' debits and credits upon endless scrolls of parchment in long columns in which, like cattle and sheep and swine herded in a pasture, marks, pounds and shillings abide together, in such confusion that none but a cloister-bred scholar could decipher them and the Archbishop himself could scarce understand? For such I have heard.'

'True enough. 'Tis my privilege and bounden duty to do all these things in mine own hand. If, Heaven forgive me, I spoke pridefully, 'tis because I love my work.'

'I'll wager thou lovest all Life. Tell me more, if the demand be not discourteous.'

''Tis a long story.'

'There be no need to shorten it. One can recite a long ballad in an hour, and thou'lt not weary me.'

'So be it.' Chaucer's eyes were twinkling. This innocent giant of a man, with his childlike interest in other people's affairs, was a type that appealed to him. 'Then, to make a beginning, I shall inform you that as a boy, garbed in a short coat and red and black breeches, I can remember myself attending the house of the Lady Elizabeth, Countess of Ulster, with some vague hopes of achieving profit and advancement. And thereafter, having greater good fortune than falls to the lot of many, I entered her service as a page. That was when my lady wedded the noble Lionel, Duke of Clarence, son of our liege Sovereign. Later, made restless by stories of the battles and knightly prowess, I asked leave to go to the Wars, and in the year of our Lord 1359 did find myself encamped near Rheims.'

The white-bearded man nodded. 'That was fourteen years since. Then, thine age——'

'A murrain upon the years—they do but serve to remind the villein when he should let his land lie fallow and the lawyer when his leases expire! To him who liveth a full and free life they have little signification.'

'True, Master Chaucer. I ask pardon that I interrupted thee.'

'In France, I say, I fought. But alack, 'twas a brief and inglorious campaign, seeing that within a few months I found myself in captivity. Natheless, thanks to the good offices and kindlieness of the King, who himself did give sixteen English pounds towards my ransom, I was soon set free again.'

'Hast not fought since?'

23

'More than once. But the gentler, subtler arts of peace have ever been more to my liking. And 'twas not long before I found myself in the King's service as—how shall I call it?—a petty ambassador, a messenger not wholly without authority to negotiate. France again I visited, and Italy, also more than once.'

'Hast been abroad of late?'

'I was at Genoa but twelve months ago, on a matter concerning a port which should serve merchants desiring to trade with us. Also in Florence, where I met the great Petrarch, and in Pisa. But for the future, good sir, what with increasing burthens of middle-age, to say nothing of wife and family, you may hazard a guess that my voyaging days are over.'

'I have no wife living,' said the big man, and sighed. 'Tell me, since thy manner and speech hint that thou art not wholly a scribe and a juggler of figures, what art or science dost practice?'

'Shrewd Sir, I have spent more time—aye, and more gold—than is seemly upon three things. Firstly, upon astrology, secondly—but let it go no further—upon alchemy; and lastly, which truth thou hast my leave to shout, an' it please thee, from the housetops, to the art of poesie.'

'Two Sciences and one Art? Strange bedfellows, Master Chaucer!'

'For the last, blame a hundred things, among them a love for my Mother-tongue, and a liking—to use no stronger word—for the society of my fellow-creatures. But as yet'—the light from the tallow dip fell upon a face that had become suddenly transfigured, that burned with new, strange fires—'as yet, I have writ no more than three trifles, one of which is a poem upon the death of the fair and virtuous Duchess Blanche o Castile. Whereas 'tis of my own people, this land, this city'—The light faded: he was the genial, commonplace citizen again. 'Tell me of thyself.'

'There be little enough to tell. I am Hugh de Grandison, having a small estate in Wiltshire, but being now come to this City upon matters of some urgency, including that of a coat of mail which needed repair. I have a stone manor-house that strangers do mistake for a church, until they discover the barns and storehouses and stables, and presently the drawbridge. And when my son cometh back from the Wars, I will make merry again at the high table in the Great Hall, with minstrels in the gallery and trumpeters to announce each dish that is brought from the kitchen. But now—now I find myself foredoomed to linger until the rogues, the artificers, have my mail ready. And that, they say, cannot be before Midsummer. Wherefore I am of a mind to go upon a pilgrimage, in company with as many worthy persons as may be willing to join me for protection and entertainment, to the tomb of the holy Thomas à Becket at Canterbury. For though, by the law, the brushwood and trees be cut back for twice an hundred yards on either side of the road, so that a traveller may have due sight and warning of highway robbers—' He broke off. 'Thy pardon, Master Chaucer; I weary thee. A dull story, as an old man's is apt to be.'

'Not so, Master Grandison, not so. Hast given me what I have been long seeking—inspiration. For that I, and perchance, Posterity, shall ever remain thy debtor.'

Geoffrey Chaucer

From PROLOGUE TO THE CANTERBURY TALES

A Frankeleyn was in his compaignye;
Whyt was his berd, as is the dayesye.
Of his complexion he was sangwyn.
Wel loved he by the morwe a sop in wyn.

. . . .

With-oute bake mete was nevere his hous,
Of fish and flesh, and that so plentevous,
It snewed in his hous of mete and drinke,
Of alle deyntees that men coulde thinke.
After the sondry sesons of the yeer,
So chaunged he his mete and his soper.
Ful many a fat partrich hadde he in mewe,
And many a breem and many a luce in stewe.
Wo was his cook, but-if his sauce were
Poynaunt and sharp, and redy al his gere.
His table dormant in his halle alway
Stood redy covered al the longe day.
At sessiouns ther was he lord and sire.
Ful ofte tyme he was knight of the shire.

Geoffrey Chaucer

From THE FRANKELEYNES TALE

'Frankeleyn, in faith, sir, wel thou knowest,
That eche of you must tellen at the lest
26

A tale or two, or breken his behest.'
'That know I wel, sir,' quoth the Frankeleyn,
'I pray you have me not in your disdain,

. . . .

'Gladly, sir hoste,' quoth he, 'I will obeye
Unto your wille; now herken what I seye;
I wil you not contrarien in no wise,
As fer as that my wittes may suffice.
I pray to God that it may plesen you,
Than wot I wel that it is good y-now.'

These olde gentile Britouns in their dayes
Of diverse aventures maden layes,
Al rymed in their firste Britoun tonge;
Which layes with their instruments they songe,
Or else redden them for their pleasaunce,
And one of them have I in remembraunce,
Which I shal seye with as goode wille as I can,
But sirs, bycause I am a common man,
At my begynning first I you beseche
Have me excused of my rude speche,
I lerned never rhetorick certayn;
That thing I speke, it wil be bare and playn;
I slepte never on the mount of Pernaso,
Ne lerned never Tullius, nor Cicero.
Colours of rhetorick non are in my hed,
But suche coloures as growen in the mede,
Or else suche as men dye with or peynte;
Colours of rhetorick be to me too quaint;
My spirit feleth nought of suche matere.
But if ye liste my tale shal ye now here.

Ther was a knight, that loved and foughte amain
In Armoryke, that cleped is Briteyne,

To serve a lady in his beste wise;
And many a labour, and many a grete emprise
He for his lady wrought, ere she was wonne;
For she was one the fairest under sonne,
And eke thereto came of so high kindred,
That scarce durst this knight for verie drede
Telle her his woe, his peyne, and his distresse.
But at the last she for his worthinesse,
And chiefly for his meke obeissance,
Hath suche a pitee felt for his penaunce,
That privily she fell into accord
To take him for her housbonde and her lord,
(Of suche lordshipe as men have over their wives);
And, for to lede the more in blisse their lyves,
Of his free wille he swor it as a knight,
That never in his wille by day or night
Wolde he upon him take the mastery
Against her wille, nor guard her jealously,
But her obey, and follow her wille in al,
As eny lover to his lady shal;
Save that the name of sovereyntee
That wolde he have because of his degree.
She thanketh him, and with ful grete humblesse
She sayde; 'Sir, since of your gentilnesse
Ye profre me to have so large a reyne,
May never God, I pray, betwize us tweyne,
For guilt of mine, bring eyther war or stryf.
Sir, I will be your humble, trewe wife,
Have here my trothe, till that myn herte fail.'
Thus be they bothe in quiete and in wele.
For one thing, masters, safely dare I seye,
That frendes al each other must obeye,
If they wille longe holde companye,
Love wil nought be constreined by mastery.
When mastery cometh, the god of love anon

Beteth his wynges, and fare wel, he is gon.
Love is a thing, as any spirit, free.
Wommen of nature loven libertee,
And nought to be constreined as a thral;
And so do men, if I the sooth say shal.
Loke who that it most pacient in love,
He is ful certes others al above.

.   .   .   .

Therefore this knight his wife for to plese
Hath promised she shal live in rest and ese;
And sche to him ful wisely gan to swere,
That never shulde ther be defaulte in her.
Here may men see an humble wyse accord;
Thus that she taken her servaunt and her lorde,
Servaunt in love, and lord in marriage.
Then was he bothe in lordshipe and servage.
Servage? Not so. In lordshipe al above,
Since that he hath his lady and his love;
His lady certes, and his wyf also,
The law of love alloweth bothe two.
And when he was in this prosperitee,
Home with his wyfe he goeth to his countree,
Nought far fro Penmark where his dwellyng was,
And ther he lyveth in blisse and in solas.

Who coude telle, but he hadde wedded be,
The joy, the ese, and the prosperitee,
That is betwixe an housebond and his wyf?
A yeer and more lasted this blissful life,
Til that this knight, of which I speke thus,
That of kindred was cleped Arveragus,
Thought for to go and dwelle a yeer or tweyne
In Engelond, that cleped eke was Bretayne,
To seek in armes worshipe and honour,

29

For all his wille was sette in such labour;
And dwelleth there two year.

Geoffrey Chaucer

From THE LEGEND OF GOOD WOMEN

And, as for me, though that my wit be lyte,
On bokes for to rede I me delyte,
And in myn herte have hem in reverence;
And to hem yeve swich lust and swich credence,
That ther is wel unethe game noon
That from my bokes make me to goon,
But hit be other up-on the haly-day,
Or elles in the joly tyme of May;
Whan that I here the smale foules singe,
And that the floures ginne for to springe,
Farwel my studie, as lasting that sesoun!

William Langland

From THE VISION OF WILLIAM CONCERNING PIERS THE
PLOUGHMAN

On Gode Fridaye fynde a felonn was ysaved
That had lyved al his lyf with lesynges and with
thefte;
And, for he beknewe on the crosse and to Cryste schrof
hym.
He was sonnere saved than seynt Johan the baptiste,
And or Adam or Ysaye or any of the prophetes
That hadde yleine with Lucyfer many longe yeres.
A robbere was yraunceouned rather than thei alle
30

With-outen any penance of purgatorie to perpetual
    blisse.
Thanne Marye Magdaleyne; what woman dede worse?
Or who worse than David that Uries deth conspired?
Or Paul the Apostle, that no pitie hadde
Moche crystene kynde to kylle to deth?
And now ben thise as sovereynes wyth seyntes in
    hevene,
Tho that wroughte wikkedlokest in worlde tho thei
    were!

John Gower

On The Lower Classes

(Written before Wat Tyler's Revolt—about 1375*: Modernised)*

The world goeth fast from bad to worse, when shepherd and cowherd for their part demand more for their
labour than the master-bailiff was wont to take in days
gone by. Labour is now at so high a price that he who
will order his business aright must pay five or six shillings now for what cost two in former times. Labourers
of old were not wont to eat of wheaten bread; their
meat was of beans or coarser corn, and their drink
of water alone. Cheese and milk were a feast to them,
and rarely ate they of other dainties, and their dress
was of hodden grey; then was the world ordered aright
for folk of this sort.

Three things, all of the same sort, are merciless when
they get the upper hand; a water-flood, a wasting fire,
and the common multitude of small folk. For these will
never be checked by reason or discipline; and therefore,
to speak in brief, the present world is so troubled by
them that it is well to set a remedy thereunto. Ha!
age of ours, whither turnest thou? For the poor and

small folk, who should cleave to their labour, demand to be better fed than their masters. Moreover, they bedeck themselves in fair colours and fine allure, whereas (were it not for their pride and their privy conspiracies) they would be clad in sackcloth as of old. Ha! age of ours, I know not what to say; but of all the estates that I see, from the highest to the lowest, each decayeth in its own degree. Poor man or lord, all alike are full of vanity; I see the poor folk more haughty than their lords; each draweth whither he pleaseth.

AT THE SIGN OF THE TABARD

CHAPTER TWO

STRATFORD TO LONDON—103 MILES

[1587]

ELIZABETH TUDOR was Queen of England. The bright, intoxicating waves of what is called the Renaissance had already swept from the west, bringing with them a new-born and passionate love of poetry, a new sensitiveness to Beauty. They imparted, mysteriously, a new ardour to chivalry, even to mere physical courage. The very air of those days gave an Englishman an access of national arrogance. He was sure of himself and his destiny, and though Philip the Spaniard had yet to wait a year or so for his drubbing, there was more contempt than fear blended with the hatred that Elizabeth's countrymen felt for him.

Elizabeth herself was in her fifty-seventh year. Already her long oblong face was heavily seamed with the lines of obstinacy and determination. Her small black eyes were undimmed; they were to remain almost as bright until that bleak day in March nearly twenty years hence when she lay dying on her cushions. The hooked nose and thin lips were the physical embodiment of the Tudor temper. The red hair piled high above the narrow forehead was still her own. The small white hands that blazed with jewels held not merely a sceptre but the powers which she wielded ruthlessly. A woman with the coolest courage and clearest head in the kingdom.

33

In that kingdom, the spirit of change was busy. Chimneys were being built to small houses as well as large. Windows were now commonly glazed. Timber was supplanting brick and stone, pewter taking the place of the wooden platter on the dining-table. Archery was decaying, young men preferring to arm themselves with rapiers and daggers. Thieves were hanged, and so were witches and wizards, except at Halifax, where they were decapitated by a primitive type of guillotine, 'though their necks be thick as oxen's'. All the equipment of the medieval torturer could still be employed to punish the wrongdoer for whom a swifter and more merciful death was not prescribed. (One William Randall, foolishly claiming to know 'where treasure was buried in the earth', was promptly executed for his boastfulness.) Most farm produce was cheap, but butter, bought by unscrupulous speculators from the farmers, was being retailed at forty pence a gallon. An embroidered velvet coat cost as much as £16, and a pair of superfine hose four guineas.

London itself had a population of less than a hundred thousand, distributed over a hundred and twenty parishes. But the growth of the City westward, especially along the river bank, was proceeding rapidly. St. Paul's, though shorn of its spire and otherwise dilapidated, was still a noble building. St. James' Park, until lately a patch of marshy land, had been transformed by his late Majesty, King Henry the Eighth, into a deer park, a bowling-green and a tennis-court. The same zealous monarch had converted a capital crowded with majestic ecclesiastical buildings into one in which large numbers of those buildings were either pulled down altogether or converted to secular uses. The great Livery Companies had been prompt to obtain halls for themselves from the spoils of the church, while Edward the Sixth, Henry's poor little disease-racked heir, had handed over the derelict Palace of Bridewell as a House of Correction for vagabonds, rogues, and refractory City apprentices. The Fleet River was an open sewer, while the tortuous and irregular streets themselves were so muddy and so badly paved that if you desired to go from one part of the City to another, it was quicker to descend to the waterside and be rowed to your destination by one of the three thousand water-men who found employment there.

It was a day of shimmering heat when William Shakespeare, a soberly-dressed youth of twenty-five, left the placid and rural loveliness of Warwickshire for London and all that London might mean. He had little money, and every groat he possessed would be needed when his journey was over. And he knew no one in London. But he was not friendless, nor was he travelling alone. He had attached himself to a troupe of actors who, banded together under the patronage of my Lord Leicester, and known as the Earl of Leicester's company, were returning to Town after what in those days must have been a formidable and exciting tour. It had lasted for the better part of two years, and in-cluded Denmark and Saxony, a halt in London in the

35

Spring, and as its final stage a provincial round which had carried them as far as Stratford. There this recruit had joined them—a recruit, but not wholly inexperienced, since he not only must have seen, as a youth, performances in his native town and in Coventry, a few miles distant, but had quite probably taken some small part in them himself.

The town was left behind. On its outskirts, Shakespeare lingered for one final, backward glance at the scattered timbered houses, the grey church by the river, the ancient Guildhall, and the Avon, flowing tranquilly through green, flower-studded woodlands. A tiny town of fourteen hundred inhabitants. But not only his parents, but Ann, his wife, and his three children were numbered among them.

The party passed through Long Compton, and climbed the stretches of barren down that separate Warwickshire from Oxfordshire. It was a bleak and unfamiliar landscape. Some miles further on came Woodstock and its park, with noble oaks and beeches stretching as far as the eye could see. Dusk fell, dusk that filled the wood with magic. The travellers found a sheltered clearing, and there Shakespeare, having supped, made a pillow of his bag, and slept the sleep of healthy and weary youth. The wild things of the woods ran no risks at his hands. He had made an end of poaching. There had been an affair in the park of Sir Thomas Lucy, only too recently, in which he had been involved. It had played no small part in sending him into exile.

The next day saw him in Oxford, city of spires and scholarship, a new world in which there was no place for him, a world that started a hundred trains of thought. The stars in their courses had made him what he was; a divinity might even now be shaping his end, but herein lay no present consolation. His father's family had sound and prosperous middle-class traditions; on his mother's—the Ardens'—side he had definite claims to gentility. But Shakespeare the elder had failed in business so lamentably that he had been unable to sustain his position as alderman or to educate his family adequately. William, the eldest living child, was leaving his native town for—what? For the career, if he was lucky, of a play-actor, for a life which stamped him socially as a rogue and a vagabond. The poorest student here would be looking on his calling with amused contempt.

The company slept at Oxford, and soon after sunrise resumed their journey. More than half of it still lay ahead ; two more days had yet to pass before they sighted the fields and hedgerows on the outskirts of London.

To the north were the hills of Highgate and Hampstead, to the south Westminster. The long road, with never a house to break its panorama of green on either side, ended at what to-day is Park Lane. From there the distant roofs of the Abbey and the Hall of Westminster were visible through the Autumn haze. Nearer stood St. James' Manor House, solitary and gloomy in its majesty. Fields and yet more fields, and then the

37

village of St. Giles. Turning south, they passed grazing cattle in the meadows, and so came at last to St. Martin's Lane. From there, weary but fascinated, overwhelmed by the nearness of the great city whose heartbeats he could already hear, William Shakespeare wandered into the Strand, and so down by Somerset Place to the River.

[1590]

A group of men are seated in a London tavern, arguing with noisy friendliness over their ale. Through the open doorway, above which swings the sign of the Cross Keys, one has a glimpse of the cobbles of Gracechurch Street. In the yard behind is erected a rough but serviceable permanent stage.

The first real theatre worthy of the name had been built in London only fourteen years before, and stood further east, in Shoreditch. Others had arisen since. They were viewed by the City fathers and the more serious-minded inhabitants with apprehension and dislike, the more especially since performances were commonly given on Sunday. It was averred that 'on the Sabbath goodly folks were enticed from the congregation of saints in church to the congregation of the devil in the play-houses'. As a result, there was a discreet tendency to erect these haunts conveniently beyond the Lord Mayor's jurisdiction, in suburban fields, on the site of old bear-pits and so forth. Performances began at three in the afternoon, and lasted two or three hours. Admission was from a penny upwards;

but for a seat in the best part of the house—in the 'rooms', or, as we should term them to-day, the boxes —as much as half-a-crown was charged. The stage itself, less than shoulder high, jutted out like a tongue into the pit; the actors delivered their lines surrounded on three sides by their audience. At the back of the stage was a balcony which served in the play for that purpose, a mountain-side, a battlement, or an upper room, as occasion might demand. A change of scene was indicated by either some trivial change in the stage properties, or alternatively, by a small boy exhibiting a strip of wood on which was painted, 'A BATTLE-FIELD', or 'A FOREST'. The scene-shifters' work was light in the sixteenth century.

No women appeared in the caste, female parts being taken by boys whose voices had not yet broken. Even among the audience a woman, if she were present, was expected to wear a mask.

.   .   .   .

A heavily-built, gawky lad stood listening to the conversation, his forehead puckered in bewildered amusement. His name was Ben Jonson. Twenty years hence he was to dominate, in another London tavern, another group of literary giants of whom only one was present now—and he the only one to leave a greater name than his. True Elizabethan, Jonson had travelled through the years with a breathless recklessness which had left him with a man's poise and self-confidence before boyhood was fairly past. Though his father—and, even more important, his stepfather—had been artisans, an ambitious mother, a passion for the classics, and the friendly patronage of Camden, historian and the head-master of Westminster School, had conspired to give him a good education. At present, under his step-father's tuition, he was learning the craft of brick-laying. Two more years had yet to pass before the theatre was to claim him.

The men seated on the bench by the fireplace were all young. The man with hazel eyes, high domed fore-head and pointed, auburn beard was Shakespeare. He had learnt much since that Autumn day when he had turned his back on Stratford. His prentice hand had become practised in the actor's art, in the technique of stage production, in the knowledge of what the theatre-goer's taste demanded. He could adapt, he could improvise. A shrewd but kindly young man, not without enemies, but with many friends too.

On his left was Kemp, the company's chief comedian. Next to him was Marlowe, the college-educated son of a schoolmaster and England's first great tragedian. A passionate and dissolute youth of Shakespeare's age, the stupid violence of his death was to cut short a career of splendid possibilities. 'Tamburlaine', lately printed, was only the first of four noble examples of his blank verse. Beside him sat Thomas Nashe, pam-phleteer, poet and wit; Nashe, whom a contemporary described as 'ingenious and ingenuous, fluent, face-tious; sharpest satyre, luculent poet, elegant orator', and who was, in fact, a journalist born out of his time, since, as he boasted, he could 'write as fast as he could trot'.

The fifth occupant of the bench was a man dressed in scholarly black, whose hair was untidy and twisted, but whose beard was 'a jolly red peak, like the spire of a steeple'. It was Robert Greene, the dissipated, the embittered; a Master of Arts, a traveller, the poet whose *Triumph of Time* was to suggest the plot of *A Winter's Tale* to his greater contemporary; a faithless but passionately penitent husband; a debtor who, dying in utter desolation and wretchedness two years later, did not forget his indebtedness to the struggling shoemaker who took him in and gave him shelter in his last illness.

A man strode hastily across the street and joined the group. It was the great Burbage himself. He had a story to tell, but it was chiefly for Will Shakespeare's ear. The Queen, wearied of Court intrigue and ceremony, had decided to go down to Greenwich. There she would fain see a play, a merry comedy which should help her to forget, at least for an hour or so, the intolerable burden of her crown. To that end she had sent for him, Dick Burbage. Cogitating, he had bethought him of the trifle which Will had lately completed, and which even now was in process of rehearsal.

' "What of the plot?" quoth the Queen'—so Burbage, flushed and excited, recounted the interview. ' "Marry, an' it please your Highness," quoth I, " 'tis a story of the King of Navarre and three of his lords, and hath no known source beyond that of the young man's own fantastical imagination. Nor is there aught in it calculated to give the smallest offence to your Highness, your Highness' Court or any of your Highness' liege subjects." "And the dialogue?" says she. " 'Tis refined," say I, "yet rich in humour, and though the majestic cadences of high tragedy may be absent, and young Master Shakespeare hath still much to learn, 'tis not a play to discredit the company." '

Upon hearing which, the Queen had been graciously pleased to signify her approbation of Master Burbage's suggestion.

. . . .

A Royal barge waits to carry Burbage and his men to Greenwich.

The company is noisy, almost riotous. Shakespeare only is silent. Sitting apart, he gazes absently at the glittering river. On the knees of the Gods lies utter failure—or success. He must brace himself to meet either. The Bridge, with the dangerous rapids that swirl under its narrow arches, is passed, the Tower; the River widens, the banks grow greener as London is left behind. At Greenwich pier the rowers ship their oars.

The Great Hall, with its temporary erection at the further end, is crowded. A multitude of the royal guard, 'every man in his hand a torch-staff', is drawn up on either side of the arras-hung stage. Behind those blue curtains—blue, because a comedy is to be presented;

had it been a tragedy, they would have been black—
are the most splendid effects that Mr. Burbage can
contrive. He has been given a free hand with the paste-
board and buckram, and the Royal tailors and car-
penters have been his to command.

The audience rises as the Queen, accompanied by her
maids, enters and takes her seat upon a raised daïs in
the centre. A flourish of trumpets announces that the
performance is about to begin. At the third clear note
the curtains are drawn.

Love's Labour Lost makes its bow to the alert, critical
little world which comprises the Elizabethan Court.

Crash after crash of laughter and applause ring
through the raftered building; the atmosphere grows
more and more vibrant with triumphant success.
Comes the final scene.

The youthful smiling figure bends low over the graciously extended hand of the Queen . . . while before
those tired, wise eyes floats a vision of a cottage in
leafy Stratford, and of the wife and children who await
him there.

William Shakespeare

From TWELFTH NIGHT

Act I. Scene I

If music be the food of love, play on;
Give me excess of it, that, surfeiting,

The appetite may sicken, and so die.—
O, it came o'er my ear like the sweet south,
That breathes upon a bank of violets,
Stealing, and giving odour.—Enough, no more;
'Tis not so sweet now, as it was before.
O spirit of love, how quick and fresh art thou!
That, notwithstanding thy capacity
Receiveth as the sea, naught enters there,
Of what validity and pitch soe'er,
But falls into abatement and low price,
Even in a minute! so full of shapes is fancy,
That it alone is high-fantastical.

William Shakespeare

From HENRY V.

AGINCOURT

O for a Muse of fire, that would ascend
The brightest heaven of invention,
A kingdom for a stage, princes to act
And monarchs to behold the swelling scene!
Then should the warlike Harry, like himself,
Assume the port of Mars; and at his heels,
Leashed in like hounds, should Famine, Sword and
     Fire
Crouch for employment. But pardon, gentles all,
The flat unraised spirits that have dared
On this unworthy scaffold to bring forth
So great an object. Can this cockpit hold
The vasty fields of France? or may we cram
Within this wooden O the very casques
That did affright the air at Agincourt?

O pardon! since a crooked figure may
Attest in little place a million,
And let us, ciphers to this great accompt,
On your imaginary forces work.
Suppose within the girdle of these walls
Are now confined two mighty monarchies,
Whose high uprearèd and abutting fronts
The perilous narrow ocean parts asunder:
Piece out our imperfections with your thoughts;
Into a thousand parts divide one man,
And make imaginary puissance;
Think, when we talk of horses, that you see them
Printing their proud hoofs i' the receiving earth;
For 'tis your thoughts that now must deck our kings,
Carry them here and there, jumping o'er times,
Turning the accomplishment of many years
Into an hour-glass.

William Shakespeare

From CYMBELINE

A DIRGE

Fear no more the heat o' the sun
    Nor the furious winter's rages;
Thou thy worldly task hast done,
    Home art gone and ta'en thy wages:
Golden lads and girls all must,
As chimney-sweepers, come to dust.

Fear no more the frown o' the great,
    Thou art past the tyrant's stroke;
Care no more to clothe and eat;
    To thee the reed is as the oak;

45

The sceptre, learning, physic, must
All follow this, and come to dust.

Fear no more the lightning-flash
    Nor the all-dreaded thunder-stone;
Fear not slander, censure rash;
    Thou hast finished joy and moan;
All lovers young, all lovers must
Consign to thee, and come to dust.

William Shakespeare

From THE SONNETS

O how much more doth beauty beauteous seem
By that sweet ornament which truth doth give!
The Rose looks fair, but fairer we it deem
For that sweet odour which doth in it live.
The Canker-blooms have full as deep a dye
As the perfumèd tincture of the Roses,
Hang on such thorns, and play as wantonly
When summer's breath their maskèd buds discloses;
But—for their virtue only is their show—
They live unwoo'd and unrespected fade,
Die to themselves. Sweet Roses do not so;
Of their sweet deaths are sweetest odours made.
    And so of you, beauteous and lovely youth,
    When that shall fade, my verse distils your truth.

.   .   .   .

When in the chronicle of wasted time
I see descriptions of the fairest wights,
And beauty making beautiful old rime
In praise of Ladies dead and lovely Knights;

Then, in the blazon of sweet beauty's best,
Of hand, of foot, of lip, of eye, of brow,
I see their antique pen would have exprest
Even such a beauty as you master now.
So all their praises are but prophecies
Of this our time, all you prefiguring;
And for they look'd but with divining eyes,
They had not skill enough your worth to sing;
For we, which now behold these present days,
Have eyes to wonder, but lack tongues to praise.

. . . .

Let me not to the marriage of true minds
Admit impediments. Love is not love
Which alters when it alteration finds,
Or bends with the remover to remove:
O, no! it is an ever-fixed mark,
That looks on tempests and is never shaken;
It is the star to every wand'ring bark,
Whose worth's unknown, although his height be taken.
Love's not Time's fool, though rosy lips and cheeks
Within his bending sickle's compass come;
Love alters not with his brief hours and weeks,
But bears it out even to the edge of doom:—
If this be error and upon me proved,
I never writ, nor no man ever loved.

William Shakespeare

WINTER

When icicles hang by the wall,
    And Dick the shepherd blows his nail,
And Tom bears logs into the hall,
    And milk comes frozen home in pail,

47

When blood is nipp'd, and ways be foul,
Then nightly sings the staring owl,
       Tu-whit!
Tu-who!—a merry note,
While greasy Joan doth keel the pot.

When all aloud the wind doth blow,
    And coughing drowns the parson's saw,
And birds sit brooding in the snow,
    And Marian's nose looks red and raw,
When roasted crabs hiss in the bowl,
Then nightly sings the staring owl,
       Tu-whit!
Tu-who!—a merry note,
While greasy Joan doth keel the pot.

Ben Jonson

From THE SAD SHEPHERD

. . . Now she is dead! of what? of thorns,
Briars and brambles? thistles, burs and docks?
Cold hemlock, yews? the mandrake, or the box?
These may grow still; but what can spring beside?
Did not the whole earth sicken when she died
As if there since did fall one drop of dew,
But what was wept for her! or any stalk
Did bear a flower, or any branch a bloom,
After her wreath was made! In faith, in faith,
You do not fair to put these things upon me,
Which can in no sort be: Earine,
Who had her very being and her name
With the first knots or buddings of the spring,
Born with the primrose and the violet
Or earliest roses blown: when Cupid smiled

48

And Venus led the Graces out to dance,
And all the flowers and sweets in nature's lap
Leaped out and made their solemn conjuration
To last but while she lived!

Ben Jonson

JEALOUSY

Wretched and foolish jealousy,
How cam'st thou thus to enter me?
   I ne'er was of thy kind:
Nor have I yet the narrow mind
   To vent that poor desire,
That others should not warm them at my fire:
   I wish the sun should shine
On all men's fruits and flowers as well as mine.

But under the disguise of love,
Thou say'st thou only cam'st to prove
   What my affections were.
Think'st thou that love is helped by fear?
   Go, get thee quickly forth,
Love's sickness and his noted want of worth,
   Seek doubting men to please.
I ne'er will owe my health to a disease.

Ben Jonson

To Celia

Drink to me only with thine eyes,
   And I will pledge with mine ;
Or leave a kiss but in the cup
   And I'll not look for wine.

49

The thirst that from the soul doth rise
    Doth ask a drink divine ;
But might I of Jove's nectar sup,
    I would not change for thine.

I sent thee late a rosy wreath,
    Not so much honouring thee
As giving it a hope that there
    It could not wither'd be;
But thou thereon dids't only breathe,
    And sent'st it back to me;
Since when it grows, and smells, I swear,
    Not of itself but thee!

Christopher Marlowe

From TAMBURLAINE THE GREAT

TO XENOCRATES

Where Beauty, mother to the Muses, sits,
And comments volumes with her ivory pen,
Taking instructions from thy flowing eyes;
Eyes, when that Ebena steps to heaven,
In silence of thy solemn evening's walk,
Making the mantle of the richest night
The moon, the planets, and the meteors, light;
There angels in their crystal armours fight
A doubtful battle with my tempted thoughts. . . .
What is beauty, saith my sufferings, then?
If all the pens that ever poets held
Had fed the feeling of their masters' thoughts,
And every sweetness that inspired their hearts,
Their minds, and muses on admired themes,

If all the heavenly quintessence they still
From their immortal flowers of poetry,
Wherein, as in a mirror, we perceive
The highest reaches of a human wit;
If these had made one poem's period,
And all combined in beauty's worthiness,
Yet should there hover in their restless heads
One thought, one grace, one wonder, at the least,
Which into words no virtue can digest.

Christopher Marlowe

From THE TRAGICALL HISTORY OF DR. FAUSTUS

Was this the face that launched a thousand ships
And burnt the topless towers of Ilium?
Sweet Helen, make me immortal with a kiss—
Her lips suck forth my soul; see where it flies!
Come, Helen, come, give me my soul again.
Here will I dwell, for heaven is in these lips,
And all is dross that is not Helena.
O, thou art fairer than the evening air,
Clad in the beauty of a thousand stars;
Brighter art thou than flaming Jupiter
When he appeared to hapless Semele;
More lovely than the monarch of the sky
In wanton Arethusa's azured arms;
And none but thee shall be my paramour!

Thomas Nashe

IN TIME OF PESTILENCE

Adieu, farewell earth's bliss!
This world uncertain is:

Fond are life's lustful joys,
Death proves them all but toys.
None from his darts can fly;
I am sick, I must die—
    Lord, have mercy on us!

Rich men, trust not in wealth,
Gold cannot buy you health;
Physic himself must fade;
All things to end are made;
The plague full swift goes by,
I am sick, I must die—
    Lord, have mercy on us!

Beauty is but a flower
Which wrinkles will devour;
Brightness falls from the air;
Queens have died young and fair;
Dust hath clos'd Helen's eye;
I am sick, I must die—
    Lord, have mercy on us!

Strength stoops unto the grave,
Worms feed on Hector brave;
Swords may not fight with fate;
Earth still holds ope her gate;
Come, come! the bells do cry;
I am sick, I must die—
    Lord, have mercy on us!

Wit with his wantonness
Tasteth death's bitterness;
Hell's executioner

Hath no ears for to hear
What vain art can reply;
I am sick, I must die—
    Lord, have mercy on us!

Haste therefore each degree
To welcome destiny;
Heaven is our heritage,
Earth but a player's stage.
Mount we unto the sky;
I am sick, I must die—
    Lord, have mercy on us!

Robert Greene

THE SHEPHERD'S WIFE'S SONG

Ah, what is love? It is a pretty thing,
As sweet unto a shepherd as a king;
    And sweeter too,
For kings have cares that wait upon a crown,
And cares can make the sweetest love to frown;
    Ah then, ah then,
If country loves such sweet desires do gain,
What lady would not love a shepherd swain?

His flocks are folded, he comes home at night,
As merry as a king in his delight;
    And merrier too,
For kings bethink them what the state require,

53

Where shepherds careless carol by the fire;
>> Ah then, ah then,
If country loves such sweet desires do gain,
What lady would not love a shepherd swain?

He kisseth first, then sits as blithe to eat
His cream and curds, as doth the king his meat;
>> And blither too,
For kings have often fears when they do sup,
Where shepherds dread no poison in their cup;
>> Ah then, ah then,
If country loves such sweet desires do gain,
What lady would not love a shepherd swain?

. . . .

Upon his couch of straw he sleeps as soun,
As doth the king upon his bed of down;
>> More sounder too,
For cares cause kings full oft their sleep to spill,
Where weary shepherds lie and snort their fill;
>> Ah then, ah then,
If country loves such sweet desires do gain,
What lady would not love a shepherd swain?

Thus with his wife he spends the year, as blithe
As doth the king at every tide or sith;
>> And blither too,
For kings have wars and broils to take in hand,
When shepherds laugh and love upon the land:
>> Ah then, ah then,
If country loves such sweet desires do gain,
What lady would not love a shepherd swain?

STRATFORD TO LONDON

Shakespeare (*English Men of Letters*)	Sir W. Raleigh
" (*Home Univ. Library*)	J. Masefield
" (*Literature Primers*)	E. Dowden
" *A Study*	D. Figgis
Shakespeare and Stratford-on-Avon	R. E. Hunter
Facts about Shakespeare	Wm. Poel
Ben Jonson (*English Worthies*)	J. A. Symonds
Poems of Greene and Marlowe	Ed. R. Bell
Elizabethan England	Ed. L. Withington
London (*Story of the English Towns*)	P. H. Ditchfield
'*Once upon a Time*'	Charles Knight

55

Chapter Three

IN THE SERVICE OF GLORIANA

[1589]

Two MEN WERE seated in a raftered room overlooking a straggling garden. The gentle Irish sunlight fell in warm splashes on the turf and on the crumbling walls of the house. Behind were thick woods dark against the lower slopes of the Galtee Mountains; in front a little lake, a wilderness of late-flowering shrubs—the month was October—and beyond, the highway running between Mallow and Limerick.

In physical appearance the two were not unlike. Both had narrow faces, with the pointed Elizabethan beard; both were obviously men of quality, and dressed in the elaborate silks and velvets proper to aristocrats of the time. Both were thirty-seven years of age. Both were men of vision, dreamers of dreams, as well as practical workers, typical products of England's Renaissance.

The taller, whose air was at once commanding and conciliatory, was Walter Ralegh, Knight, until a few years ago a poor adventurer, now Warden of the Stannaries, Lord Lieutenant of Cornwall, Captain of the Bodyguard of Queen Elizabeth—with the weighty responsibility of personal attendance upon Her Highness; owner of forty thousand acres in Cork, Waterford and Tipperary, and of other estates in Lincolnshire, Nottinghamshire and Derby, and one of the wealthiest of the courtiers who stood in the fierce light which beat

about the Tudor Throne. He had other claims, beside
the legendary incident of the puddle and the doffed
cloak, to Elizabeth's favour. It was he who had first
suggested the colonization of America. He hated and
baited Spain with Elizabethan vigour and unscrupu-
lousness. (Not until a later reign was the much-tor-
mented Philip able to enjoy his revenge, and see
Ralegh go to the scaffold under a grotesque charge
ten years old.) But recently he had removed himself
from the court to his Irish manor-house at Youghal, at
the mouth of the Blackwater. From there it was but a
few miles to the pleasant room in Kilcolman Castle,
where he now sat chuckling with amusement at the
Castle's owner.

Edmund Spenser, slight, dark and dapper, was not
chuckling. He looked pale and unhappy. His unhappiness was recent; for an hour they had been talking of
politics and war; cautiously and in undertones of the
Queen's swift-changing moods; of Burleigh's fox-like
counsels, of the reckless and arrogant Essex and his
swift ascent to power; of King Philip and his eternal
plotting; of the Pope. Then, more boldly, they had discoursed of warfare, both by land and by sea; more
especially of the Armada, which a year ago had
threatened England, and threatening, perished by the
Grace of God and the fact that the Spaniards sent
soldiers to win a sea-battle while the English sent
fishermen. At which point Ralegh, smiling, had produced his gift—and Spenser had accepted it—a long
tube of wood ending in a silver bowl. Into this bowl

57

Ralegh had packed not more than a thimbleful of a dried herb of strange odour, fired it, and bid his friend inhale, with the result that within five minutes the unhappy Spenser's eyes were red-rimmed and full of tears and his voice husky with coughing.

The pitying exponent of the art of smoking produced and lit a pipe of his own.

'Should'st use the weed *thus*—and *thus*,' he said.

''Tis Nature's own Inquisition, and the sentence death by slow suffocation!' gasped Spenser.

''Tis Nature's own sedative, growing freely in the wilds of Virginia. All unknown to English lips and throats until the day when, as I've told thee, my man Harriot, whom I had despatched thither with the expedition, did acquire from the natives not only the habit, but pipes and a supply of tobacco itself. And he, returning, did instruct me in the art, which I now impart to thee.'

'Would he had married a native wife, and forgotten it!'

'Speaking as one bachelor to another, I'll swear that no wife, white or native, will ever make a man forget his earlier love—if her name be Nicotina! Meanwhile, what of this poem thou would'st read me?'

Spenser put aside the pipe and leaned forward, his small, almost effeminate, hands gripping the table-edge.

'It is one which hath been in my mind, Walter, for a long time past. Indeed, 'tis nine years since I spoke of it to Master Gabriel Harvey.'

58

'So long?'

'Aye. And three years—nay, four—since 'twas discussed at the house of Master Ludowick Bryskett, who held office before me in the service of the Council of Munster. There was with him a company of others concerned in the governance of this inhospitable and savage island. I recall His Grace of Armagh, Sir Robert Dillon, the brothers Norreys, Captain Carlish —he who was son-in-law to Walsingham—'

'Have done, man, with thy catalogue of notables. Let us hope that this over-hatched egg of thine be not addled!'

'Jest not.' Spenser spoke fiercely.

'Beseech you pardon my unmannerliness. Read on.'

The poet crossed to a bureau on the far side of the room, and extracted a thick volume. The covers were plain boards, secured by a clasp. Between them were many quires of manuscript. He unlocked the clasp, opened the covers, and hesitated.

'I wait,' said Ralegh.

'Swear, then, thou'lt not fill the room with thine accursed smoke.'

'See, my pipe hath nought in it but ash.'

Spenser took up the first sheet, and began to read.

.   .   .   .

The short Autumn afternoon grew mellower. It passed into twilight, and from twilight into dusk. A fiery sunset died down into cool greys and blues. The birds in the garden ceased their twittering. From some-

59

where overhead came the sound of a woman crooning an Irish lullaby to herself. Darkness fell. Spenser would have ended the reading, but Ralegh impatiently demurred. Lights were brought; the gentle cultured voice resumed. . . . There were still many pages unturned when at last it died away.

'Wilt return with me to England,' said Ralegh, breaking a long silence. 'This masterpiece of thine shall be laid at the feet of Her Highness—t'were treason otherwise. God hath given thee genius, Edmund, and when that genius be manifest, thy fellow-countrymen shall honour both him and thee.'

.   .   .   .

So London engulfed them—Ralegh, the Adventurer, and Spenser, the Poet. The two travelled there from Southampton, with Ralegh's servants in attendance as an escort and for protection.

The Queen was at the Manor House of St. James'. (It had not then acquired the title of Palace.) With her was the Court, that strange firmament in which she blazed, sunlike, while about her her satellites flashed and wheeled for a few short years of brilliance and power, until her displeasure brought extinction—imprisonment, exile or the grave. Lord Treasurer Burleigh; Hatton, the Chancellor; Walsingham, perhaps the most honest among them, now very near his death; Oxford, Northumberland, Howard of Effingham—warriors, diplomats and place-seekers, all cynically aware that neither wisdom nor cunning, simplicity nor honour, learning nor wealth would avail them when their hour had come; when Elizabeth the Queen had no more work for them to do or Elizabeth the Woman was awearied.

At present the newest, brightest star was Essex, whose dizzy rise was to end in futility and eclipse a few years later under the cold eyes of Ralegh himself. Ralegh had left for Ireland because his rival's insolence and the Queen's growing coldness had made any further lingering at the Court as dangerous as it was humiliating. Now, he explained to Spenser, as, dismounting, they passed through the gateway with its halberded sentries, there was a chance—nay, more than a chance —that this new and magnificent tribute the poet was laying at her feet might bring both of them into Royal favour again. The Queen craved flattery; here it was none the less gross because of the rainbow loveliness of the language. Gloriana, Belphoebe, Britomarte—as such she was depicted, while her enemies were monsters as evil as their fates. Spenser listened uneasily; perhaps, the poet predominating over the courtier, a little shamefaced. He was less sanguine. He could afford to be. He had less to lose.

Their names were taken into the Queen. Presently the messenger returned. Her Highness would deign to see Sir Walter and Mr. Spenser.

They followed him, plumed hats in hand. Under Spenser's left arm he carried the book. Their footsteps seemed to echo the beating of his own heart. The two passed beneath purple velvet curtains into the Presence.

Elizabeth was seated on a dais at the far end of the room. Her narrow face was puckered and pale. (Did not that same pallor impel her to order that her maids should rub their cheeks with tallow, that the too-attractive pink-and-whiteness of their complexions should not emphasize the ravages of old age upon her own?) She had ruled England inflexibly for more than thirty years. Though she did not know it, and even Burleigh himself would never have dared to hint it, her life's work was done. Those thirty years were to become forty-five before the sceptre slipped from her tired old hands—but already Philip and all that he stood for was broken and impotent. Her kingdom was sound and safe; if the plotting brain that had saved it had let her she might have rested. But Elizabeth could not rest. She was to plan and scheme, lie and manœuvre, to the end.

The men, closely watched by the little group of courtiers, made their obeisances.

'Your business, Sir Walter?' demanded the harsh but not unkindly voice.

Ralegh explained. Spenser needed no introduction; apart from his reputation as a poet, he had already had contact with the Court as a Crown employee. But here, in the very presence of Gloriana, with her background of jealousy, backbiting, and perpetual intrigue, he was tongue-tied.

Her Highness listened, a frown wrinkling her high forehead, the thin lips peevish. She was, in truth, suffering from a surfeit of over-honeyed phrases, elaborate and fantastic compliments, homage passing all bounds of adulation. Her fan tapped the arm of her seat impatiently; now and again the dark eyes shot a fierce challenge at her courtiers, as though seeking to catch them off their guard, sneering. . . . Her Highness continued to listen. The frown faded, the twitching hands were still. Master Spenser might leave this strange poem of his. Perchance she might peruse further. He should be instructed concerning the hour at which he might present himself at St. James' again.

That second visit was paid two days later. It ended in splendid unequivocal triumph. Elizabeth had surrendered utterly to the splendours of the 'Faerie Queen'. She had recognized, as a woman so intellectual and cultured was bound to recognize, genius which had no affinity with mere talent. The poem—or, more exactly, so much of it as was written—should be dedicated to her. A pension, whittled down by the frugal-minded Lord Treasurer to fifty pounds a year, but a pension, nevertheless, was conferred upon the author. And Ralegh himself was in favour again.

'How can I thank thee, Walter?' cried Spenser, as they left the royal precincts.

'With that largesse which none other can bestow so fittingly,' answered Ralegh with gay arrogance. 'A poem setting forth, an' thou wilt, what small deeds I may have performed in the service of Gloriana and her Kingdom.'

'Here's my hand on it,' said Spenser.

That night, lodging nobly in the house of his friend, he sat at his casement watching the tranquil sky.

63

As he watched, a star blazed across the heavens, to expire in aching blackness in the west.

In the west lay Ireland.

[1598]

It was October again, nine years later. And though Kilcolman Castle, once the home of the Desmonds, was still the home of Edmund Spenser, much had happened since Elizabeth had smiled approval upon the first book of the 'Faerie Queene'. He was recognized as England's greatest living poet, her 'sweetest singer'. But there was another Spenser, the hard-working, bigoted and intolerant administrator, lately appointed Sherriff of Cork, and who, like his chief, Lord Grey, was hated fiercely by the Irish he ruled. Their hatred was repaid with contempt. They were barbarians without rights, cattle to be controlled and driven by their English masters.

There were other changes. Spenser was now a married man. It was not—alas for romance!—his first falling in love. But it was the first time his wooing had been successful. A country maiden named Elizabeth, who in the beginning was unkind, but later changed her mind, became Mistress Spenser in 1594, and the most exquisite wedding ode in any language had testified to her husband's happiness. Four children had been born to them, the youngest only a month or so before. Its cries came faintly to Spenser as he stood on the threshold of his house staring into the darkness. Though long

64

past sunset, the heavy clouds on the horizon were glowing redly. The Ireland whose green and beautiful landscapes he loved as deeply as he detested her people, had suddenly risen in a rebellion which was sweeping the land with savage violence.

Spenser had been warned that the storm was about to break. But until that night he had been sceptical and contemptuous. He had made no preparations. Now he was faced with only two alternatives, a siege or flight. But for the first he had no adequate defences, either in men or material; for the second, he was hopelessly handicapped by his wife and the children. The risks of taking them through a wild and enemy-infested countryside were enormous. It was not through fear that he hesitated, but through sheer indecision.

The hour grew later; the glow in the sky brighter. A reek of burning homesteads tainted the air. Through the thick woodland behind the house a servant from the neighbouring estate of a fellow Englishman named Piers crept with a last urgent warning. The rebels, exasperated by a hundred stories of injustice and oppression, had sworn that if a Desmond might not rule in his castle, no other should. . . . Spenser, with heavy steps, went back to make the final plans for flight.

$$\bullet \quad \bullet \quad \bullet \quad \bullet \quad \bullet \quad \bullet \quad \bullet \quad \bullet \quad \bullet$$

The night wore on, a night filled with scenes of horror and agony. Scenes of a sudden maddened rush by the Irish hordes, of the house surrounded and in flames before the trapped inmates could assemble the barest

65

necessaries. Of Elizabeth Spenser, still weak from child-birth, being carried in a swoon down the crackling stairs and out to where a wagon and horse were wait-ing. Of the little nursemaid who heroically brought three screaming children from their beds, discovered that the youngest was not with its mother, went back for it . . . and did not return.

There were merciful blanks, else the end would have been madness. Of the journey itself he had no clear memories. The rebels, overwhelmed, shocked, perhaps, by the frightful completeness of their re-venge, had allowed the forlorn little party to escape unmolested. Cork, in the person of Sir Thomas Norris, received the stricken family kindly. But perfunctorily; Norris himself was under a cloud. As President of Munster, he had shown indecision and feebleness—and indecision and feebleness in an Englishman were crimes which Elizabeth did not pardon. '*You might have better resisted than you did,*' she wrote, '*considering the many defensible houses and castles possessed by the settlers, who, for aught we can hear, were by no means comforted nor supported by you, but either from lack of comfort from you, or out of mere cowardice, fled away from the rebels on the first alarm.*'

In Cork, Spenser and his family remained while Norris, still vacillating, still trying to discover excuses for the inexcusable, drew up a long report of the pro-gress of the rebellion. This, on the ninth of December, he gave to Spenser, with instructions to seek out the Queen personally and add his own views on the situa-tion. Did he think that the grief-ravaged man would

66

add life and colour to the cold official document?
Perhaps.

Burghley's note at the foot of that futile document
shows that it reached his hands on Christmas Eve. But
Spenser himself did not see the Queen. Gloriana was
never again to hear honeyed compliments from the
dapper little man with the soul of a great poet. He was
ill, too ill even to ask an audience. And in a shabby
upper room in King Street, Westminster, his arrival
in the city almost unknown, he died on Saturday the
16th of January, 1599—not for lack of bread, as picturesque tradition afterwards averred, nor from the
physical sufferings of those last ghastly days, but from a
broken heart.

He died—and abruptly all England knew of his
tragedy. Elizabeth herself, shocked out of her royal
callousness towards those who could no longer be of
service to her, decreed burial in the Abbey, a few yards
from the grave of Chaucer, and ordered that a monument should be erected at her expense. (That an avari-
cious courtier should intercept the order, and that
Spenser's monument should be erected twenty years
later by another donor, is one of the minor ironies of
death.) Essex, with typical generosity, bore the cost
of the funeral; Shakespeare and Jonson, with a company of other poets, followed the body to its last resting-
place.

Ireland was to remain unconquered. Elizabeth
Spenser was to wed again. The flames that left Kilcolman a blackened ruin devoured the last-written

67

pages of the 'Faerie Queene'. But the lovely fragment
that remains is beyond destruction or oblivion.

Edmund Spenser

From The FAERIE QUEENE

THE CAVE OF DESPAIR

Ere long they come, where that same wicked wight
His dwelling has, low in a hollow cave,
Far underneath a craggy cliff ypight,
Dark, doleful, dreary, like a greedy grave,
That still for carrion carcases doth crave;
On top whereof ay dwelt the ghastly owl,
Shrieking his baleful note, which ever drave
Far from that haunt all other cheerful fowl;
And all about it wandering ghosts did wail and howl.

And all about old stocks and stubs of trees,
Whereon nor fruit nor leaf was ever seen,
Did hang upon the ragged rocky knees;
On which had many wretches hanged been,
Whose carcases were scattered on the green,
And thrown about the cliffs. Arrived there,
That bare-head Knight, for dread and doleful teene,
Would fain have fled, ne durst approachen near;
But the other forced him stay, and comforted in fear,

That darksome cave they enter, where they find
That cursed man, low sitting on the ground,
Musing full sadly in his sullen mind;
His grisly locks, long growen and unbound,
Disordered hung about his shoulders round,
68

And hid his face; through which his hollow eyne
Looked deadly dull, and stared as astound;
His raw-bone cheeks, through penury and pine,
Were shrunk into his jaws, as he did never dine:

His garment, nought but many ragged clouts,
With thorns together pinned and patched was,
The which his naked sides he wrapped abouts:
And him beside there lay upon the grass,
A dreary corse, whose life away did pass

. . . .

Which piteous spectacle approving true
The wofull tale that Trevisan had told,
When as the gentle red-cross knight did view,
With fiery zeal he burnt in courage bold,
Him to avenge before his blood was cold:
And to the villain said, 'Thou damned wight,
The author of this fact we here behold,
What justice can but judge against thee right,
With thine own blood to price his blood, here shed in
    sight?'

'What frantic fit,' quoth he, 'hath thus distraught
Thee, foolish man, so rash a doom to give?
What justice ever other judgment taught,
But he should die who merits not to live?
None else to death this man despairing drove,
But his own guilty mind deserving death.
Is't then unjust to each his due to give?
Or let him die that loatheth living breath?
Or let him die at ease, that liveth here uneath?

'Who travels by the weary wandering way,
To come unto his wished home in haste,

And meets a flood that doth his passage stay,
Is't not great grace to help him over-past,
Or free his feet, that in the mire stick fast?
Most envious man, that grieves at neighbours' good,
And fond, that joyest in the woe thou hast;
Why wilt not let him pass, that long hath stood
Upon the bank, yet wilt thyself not pass the flood?

'He there does now enjoy eternal rest
And happy ease, which thou doest want and crave,
And further from it daily wanderest;
What if some little pain the passage have,
That make frail flesh to fear the bitter wave?
Is not short pain well borne, that brings long ease,
And lays the soul to sleep in quiet grave?
Sleep after toil, port after stormy seas,
Ease after war, death after life, doth greatly please.'

The knight much wondered at his sudden wit,
And said, 'The term of life is limited,
Nor may a man prolong nor shorten it;
The solder may not move from watchful sted,
Nor leave his stand, until his captain bid.'
'Who life did limit by almighty doom,'
Quoth he, 'knows best the term established;
And he, that points the sentinel his room,
Doth license him depart at sound of morning drum.

'Is not his deed, whatever thing is done
In heaven and earth? did not he all create
To die again? all ends that are begun:
Their times in his eternal book of fate
Are written sure, and have their certain date.
Who then can strive with strong necessity,
That holds the world in his still changing state?

Or shun the death ordained by destiny?
When hour of death is come, let none ask whence nor
    why.'

Edmund Spenser
From Muiopotmos

THE BUTTERFLY

The woods, the rivers, and the meadows green,
With his air-cutting wings he measured wide,
Nor did he leave the mountains bare unseen,
Nor the rank grassy fens' delight untried;
But none of these, however sweet they been,
Mote please his fancy, or him cause to abide;
His choiceful sense with every change doth flit;
No common things may please a wavering wit.

To the gay gardens his unstaid desire
Him wholly carried, to refresh his sprights;
There lavish Nature, in her best attire,
Pours forth sweet odours and alluring sights,
And Art, with her contending doth aspire,
To excel the natural with made delights;
And all that fair or pleasant may be found,
In riotous excess doth there abound.

There he arriving, round about doth flie,
From bed to bed, from one to the other border,
And takes survey with curious busy eye,
Of every flower and herb there set in order,
Now this, now that, he tasteth tenderly,
Yet none of them he rudely doth disorder,
Ne with his feet their silken leaves displace,
But pastures on the pleasures of each place.

71

And evermore with most variety
And change of sweetness (for all change is sweet)
He casts his glutton sense to satisfy,
Now sucking of the sap of herbs most meet,
Or of the dew which yet on them doth lie,
Now in the same bathing his tender feet;
And then he percheth on some branch thereby
To weather him and his moist wings to dry.

And then again he turneth to his play,
To spoil the pleasures of that paradise;
The wholesome sage, the lavender still grey,
Rank-smelling rue, and cummin good for eyes,
The roses reigning in the pride of May,
Sharp hyssop good for green wounds' remedies
Fair marigolds, and bees-alluring thyme,
Sweet marjoram and daisies decking prime.

Cool violets, and orpine growing still,
Embathed balm, and cheerful galingale,
Fresh costmary and breathful camomill,
Dull poppy and drink-quickening setuale,
Vein-healing vervain and head-purging dill,
Sound savoury, and basil hearty-hale,
Fat coleworts and comforting perseline,
Cold lettuce, and refreshing rosemarine.

Edmund Spenser

From EPITHALAMION

Tell me, ye merchants' daughters, did ye see
So fayre a creature in your towne before;
So sweet, so lovely, and so mild as she,
Adornd with beautye's grace and vertue's store?

Her goodly eyes lyke Saphyres shining bright,
Her forehead ivory white,
Her cheeks lyke apples which the sun hath rudded.

.   .   .   .

But if ye saw that which no eyes can see,
The inward beauty of her lively spright,
Garnisht with heavenly gifts of high degree,
Much more then would ye wonder at that sight
And stand astonisht lyke to those which red
Medusæs mazeful hed.
There dwels sweet love, and constant chastity,
Unspotted fayth and comely womanhood,
Regard of honour and mild modesty;
There vertu raynes as Queene in royal throne,
And giveth lawes alone,
The which the base affections doe obay,
And yeeld theyr services unto her will;
Ne thought of thing uncomely ever may
Thereto approach to tempt her mind to ill.
Had ye once seene these her celestial threasures,
And unrevealed pleasures,
Then would ye wonder, and her prayses sing,
That al the woods should answer, and your echo ring.

Sir Walter Ralegh

A Vision upon this Conceipt of the Faery Queen

Methought I saw the grave where Laura lay,
Within that temple where the vestal flame
Was wont to burn; and passing by that way,
To see that buried dust of living fame
Whose tomb for Love and fairer Virtue kept,

73

All suddenly I saw the Faery Queen:
At whose approach the soul of Petrarke wept,
And from thenseforth those Graces were not seen
(For they this Queen attended); in whose stead
Oblivion laid him down on Laura's hearse.
Hereat the hardest stones were seen to bleed,
And groans of buried ghosts the heavens did perse;
    Where Homer's spright did tremble all for grief,
    And curst the access of that celestial thief.

Sir Walter Ralegh

From a Historie of the World

The Kings and Princes of the world haue alwaies laid before them, the actions, but not the ends of those Great Ones which preceded them. They are always transported with the glorie of the one, but they neuer minde the miserie of the other, till they finde the experience in themselues. They neglect the aduice of God, while they enjoy life, or hope it; but they follow the counsell of Death, vpon his first approach. It is hee that puts into man all wisedome of the world, without speaking a word; which God with all the words of his Law, promises, or threats, doth infuse. Death, which hateth and destroyeth man, is beleeued; God, which hath him and loues him, is alwaies deferred. I haue considered (saith Solomon) all the workes that are vnder the Sunne, and behold, all is vanitie, and vexation of spirit: but who beleeues it, till Death tells it vs? It was Death, which opening the conscience of Charles the fift, made him enioyne his sonne Philip to restore Nauarre; and King Francis the first of France, to command that iustice should be done vpon the Murderers

74

of the Protestants in Merindol and Cabrieres, which til then he neglected. It is therefore Death alone that can suddenly make man to know himselfe. He tells the proud and insolent, that they are but Abjects, and humbles them at the instant; makes them crie, complaine, and repent, yea, euen to hate their forepassed happinesse. He takes the account of the rich, and proues him a beggar; a naked beggar, which hath interest in nothing, but in the grauell that fills his mouth. He holds a glasse before the eyes of the most beautifull, and makes them see therein, their deformitie and rottennesse; and they acknowledge it.

O eloquent, iust, and mighty Death! whom none could aduise, thou hast perswaded; what none hath dared thou hast done; and whom all the world hath flattered, thou only has cast out of the world and despised; thou hast drawne together all the farre stretched greatnesse, all the pride, crueltie, and ambition of man, and couered it all ouer with these two narrow words, *Hic iacet.*

Sir Walter Ralegh

Letter to SIR ROBERT CAR

After many losses and many years sorrows, of both which I have cause to fear I was mistaken in their ends, it is come to my knowledge, that yourself (whom I know not but by an honourable favour) hath been persuaded to give me and mine my last fatal blow, by obtaining from his majesty the inheritance of my children and nephews, lost in law for want of a word. This done, there remaineth nothing with me but the name of life. His majesty, whom I never offended (for I hold it unnatural and unmanlike to hate goodness), staid

75

me at the grave's brink; not that I thought his majesty thought me worthy of many deaths, and to behold mine cast out of the world with myself, but as a king that knoweth the poor in truth, hath received a promise from God that his throne shall be established.

And for you, sir, seeing your fair day is but in the dawn, mine drawn to the setting; your own virtue and the king's grace assuring you of many fortunes and much honour; I besseech you begin not your first building upon the ruins of the innocent, and let not mine and their sorrows attend your first plantation.

Sir Walter Ralegh

Last Lines

(Believed to have been written in his Bible the night before his execution, October 29th, 1618.)

> Even such is time, that takes in trust
> Our youth, our joys, our all we have,
> And pays us but with earth and dust;
> Who, in the dark and silent grave,
> When we have wandered all our ways,
> Shuts up the story of our days;
> But from this earth, this grave, this dust,
> My God shall raise me up I trust.

IN THE SERVICE OF GLORIANA

Spenser (English Men of Letters)   R. W. Church
Great Authors of English Literature   W. S. Dalgleish
Ralegh   Louise Creighton

Chapter Four

CRABBED AGE AND YOUTH

[1673]

CHARLES THE SECOND, cleverest, laziest and luckiest of the Stuarts, lolled upon the throne of England. (Some also insist that he was the wickedest of his line. But any discussion of that point would carry us into limitless realms of speculation.)

It was a period when the patriot might join the moralist in lamentations; when Britannia's grasp of her trident was uncertain and her helmet rakishly and precariously balanced on her bewildered brows. The navy, as Macaulay acidly remarks, was run by gentlemen and sailors, but the gentlemen were not sailors and the sailors were not gentlemen. Ships which should have been soundly built of good English oak were constructed with such a flagrant disregard for anything but the contractors' pockets that they were unfit to float, much less to fight. A regular army, apart from the King's Guards, was practically non-existent. His Catholic Majesty of France did his best to dictate England's foreign policy what time his Protestant Majesty of England dallied with the baby-faced Mademoiselle de Querouaille, whom his people called 'Mrs. Carwell', and heartily hated. But Nell Gwynne, the Drury Lane orange-girl, they loved. As free with her tongue as with her purse, and to the end of her life incapable of signing her name—the initials 'E.G.' with dots to show her

77

where to begin and where to end each letter, were the utmost she could achieve—Nelly had no enemies among her own countrymen.

Thirteen years had passed since the glorious Restoration, its glories now so demonstrably tarnished. Eight years had passed since that sweltering summer when, to an accompaniment of clanking bells and cries of 'Bring out your dead', the death-carts had rumbled over the desolate and grass-grown cobbles of London's streets, and the Great Plague had struck down seventy thousand victims. Seven years had passed since the Great Fire had done its cleansing task. Both afflictions might be attributed by the godly to the sins of the King and his Court; impartial historians trace the Plague— incidentally the twelfth and worst of its kind to visit the City—to infection brought from the Levant in a bale of figs in the previous year, and the Fire to the drought, the narrowness and crookedness of the streets, the tinder-like qualities of the houses, and the absence of any fire-fighting organization worth mentioning. Certain it is that the burning of the City did not owe its origin to a Catholic conspiracy, as once stated on the Monument, to the exasperation of Mr. Alexander Pope.

At the Admiralty, a stout gentleman of forty occupied the Secretary's apartment. He had other qualities beside stoutness, being a distinguished, not to say an amazing gentleman, as well as a notable example of what progress may be achieved when personality is allied to brains under the patronage of the great. When, through the influence of his kinsman, Lord Sandwich,

78

the youthful Samuel Pepys began his governmental career as a humble clerk of the Acts in the Navy Office, he was ignorant not only of business routine, but of the multiplication table. Yet thereafter his official and social progress was swift and honourable—Clerk to the Privy Seal, Justice of the Peace, Younger Brother of Trinity House, Elder Brother of Trinity House, Commissioner for Managing the affairs of Tangier (the oddest dowry an English queen ever brought her husband), Surveyor-General of Victualling, Fellow of the Royal Society, and now Secretary to the Navy and high in the confidence of the Merry Monarch and the Merry Monarch's far from merry brother, the Duke of York, High Admiral of England. Though still lamenting the death of his wife, and suffering from the effects of eye-strain and other intermittent bodily discomforts, he sought—and found—consolation in his books, his music, and his innumerable friends. An estimable citizen. But one with a secret.

In the whole history of authorship there is no secret quite so odd. A diary in cipher, bequeathed as such to posterity by the writer, who overlooked the fact that he had at the same time provided a key. A diary of incredible interest and naïve intimacy, left for a hundred and forty years lying un-decoded in its case at Magdalene College, Cambridge, before, by mere chance, the secret was discovered, and it took its unique place in English literature. . . . Now, in 1673, the last incomparable comment on seventeenth century follies and vices was already four years old.

So much for Charles the Second; so much for Samuel Pepys, Esquire, F.R.S. One turns, not without reluctance, to other actors upon the Stuart stage, the scene being a London street.

The street belonged to a section of the city which from the middle of the 16th Century till the beginning of the 18th was a Mecca for the collector and student of books and prints. By 1800 most of its glories had faded; to-day, they are forgotten, in the later reputations of Wych Street, Paternoster Row and Charing Cross Road. But in the time of Charles the Second all learned London knew and visited Little Britain.

Originally Britain, or Bretagne Street, it took its name from the mansion of the Duke of Bretagne, which stood near St. Botolph's Church. Other members of the nobility had houses there, and the whole of the east side was occupied by a mansion belonging to Lord Montagne. (Duke Street, by the gate, was once Duck Lane, originally Duc Lane, after the Duc de Bretagne.) Among the multitude of dealers there, the man with the pleasantest claim upon Londoners of to-day was one Millington, and that because of his friendship with one of the greatest Londoners of all time.

Millington was a shrewd tradesman, but he was something of a scholar too, as indeed, no man who deals in books, and whose heart is in his work, can fail to be. And he had sheltered in his house another scholar whose learning was lit by genius and impelled into action by fanatical honesty. A Puritan who could be neither gagged nor bribed, an enemy to the Government upon whose head a price had been set. . . . Since then the ban had been lifted; the proud and rebellious spirit was free to walk unhindered through the London streets he loved. But the good Millington's friendship was still needed, Millington's right arm was still at his service, Millington's voice still ready to counsel. For the patriot was blind.

He was a man of middle height, with ringlets of silky hair which in his youth had been a warm brown. Under the broad forehead and arched temples were deep sockets from which the sightless but unblemished eyes faced the passing world. Upon a feminine delicacy of feature adversity and physical suffering had imposed heavy lines; the pouting mouth, which drooped a little querulously in repose, could stiffen indomitably. The whole expression was one of fortitude blended with un-utterable sorrow. He was dressed very soberly in black, with knee-breeches and wide silver-buckled shoes, and carried a staff in his disengaged hand.

John Milton was now in his sixty-fifth year. He had lived through troubled and dangerous times, asking nothing of his enemies, conceding nothing. Old age, though it had not changed his views and beliefs, had softened him, had made him less eager to strike with the terrific force of his pen, though none the less expert in its use. To-day he had come from his home in Artillery Walk, near by, to browse among, though he might not read, the books he loved.

Of 'Paradise Lost', the noblest epic poem in our Eng-glish tongue, you may still see the agreement between the author and the printer—one Samuel Simon—by which the author was to receive five pounds down, and three other sums of like amount upon the sale of the second, third and fourth editions respectively. That agreement was dated March 27th, 1667, and the work, conceived and planned nearly thirty years earlier, was published during the same year. But Milton lived only long enough to receive the second instalment.

. . . .

The April sky clouded, and presently a heavy shower drove the friends towards a neighbouring bookshop. There was scarcely room for them; too many others had already crowded into the same shelter. A gawky youth of fourteen or fifteen glanced at the blind man and his companion and slipped out on the pavement again.

'There'll be space for both of you if I go,' he said, with a friendly grin. 'And I've naught that's like to suffer from a few raindrops.'

'My thanks,' said Millington.

'And mine,' added John Milton. He turned his intent, sightless gaze towards the youth, who was edging away. 'Though I know not to whom I tender it.'

'I am Daniel Foe.'

'And thy father?'

'James Foe, the butcher, of Fore Street.'

'He hath a well-mannered son.'

''Twould have been something worse than ill-mannered to shelter while Master Milton endured the elements.'

82

The austere mouth quavered in a smile. 'Thy family hath learnt to deal in courtly phrases as well as beef and mutton. How didst know my name?'

'My father has pointed you out to me, more than once, when he and I have been walking together.'

'Hast a leaning towards books and book-learning?'

Young Foe hesitated. 'Of certain sorts, Master Milton. Of peoples and places I shall never live to see. . . . Yet there be so many things which happen from day to day in a great city such as this—'

'I understand. Wouldst learn from life itself, a study which is more than lifelong.' John Milton sighed, and for a moment was silent. Then, as the boy was moving hesitatingly away, he turned abruptly to Millington. 'Friend, I would ask a favour. The rain is ceasing, if it hath not ceased already. I can feel the sun upon my face. Do you go back to your business; this lad, if he be willing and hath no other claims upon him, shall guide me home.'

Millington raised no objection; though he was cheerfully and proudly prepared to sacrifice his time to an old friendship, that time had its value. And a delighted, 'Aye, willingly and proudly,' was answer enough from young Foe.

They walked, without undue hurry, back to Milton's house in Artillery Walk, near Bunhill Fields.

It was a pleasant house, built in one of those little oases of quiet which may still be discovered here and there in London's desert of noise. In front was open ground; behind, flower-beds and a stretch of sward.

83

Milton, with the assurance bred of eleven years' occupation, unlatched the door, and led the way into the house. A woman, hearing his step, emerged from a door on the right. She was golden-haired and still youthfully pretty; it was difficult to realize that she was now thirty-five. Elizabeth Minshull had been less than half John Milton's age when she became his third wife. It had been a union arranged by a mutual friend, but a deep and tranquil affection had grown up between the two, and her coming brought happiness into a home where discord and bitterness had reigned before.

Young Foe was introduced. He found himself ushered into a sunny, raftered room in which the scent of Spring flowers blended with that of the leather bindings. For many books lined the walls. Near the window was a small organ, and leaning against it a bass viol. Both these instruments the blind poet played; he and Mistress Milton loved cheerful music.

The boy was invited to remain to the midday meal. Hardly able to credit his own good fortune, he accepted the invitation. Afterwards Milton, his long clay pipe held between his thin, sensitive fingers, held forth on his life's work, as elderly, reticent men sometimes will in the presence of youth. That work was almost ended now, and he had few regrets. He had been a diligent and loyal servant of the Commonwealth. His had been the pen which drafted letters of state in Latin, the diplomatic language of the period, and translated the replies into English. Had he been content to be a mere scribe, he might still have held office. But the Puritanism he had fought for had become a thing to sneer at, the Commonwealth a tradition. He had seen Cromwell the Little succeed Cromwell the Great and let the reins of power slip from his careless, drunken fingers. Milton, fiercely championing a lost cause, had gone too far. A price had been set upon his head. How and why he escaped imprisonment, to say nothing of the worse fate which overtook so many of the anti-Royalists, remains to this day one of the minor historical mysteries. There is a legend that Sir William Davenant, the Poet-Laureate, had been saved from imprisonment by Milton's influence in 1650, and that Davenant was glad to repay the debt when the opportunity arose. Andrew Marvell, another poet, was also said to be involved in Milton's escape. But one would rather think that those who might have ruined him utterly tempered Restoration justice with more than Puritan mercy, as a tribute to a genius too great to be arraigned before any political tribunal.

The three rebellious daughters, children of his earlier marriages, had left home to earn their own livings. The sympathetic chronicler dwells unwillingly upon their upbringing. Paternal discipline was severe and undisputed in those days, but there was a streak of almost savage autocracy in John Milton's nature which no feminine adolescence could be expected to accept. He had, for example, decreed that, as mere women, his daughters should learn no language beyond their own; yet at the same time he insisted that they should read aloud to him in half-a-dozen languages—and so combine complete uncomprehension with boredom. Ann, the eldest of the band of malcontents, was lame. She had, too, an impediment in her speech. She had no sympathy with her father's views, and upon the two other girls, Mary and Deborah, had fallen most of the task of attending to the needs of the blind and intolerant old man. They hated it, neglected him when they dared, and revenged themselves by selling some of his books and keeping the proceeds. Now all that was past. Elizabeth Milton was mistress of the household. She had a servant for the rough work; her husband had his own amanuensis. Age softened the blind poet's bitterness and asperity. The visits of friends brought variety into the household, but did nothing to spoil its new and happy serenity.

.   .   .   .

The afternoon passed. The dark-haired boy with eager eyes listened and was happy. An incredible dream had come true. Presently, under gentle encouragement, he was speaking of himself, his hopes, his plans. Milton listened, cheek on hand. Were his thoughts of the boy baby whose name he had inscribed in the family Bible twenty-seven long years ago? *'My son John was born on Sunday March the 16th about half past nine at night 1650.'* So, with paternal pride, he had written. But little John had followed his mother into the darkness of the grave two years later.

'And thy father would make thee a preacher?' he asked.

'Aye, Master Milton. Only last year, I left school to go

86

to the Academy kept by the Reverend Morton, of Stoke Newington.'

'I have heard of him. A worthy minister whom the Act of Uniformity has made into a pedagogue.'

'Worthy indeed. But while there be some learning I love'—the boy made a wry face—

'The steps that lead to the pulpit are too dull and dusty for thy young feet? Well, well, thou art lucky.'

'In what wise, Master Milton?'

'Hast discovered in youth what did not come to me until mine old age—that creed and canon and dogma matter little, and that a man may shackle his soul to none of them, and still serve and praise his Maker faithfully. Are there others of like mind at friend Morton's academy of learning?'

Foe chuckled. 'Not many. They be too wrapped in theological doctrines and their own salvation. Why, there be one, Timothy Crusoe by name, who is so great a textuary that he will, I'll warrant you, pray for two hours together in Scripture language! While I —I be interested in the streets and highways, and those who live therein.'

'Streets and highways, hey?'

'I would be a chronicler,' persisted the lad doggedly, 'setting down faithfully all I have seen and heard. Or so much of it as I can recall.'

'That cannot be much—yet.'

'I can remember the Restoration, and the Great Pestilence, and the Fire, while to-day—to-day, have I not sat at meat with Master John Milton?'

Milton gave one of his rare laughs. 'His Majesty's Court, methinks, where there is ever advancement for subtle arguments and a flattering tongue, should be *thy* sphere, boy. But whatever thy destiny, ply thy pen faithfully, and take with thee a blind old man's blessing.'

[1731]

Again London glittered and toiled in the April sunshine. But it was fifty-eight years later—and the loom of History spins fast. The Merry Monarch long ago made his last jest, his Papist brother his last confession. Dour Dutch William, who followed, with Mary his wife, and Anne, and the first George—all were shadows now.

George the Second reigned.

In Ropemakers' Alley, Moorfields, whither he had come from Kent in the previous year, an old, tired man was lodging; '*a middle-sized, spare man*'—so a Government handbill had once described him, '*of a brown complexion and dark-brown coloured hair, a hooked nose, a sharp chin, and a large mole near his mouth.*' The dark-brown coloured hair was grey and sparse, the hooked nose thin and fierce as a beak, the cheeks sunken. For he was over seventy now. The magnet of the City in which he had spent his boyhood, whose alleys and squares had been his playground, had drawn him from the peace and silence of green fields. Fore Street itself was near, though none living there now would recognize him.

He was alone, not merely physically, but mentally. He who for fifty years had been exploiting human nature, he, the cynic who had played without scruple on his fellow-creatures' credulity and ignorance, had now no friend whom he could trust. Even his children he suspected and avoided.

He lay upon a bed, his half-open eyes fixed on the ceiling. He had been ill from a fever, but that had gone, and only lethargy, not in itself unpleasant, remained.

The door opened, and the landlady's son came in, a loose-limbed lout of about fourteen.

'My mother's respects, Mr. Defoe, and is there aught you need?'

The man on the bed turned. 'Has any message come?'

The boy shook his head.

'I had thought, perchance, that my daughter Sophy —What's thy name?'

'Jack, Sir.'

'Ah. Many years since I wrote a book called *Colonel Jack*. A writer may choose what names he will for his characters. Nay, he may even change his own, if he have the mind. My father's name possessed but one syllable, but "Defoe" possessed more weight and dignity. Hence I am as you know me.'

The boy stood listening awkwardly to the weary old voice. He had neither the tact to go, nor skill enough to change the subject to another which was consuming him with curiosity.

'Mother says—' he made the effort at last, 'that the adventures of the mariner, Robinson Crusoe, were

89

writ by your hand, she having read the story of them first in a printed sheet, and afterwards in a book lent her by my uncle Peter, who is a bookseller. He himself sat reading it from dusk to cockcrow, to the anger of my Aunt Ellen. He told us, too——'

The man on the bed interrupted. 'Mr. Selkirk, of Juan Fernandez—'tis he whom you have to thank for the notion of the story. Though much of the latter part, mark you, was writ as an allegory. They've taught you at school what an allegory is, hey?'

'I—I have heard the word, Mr. Defoe.'

'When I was your age I spoke with John Milton. He had a fine house not far from here. With a garden. His wife was young. His daughters were ungrateful, and hated him. . . . An' I hear from Sophy, I'll die a happier man. He warned me to wield a faithful pen. Mine has been faithless many times, but how shall a man serve his country if the country be corrupt and the man inflexible? Inflexible—d'ye know what that means, boy? Unbending. John Milton did not bend. And they could not break him. But I, who am shortly leaving this earthly kingdom for one where there is no strife, am a broken man. . . . I can remember the Great Pestilence and the Fire that followed. So I told Master Milton when, having heard that I would become author, he asked what I would write about. And I said, too, "Have I not sat at meat with *thee*!" That pleased him mightily. He was blind, but not in utter darkness, the darkness which is profound as the grave. . . . If word should come from my daughter, and come too late, I charge

90

you tell her that I loved her above all else to the last breath.'

The voice of the old man dwindled to a murmur and the murmur into silence.

The boy lingered for a moment and then stole on tiptoe from the room.

Samuel Pepys

From The Diary

May 1st. Up betimes and my father with me. . . . After dinner we all took horse, and I, upon a horse hired of Mr. Game, saw him out of London, at the end of Bishopsgate Streete, and so I turned and rode, with some trouble, through the fields, and then Holborne etc., towards Hide Parke, whither all the world, I think, are going; and in my going, almost thither, met W. Howe coming galloping upon a little crop black nag; it seems one that was taken in some ground of my Lord's, by some mischance being left by his master, a thiefe; this horse being found with black cloth eares on, and false mayne, having none of his owne; and I back again with him to the Chequer, at Charing Crosse, and there put up my owne dull jade, and by his advice saddled a delicate stone-horse of Captain Ferrers's, and with that rid in state to the Parke, where none better mounted than I almost, but being in a throng of horses, seeing the King's riders showing tricks with their managed horses, which were very strange, my stone-horse was very troublesome, and begun to fight with other horses, to the dangering him and myself, and with much ado I got out, and kept myself out of harm's way. Here I saw

nothing good, neither the King, nor my Lady Castle-
maine, nor any great ladies or beauties being there,
there being more pleasure a great deal at an ordinary
day; or else those few good faces that there were choked
up with the many bad ones, there being people of all
sorts to some thousands, I think. Going thither in the
highway, just by the Parke gate, I met a boy in a
sculler boat, carried by a dozen people at least, rowing
as hard as he could drive, it seems upon some wager.
By and by, about seven or eight o'clock, homeward;
and changing my horse again, I rode home, coaches
going in great crowds to the further end of the towne
almost. In my way, in Leadenhall Streete, there was
morris-dancing, which I have not seen a great while.
So set my horse up at Game's, paying 5s. for him, and
went to hear Mrs. Turner's daughter play on the
harpsicon; but, Lord! it was enough to make any man
sicke to hear her; yet I was forced to commend her
highly. So home to supper. This day Captain Grove
sent me a side of pork, which was the oddest present,
sure, that was ever made any man; and the next, I
remember I told my wife, I believe would be a pound
of candles, or a shoulder of mutton; but the fellow do it
in kindness, and is one I am beholden to. So to bed
very weary.

John Milton

From L'ALLEGRO

Haste thee, nymph, and bring with thee
Jest and youthful Jollity,
Quips, and cranks, and wanton wiles,
Nods, and becks, and wreathèd smiles,

Such as hang on Hebe's cheek,
And love to live in dimple sleek;
Sport that wrinkled Care derides,
And Laughter holding both his sides.
Come, and trip it as you go
On the light fantastic toe;
And in thy right hand lead with thee
The mountain nymph, sweet Liberty;
And, if I give thee honour due,
Mirth, admit me of thy crew,
To live with her, and live with thee,
In unreproved pleasures free;
To hear the lark begin his flight,
And singing startle the dull night,
From his watch-tower in the skies,
Till the dappled dawn doth rise;
Then to come, in spite of sorrow,
And at my window bid good-morrow,
Through the sweet-brier, or the vine,
Or the twisted eglantine.
While the cock with lively din
Scatters the rear of darkness thin,
And to the stack, or the barn-door,
Stoutly struts his dames before:
Oft listening how the hounds and horn
Cheerly rouse the slumbering morn,
From the side of some hoar hill,
Through the high wood echoing shrill:
Sometime walking, not unseen,
By hedge-row elms, on hillocks green,
Right against the eastern gate
Where the great Sun begins his state
Robed in flames and amber light,
The clouds in thousand liveries dight;
While the ploughman, near at hand,

93

Whistles o'er the furrowed land,
And the milkmaid singeth blithe,
And the mower whets his scythe,
And every shepherd tells his tale
Under the hawthorn in the dale.

.   .   .   .

Hard by, a cottage chimney smokes
From betwixt two aged oaks,
Where Corydon and Thyrsis, met,
Are at their savoury dinner set
Of herbs, and other country messes,
Which the neat-handed Phillis dresses;
And then in haste her bower she leaves,
With Thestylis to bind the sheaves;
Or, if the earlier season lead,
To the tanned haycock in the mead,
Sometimes with secure delight
The upland hamlets will invite,
When the merry bells ring round,
And the jocund rebecks sound
To many a youth and many a maid,
Dancing in the chequered shade;
And young and old come forth to play
On a sunshine holiday,
Till the live-long day-light fail;
Then to the spicy nut-brown ale,
With stories told of many a feat,
How Faery Mab the junkets eat:—
She was pinched and pulled, she said;
And he by Friar's lantern led;
Tells how the grudging goblin sweat
To earn his cream-bowl duly set,
When in one night, ere glimpse of morn,
His shadowy flail hath threshed the corn,

That ten day-labourers could not end;
Then lies him down the lubber fiend,
And, stretched out all the chimney's length,
Basks at the fire his hairy strength;
And crop-full out of doors he flings,
Ere the first cock his matin rings.

Thus done the tales, to bed they creep.
By whispering winds soon lulled asleep.

John Milton

From SAMSON AGONISTES

This, this is he; softly a while;
Let us not break in upon him.
O change beyond report, thought, or belief!
See how he lies at random, carelessly diffused
With languished head unpropt,
As one past hope, abandoned,
And by himself given over,
In slavish habit, ill-fitted weeds
O'er-worn and soiled.
Or do my eyes misrepresent? Can this be he,
That heroic, that renowned,
Irresistible Samson? whom unarmed
No strength of man or fiercest wild beast could with-
     stand;
Who tore the lion, as the lion tears the kid;
Ran on embattled armies clad in iron,
And, weaponless himself,
Made arms ridiculous, useless the forgery
Of brazen shield and spear, the hammered cuirass,
Chalybean-tempered steel, and frock of mail

95

Adamantean proof;
But safest he who stood aloof,
When insupportably his foot advanced,
In scorn of their proud arms and warlike tools,
Spurned them to death by troops. The bold Ascolanite
Fled from his lion ramp; old warriors turned
Their plated backs under his heel,
Or grovelling soiled their crested helmets in the dust.

John Milton

On His Blindness

When I consider how my light is spent
   Ere half my days, in this dark world and wide,
   And that one talent which is death to hide
Lodged with me useless, though my soul more bent
To serve therewith my Maker, and present
   My true account, lest He returning chide,—
   Doth God exact day-labour, light denied?
I fondly ask:—But Patience, to prevent
That murmur, soon replies: God doth not need
   Either man's works, or His own gifts: who best
   Bear His mild yoke, they serve Him best: His state
Is kingly; thousands at His bidding speed
   And post o'er land and ocean without rest:
   They also serve who only stand and wait.

Daniel Defoe

From Robinson Crusoe

It would have made a Stoick smile to have seen me
and my little Family sit down to Dinner; there was my
Majesty, the Prince and Lord of the whole Island; I

96

had the Lives of all my Subjects at my absolute command. I could hang, draw, give Liberty, and take it away, and no Rebels among all my Subjects. Then to see how like a King I din'd, too, all alone, attended by my servants; Poll, as if he had been my favourite, was the only Person permitted to talk to me. My Dog, who was now grown very old and crazy, and had found no Species to Multiply his Kind upon, sat always at my Right Hand, and two Cats, one on one Side the Table, and one on the other, expecting now and then a Bit from my Hand, as a mark of special Favour.

Daniel Defoe

From COLONEL JACK

When he (my comrade) had got it (the Bag of Money) he came out to me, who stood at the Door; and pulling me by the sleeve, Run, Jack, says he, for our lives; and away he scours, and I after him, never resting, or scarce looking about me, till we got quite up into Fenchurch-Street, through Lime-Street, into Leadenhall-Street, down St. Mary-Axe, to London-Wall, then through Bishopsgate-Street, and down Old Bedlam into Moorfields. By this time we were neither of us able to run very fast, nor need we have gone so far, for I never found that anybody pursued us. When we got into Moorfields, and began to take breath, I ask him, what it was frighted him so? Fright me, you Fool, says he, I have got a devilish great Bag of Money. A bag! said I; Ay, ay, said he, let us get out into the fields where nobody can see us, and I'll show it to you. So away he had me through Long-Alley, and across Hog-Lane, and Holywell-lane, into the middle of the great Field, which, since that, has been called the Farthing

97

Pie-house Fields. There we would have sat down, but it was all full of Water; so we went on, crossed the road at Anniseed Cleer, and went into the Field where now the great Hospital stands; and finding a bye place, we sat down, and he pulls out the Bag.

Daniel Defoe

From A Tour through the Whole Island of Great Britain

Gravesend

When a Merchant Ship comes down from London (if they have the Tide of Ebb under Foot, or a fresh gale of Wind from the West, so that they have, what they call Fresh-Way, and the Ships come down apace), they generally hand some of their sails, haul up a Fore-Sail, or Main-Sail, or lower the Fore-top-Sail; so to slaken her way, as soon as they come to the Old Man's Head; when they open the Reach, which they call Gravesend Reach, which begins about a mile and a half above the Town, they do the like, to signify that they intend to bring too as the Sailors call it, and come to Anchor.

As soon as they come among the Ships that are riding in the Road (as there are always a great many) the Centinel on the Block-House, as they call it, on Gravesend side, fires his musquet, which is to tell the Pilot he must bring too; if he comes on, as soon as the ship passes Broad-side with the Block-house, the Centinel fires again, which is as much as to say, why don't you bring too? If he drives a little further, he fires a Third Time, and the Language of that is Bring too immediately, and let go your Anchor, or We will make you.

98

If the Ship continues to drive down, and does not let
go her Anchor, the Gunner of the Fort is fetched, and
he fires a Piece of Cannon tho' without Ball; and that
is still a Threat, tho' with some Patience, and is to say
Will you come to an Anchor, or won't you? If he still
ventures to go on, by which he gives them to understand he intends to run for it; then the Gunner fires
again, and with a Shot, and that Shot is a Signal to
the Fortress over the River (viz.) Tilbury Fort (which I
described in my account of Essex) and they immediately let fly at the Ship from the Guns on the East
Bastion; and after that from all the Guns they can
bring to bear upon her; it is very seldom that a Ship
will venture their Shot, because they can reach her all
the way unto the Hope, and round the Hope-Point
almost to Hole-Haven.

Daniel Defoe

From THE TRUE-BORN ENGLISHMAN

These are the Heroes who despite the *Dutch*,
And rail at new-come Foreigners so much;
Forgetting that themselves are all deriv'd
From the most Scoundrel Race that ever liv'd,
A horrid Crowd of Rambling Thieves and Drones,
Who ransacked Kingdoms and dispeopled Towns.

The *Pict* and Painted *Britain*, Treach'rous *Scot*,
By Hunger, Theft, and Rapine, hither brought.
Norwegian Pirates, Buccaneering *Danes*,
Whose Red-hair'd Offspring ev'ry where remains.
Who, join'd with *Norman-French*, compound the
    Breed
From whence your *True-Born-Englishmen* proceed!

99

CRABBED AGE AND YOUTH

Milton (*Bell's Miniature Series*)	G. C. Williamson
,, (*Great Writers Series*)	Richard Garnett
" Once Upon a Time "	Charles Knight
The Story of Nell Gwynne	Peter Cunningham
England's Antiphon	George Macdonald
Daniel Defoe	Wilfred Whitten
Votive Tablets	Edmund Blunden

CHAPTER FIVE

THE COMET AND THE STAR

[1727]

LONDON WAS ALMOST INTOLERABLY hot and quite intolerably noisy. But it was easy to outdistance the raucous voice of that hobbledehoy of a City, and twelve miles from Charing Cross one achieved rural isolation —two centuries ago.

There, in his beloved 'Twittenham', Mr. Alexander Pope had dwelt these eight years past, having amassed a comfortable fortune from a metrical translation of the *Iliad* which was possibly his own work, and another of the *Odyssey* which quite certainly was not. Neither, whatever their merits as poetry, was Homer, which in view of Pope's almost complete ignorance of Greek was hardly surprising. But as translations they exactly suited the early eighteenth-century intelligentsia, and the intelligentsia backed its fancy to the tune of about eight thousand pounds. There, in a demesne which began in a straggling little spinney, plunged underground for the width of the road, and emerged upon a lawn and the river bank, the poet nursed his frail body and his vigorous enmities, received his admirers and their homage, and exhibited, in short, all the qualities which belonged so typically to himself and the century.

Three men paced side by side in the semi-darkness of the celebrated grotto which linked the genteel villa with the genteel river. Frequently they halted, not because they were unfamiliar with the singular collection of objects which diversified the walls, but because the grotto, together with its temple 'wholly composed of shells in the rustic manner', was the delight and pride of their host. 'A perpetual rill of the clearest water' echoed there, and when the grotto was lighted up 'rays of light were reflected with pieces of looking-glass of angular form'. And in the ceiling was a star-shaped mirror from which hung an orb-shaped lamp of thin alabaster.

Pope's friends had been invited to contribute towards the grotto's bizarre adornments. They had responded with more enthusiasm than good taste. Her Dowager Grace of Cleveland had sent amethyst and spar from Raby; Borlase, the antiquary, semi-precious stones from Cornwall and Devon; Mr. Spence, lava from Mount Vesuvius and a fragment of marble from the grotto of Egeria; others had added gold and silver ore from Peru and old Spain, crystals from the Hartz Mountains, coral, and petrified moss. There were even humming-birds, complete with their nests, to confuse the student of mineralogy and confound the ornithologist. Upon this retreat Pope himself had spent a thousand pounds and written a poem which included *The feast of reason and the flow of soul* among its lines. In common with the garden and house which it linked, it was his solace and his escape. He possessed his own waterman, as well as his own gardener—'Honest John Searle', who has left us his own plan of the Grotto, which to the end of his life was merely 'The Underground Passage'.

In the garden itself Pope had contrived to include, amid winding walks, 'a large mount, a vineyard, two smaller mounts, a bowling green, a wilderness, a grove, an orangery, a garden-house and a kitchen-garden'—a truly staggering example of *multum in parvo* which cost, from first to last, another four thousand pounds.

If the three friends formed an odd trio, Pope himself was the oddest. His own whimsically exaggerated description of himself as President of the Little Club may serve as an introduction. 'Elected President not only because he is the shortest of us all, but because he has entertained so just a sense of his stature as to go generally in black, that he may appear yet less; to that perfection is he arrived that he stoops as he walks. . . . He is a lively little creature, with long arms and legs; a spider is no ill emblem of him; he has been taken at a distance for a small windmill.' Like most people who jest at their own deformities, he was sensitive to caricatures by his enemies. But no caricatures, self-sketched or not, could defraud him of those quick and piercing eyes and nobly intellectual forehead. A complex character, displaying generosity and pettiness, a sense of humour and a pompous secretiveness, a masculine clarity of thought with a feminine concentration upon irrelevant trivialities. His voice was clear and boyish, his manner authoritative. The note of authority was justified. For more than thirty years out of his compara-

tively short life Pope was so completely and unequivo-
cally the focus of poetical thought in England that he
might almost be said to comprise the poetry of his
period.

On his left was a ruddy, tubby little man with a
double chin, very modishly dressed and carrying a
tasselled cane. He was John Gay, dramatist, poet and
dandy. He had formed the acquaintance of Pope as
long ago as 1711, and when, two years later, he had
published *Rural Sports*, his first work of any importance,
he had dedicated the book to Pope. Pope was physically
incapable of any sports at all—he had, he confessed, 'a
crazy carcase', and could not even stand until he had
been laced in a sort of armour—while Gay himself
'could not distinguish rye from barley, or an oak from a
crab-tree', and 'his highest country skill was fishing for
gudgeon'. Nevertheless the book was a success.

A play, a 'tragi-comic pastoral farce' entitled *The
What D'ye Call It?* and a picturesque poem *Trivia* were
his only real successes in several lean years. Drifting
from friend to friend, and half-starving when no
friend's hospitality was available, John Gay must
have been in need of all his happy-go-lucky
philosophy. But in 1720 his poems, published in a
quarto volume, brought in a profit of a thousand
pounds. The jubilant author invested the money in
shares which soared until, on paper, his capital
amounted to twenty thousand pounds. Alas, the times
were unlucky for far shrewder investors than Gay. The
'South Sea Bubble', originating in 1711 as an honest

trading concern, had developed into a series of crazy speculations, and ended in disaster which ruined not merely those who took the risks with their eyes open, but the unfortunate annuitants who had been induced to exchange sound Government stock for its shares. Great reputations, including those of the Chancellor of the Exchequer, Lord Sunderland and Lord Stanhope, were dragged in the mud: Gay, the amiable, merry, greedy and charming Gay, lost every penny of his thousand pounds.

He turned to a great lady for help and comfort, and his luck did not fail him. The Duchess of Queensberry became his patroness. Once more he achieved leisure and freedom. He wrote a book of fables, he studied Life, he kept warm his friendships.

In *Trivia* he had collaborated with the third of the trio—a fantastic partnership, for the third man was one whose humour was savage satire, and whose pen was impelled by hate and tipped with venom. A man whom the Fates taunted intolerably, and from whom even Death, merciless as Life, stood aloof until long after the magnificent intelligence had crumbled and was in ruins. A massive forehead, dark eyebrows arched above full-lidded, prominent eyes of burning blue, an aquiline nose, a firm, handsome mouth—thus one sketches, in his sixtieth year, the Very Reverend Jonathan Swift, Master of Arts and Doctor of Divinity, Vicar of Laracor by Trim in the Diocese of Meath in the Kingdom of Ireland, Prebendary of Dunlavin in St. Patrick's Cathedral. Of English parentage, cousin to Dryden—

dead now a generation—and kinsman to Herrick, Swift was born in Ireland, and by Ireland, which was fated to adore him as he was fated to detest her, was claimed and enslaved. From a school in Kilkenny and an embittered career at Trinity College he had escaped for a few brief years to Moor Park. There Sir William Temple, another kinsman, yawned over his library, dabbled with cautious and courtly reserve in politics, and amusedly tolerated the insubordinate temper of his poor relation and secretary. There that poor relation had met a child named Esther Johnson. He had taught her, re-named her 'Stella', and sown the seeds of a love that was to blossom into one of the romances of all time. Sir William had died in 1699, Stella, now a middle-aged woman, was living near the Deanery which marked the summit of Swift's progress in the Church, and Swift himself was the possessor of a reputation as a pamphleteer, satirist and wit which was now at its zenith. Long ago Addison had presented him with a book inscribed, '*To Dr. Jonathan Swift, the Most Agreeable Companion, the Truest Friend, and the Greatest Genius of the Age.*' But the times had changed, and Swift had changed with them. He had left Addison and his other Whig friends for the opposite camp. As a Tory he had vehemently attacked them. If Anne had trusted, instead of detested him, the coveted bishopric might have rewarded him. And with her death the Whigs came again into power. Three steeds he harnessed to his chariot—Politics, the Church and Literature, and in the end paid the penalty which intellect inexorably pays when there is no greatness of character to support it. And contributing to the final ruin must be added that unexplained and inexplicable attraction which drew women to him as to a magnet, to their torment and his own.

Frustrated in politics Swift might be. But he had paid this visit to England under no cloud so far as his friendships were concerned, from the Princess of Wales downwards. To Mrs. Howard, her lady-in-waiting, he wrote with gay familiarity, 'I desire you will order H.R.H. to go to Richmond as soon as she can this summer because she will have the pleasure of my neighbourhood'. And twice afterwards, by the Princess' own request, he met her. But the death of George the First suddenly and unexpectedly turned the tables. The Princess of Wales became Queen of England and its real ruler. As Queen, she turned, after a brief interval, to the leadership of Walpole, Swift's inexorable enemy. Swift withdrew to the oblivion of lodgings in London and the hospitality of the villa at Twickenham.

. . . .

The three friends emerged from the twilit grotto into daylight, and for a space lingered on the green slope that led down to the river.

''Tis passing strange,' meditated Swift, 'that Pope here, who has been spurred into winning so large a fortune with his pen that he need ask nothing of the great, and so can meet 'em as his equals, yet hateth the whole tribe. While thou, Jack—' he clapped a kindly

107

hand on Gay's shoulder—'with an understanding of low life and an affinity with them that live it which should get thee crowned Laureate of the Kingdom of Them That Have Nothing, must, through poverty and other frailties, forever dog the steps of the wealthy and influential.'

'And Doctor Swift himself?' snapped Pope.

'I?' The Dean's lips curved in a half-smile. 'I must needs spend such hours as I can spare from the study of Nature in the study of Nature's most ignoble product—man, lest I might forget my contempt for the species.'

'The poor have fewer vices—and the greater excuse for possessing every vice,' murmured Gay.

'True. Wherefore—' Swift abruptly abandoned his philosophy—'write a pastoral, painting as intimately as may be the rural follies of Seven Dials, the amiable peccadillos of Drury Lane, the innocent diversions of Newgate, and concluding with a fandango of the merriest nature at Tyburn!'

'Low Life, with a Beggars' Chorus!' cried Pope. 'What more fitting enterprise for thy pen!'

Gay turned his plump, cheerful face from one friend to the other.

'A pastoral,' he mused. 'Perhaps. And yet——'

'There need be no "perhaps" '—Pope shook a minatory finger—'though idleness may clog the pen. Ah, Jack, Jack, unless a day come when a poet can spell out his lines by the mere touch of a finger-tip upon a key, and ink and quills become as obsolete as chain-mail,

I'll warrant old age will have claimed thee before the first stanza be set down!'

'You do me injustice. Have I not already written many——'

'Pages, quires and reams?' Swift raised mocking brows. 'Verily. But never a footman's, porter's or chairman's pastoral among them. And did I not bring forward the theme seven long years ago?'

'It has possibilities. But I cannot see it as a pastoral.'

'A drama, then. With the scene a tavern, friend Quin as hero, and a drinking-chorus, by a rabble of pickpockets and cut-throats.'

''Tis an idea. And if ever 'tis produced, I'll remit my indebtedness with a dedication.'

A spatter of rain fell. Pope, who had a cat-like detestation of getting wet, moved towards the house.

'Come,' he said, and led the way into the stone-paved hall, 'lest a shower fatally chill the new-born ardour of our Beggars' Laureate.'

·　　·　　·　　·　　·　　·　　·　　·　　·

The afternoon had passed into the dusk of the evening. Gay had returned to London, borrowing Pope's chaise —the chaise in which the owner was irreverently nicknamed 'Homer in a walnut-shell'. Swift and Pope were seated on either side of the empty fireplace.

If Swift had wanted conversation, he would have drawn up his chair on his host's left, since his right ear was the one which heard best. But now the two old friends were silent, each lost in memories.

Pope sat huddled in a chair which engulfed his little monkey-like figure. His face was drawn; the lines in his forehead—noted afterwards by a shrewd French sculptor to whom the poet gave a sitting—had deepened. Physical suffering, never far distant, had suddenly tightened its grip on that frail body. But there was a malicious sparkle in his eyes. With Swift, Arbuthnot and Gay as fellow-contributors, he had lately completed the first two volumes of the *Miscellanies*, and therein at least was material warranted to sting to fury the lesser men of letters who imitated, sneered at, vilified and envied the little dictator, so secure in his eminence and his country retreat. They would attack; he, in turn, would retaliate. Their own generation should laugh them out of court; posterity should remember them only to jeer. The lips that were never known to part in a laugh curved in a malicious smile. He flashed a glance at Swift, motionless, silent, an admirable companion for a man whose vitality habitually ebbed as the day wore on, until by nightfall he was torpid and only half awake. (Did not Pope fall asleep on the very afternoon when His Royal Highness the Prince of Wales deigned to visit him, and not only to visit him, but to hold forth on the art of Poetry!)

$$\cdot \quad \cdot \quad \cdot \quad \cdot \quad \cdot \quad \cdot \quad \cdot \quad \cdot$$

Swift was seated with eyes half-closed, head thrown back and hands clasped behind it, wig awry. His thoughts, like those of his friend, were bitter. But there was no saving humour to mitigate the bitterness. *The*

Travels of Lemuel Gulliver, M.D., that strange and savage satire which (final irony), its satire forgotten, was to confer upon him immortality as the inventor of a children's classic; that, just published anonymously, was not in his thoughts. Stella's face haunted him, Stella's voice echoed in his tired brain. She was in Dublin, he in England. And more than the grey and rolling waste of the Irish Channel sundered them. . . . Stella, whom he had taught in the days when he was a gauche and scowling hobbledehoy earning twenty pounds a year and his keep at Moor Park, a paid dependent at whom the very lackeys sneered. Stella, uncomplaining, adoring. . . .

There had been another woman, another slave, another worshipper—'Vanessa'—again Swift's own half-poetic, half-mocking name—Esther Vanhomrigh to the rest of the world. Less feminine, more assertive, an Amazonian spirit whom only her passion for Swift subdued and made abject. He had met her and her mother in London; the Fates had brought her to Ireland within a mile or so of Stella. Too late Swift had struggled to return to the pleasant shallows of their early friendship. Unhappy, tormented Vanessa! Her letters wring the soul with their poignant appeals for the love which Swift could not bestow, perhaps because such love as he had was already Stella's, perhaps because there was no capacity for its bestowal. He might write playfully, charmingly; so he wrote, too, to Stella. He might plead his infirmities and suggest younger and more fitting partners. But she refused to be cheated. She discovered her rival, and wrote, demanding a plain answer concerning Stella's relationship to Swift. Swift saw and read the letter (some say it was addressed direct to himself). The incarnation of fury, he rode back with it to the writer, flung it before her, and without a word rode away again. . . . Vanessa wrote no more, asked no more indiscreet questions. The shock of that last encounter killed her.

That was a four-year-old story now. Stella still lived, her eyesight failing, her health failing, happy only when he was near, loving him unwaveringly. Though he might be punctiliously cold, remote, even harsh, she asked no other companionship. Enough that she might come from her lodgings to his house, and there on Sunday evenings play hostess to his friends. Swift, 'most unhappy of men', carried the secret of their relationship to the grave with him. If he had no right to a closer human tie, Stella was his in spirit. In his contact with the world, in the society of learned men who were petty and great men who were dull, of the wits and fops who presented themselves, sheep-like, for the flashing blade of his scorn, she was the one human being who never changed, who never failed him. The Irish might hail him as a champion of their liberties. But Swift shrank scornfully from their homage. What mental stimulus he sought was to be found in England.

He had paid a visit there the year before. Then, as now, Stella had called him, a voiceless, unwritten call. He had answered it, and she had recovered. Now she called again.

He would not go.

He drifted into a doze. His strange, incurable giddiness left him, his deafness vanished. He was in his study at the Deanery. The door opened silently; Stella entered. She smiled. Her dear arms clung about his neck. Then, suddenly, Vanessa came. Agony stabbed him; he awoke, to discover a sharp angle of the chair cutting his side.

'A mighty restless sleeper!' commented Pope mockingly from his seat. 'Has Walpole snatched another bishopric from those twitching fingers?'

Swift straightened his wig and rose unsteadily to his feet. 'I am growing aged and afflicted,' he grumbled, 'whilst you are younger, but no less afflicted. For which reasons I will betake me to London again, where we may not add to the sum of human misery by wearying each other.'

Pope did not dispute the point. Himself a paradox, he understood Swift, a greater paradox, as probably no other man understood him.

'Perhaps you are right. But here comes Honest John with the mail.'

'He brings no good news for me,' muttered Swift. His face paled as Pope handed him a letter. For a long time he could not bring himself to break the seal.

Stella, ran the message, was at the point of death.

. . . .

He did not go to her, though he was wrenched by grief. Heaven alone knew why he delayed, or what struggles the delay cost him. Possibly it was merely his own physical wretchedness which made him shrink from the journey. Noon on the following day found him in his London lodgings. The house at Twickenham, with its grotto and pleasant garden, was left behind, never to be seen by those fierce blue eyes again.

From London he wrote to Sheridan, a friend in Ireland.

'I have just received yours of August 24th. I kept it an hour in my pocket with all the suspense of a man who expected to hear the worst news that fortune could give. . . . What have I to do in the world? I am able to hold up my sorry head no longer.'

Pope, too, wrote to Sheridan. He and a certain Doctor Arbuthnot had been so troubled about Swift that they had tracked him to London. What they feared as the outcome of his sullen and desperate wretchedness may be guessed. But the worst did not happen. '*His physician, Dr. Arbuthnot, assures me that he will soon be well,*' so reported the devoted Pope. '*I will not leave him a day, until I see him better.*'

Swift's illness abated. Stella did not die. He decided to go back to Dublin, despite a broad hint from Mrs. Howard, the Queen's favourite, that his departure just then would mean ruin to his last chances of promotion. He had finished with Court intrigues for ever. He left behind him at his lodgings a farewell letter for Pope.

During the homeward journey he recovered his hearing. There is still extant a joint letter from Pope and Gay, whose anxiety on his account had been acute. Its very levity bears witness to their relief. '*No doubt,*' they wrote, '*your ears knew well that there was nothing worth hearing in England.*'

Swift reached Holyhead only in time to discover that the packet for Dublin had just left. There was nothing for it but to spend a week in smoky lodgings, while the shipmaster of the next boat awaited calmer weather and a fresh cargo of passengers. The Dean filled in the interval by setting down in diary form a record of his wretched surroundings and the wearying succession of trivialities which filled his hours. He described in detail the solitary visitor to Holyhead, the behaviour of the shipmaster, an indigestible dinner of tough fowl and sour wine, and the dream about Bolingbroke and Pope which followed.

At long last the ship sailed, though the weather was still stormy. He reached Dublin safely.

Stella still lived to welcome him. The old routine was resumed.

He heard from Pope. The letter left in Swift's London lodgings had moved that cynical little autocrat to tears. He was grieved that Swift should find himself '*easier in any house than mine*'. To which Swift wrote in reply, '*I thought it best to return to what fortune had made my home. Two sick friends never did well together; such an office is fitter for servants and humble companions, to whom it is wholly indifferent whether we give them trouble or not.*'

Later he wrote, '*If it pleases God, I shall readily make a third journey*'. It was a futile hope; God did not please. The rest of his life was to be spent in Ireland. There, fulfilling his own exceeding bitter prophecy, he was to perish 'like a poisoned rat in a hole'.

Stella died three months after his return. The end came so suddenly that Swift was actually entertaining a dinner-party at the Deanery when the news reached him. The party did not break up; it was midnight before the giver of the feast found himself alone. . . . Then, when the guests were gone, when the last wine-glass had been drained, and the last jest had rippled its way along the table, Swift retreated to his study. And there, among dusty regiments of folios and quartos, with the shelves of smaller volumes above them (but never one of English fiction), he took quill and paper and wrote.

Of Stella; of her tenderness and wistful grace; of her beauty of soul and body. Of how she had been to him his good angel, his better self, his guiding star. . . . Until at last the weary hand could write no more, and the scratching of the pen ceased and Swift slept—to dream of the long-ago days when he had written not of Stella, but to her, in the baby language which was one of the little, exquisite bonds between them. Letters in which, from a London lodging, he had chronicled the happenings of a time when the world—their world—held happiness, and perhaps hope of greater happiness. A world in which all the harshness and bitterness and futile strivings after power and position might cease and be forgotten.

．　．　．　．　．　．　．　．　．

Thus he dreamed, his cheek resting upon a folded

packet he had taken from his bureau. The packet held little—'*Only a woman's hair*', Swift had written, long ago, on the back.

Yes, but Stella's hair.

Alexander Pope

From An Essay on Man

Heav'n from all creatures hides the book of Fate,
All but the page prescribed, their present state;
From brutes what men, from men what spirits know:
Or who could suffer Being here below?
The lamb thy riot dooms to bleed to-day,
Had he thy Reason, would he skip and play?
Pleas'd to the last, he crops the flow'ry food,
And licks the hand just rais'd to shed his blood.
Oh, blindness to the future! kindly given,
That each may fill the circle mark'd by Heav'n;
Who sees with equal eye, as God of all,
A hero perish, or a sparrow fall,
Atoms or systems into ruin hurl'd,
And now a bubble burst, and now a world.

Hope humbly then; with trembling pinions soar;
Wait the great teacher Death; and God adore.
What future bliss, he gives not thee to know,
But gives that Hope to be thy blessing now.
Hope springs eternal in the human breast;
Man never Is, but always To be blest;
The soul, uneasy and confined from home,
Rests and expatiates in a life to come.

Lo, the poor Indian! whose untutor'd mind
Sees God in clouds, or hears him in the wind;

His soul, proud Science never taught to stray
Far as the solar walk, or milky way;
Yet simple Nature to his hope has giv'n,
Behind the cloud-topt hill, an humble heav'n;
Some safer world in depth of woods embrac'd,
Some happier island in the wat'ry waste,
Where slaves once more their native land behold,
No fiends torment, no Christians thirst for gold.
To Be, contents his natural desire,
He asks no Angel's wing, no Seraph's fire;
But thinks, admitted to that equal sky,
His faithful dog shall bear him company.

.   .   .   .

Cease then, nor ORDER Imperfection name:
Our proper bliss depends on what we blame.
Know thy own point: This kind, this due degree
Of blindness, weakness, Heav'n bestows on thee.
Submit.—In this, or any other sphere,
Secure to be as blest as thou canst bear:
Safe in the hand of one disposing Pow'r,
Or in the natal, or the mortal hour.
All nature is but Art, unknown to thee;
All Chance, Direction, which thou canst not see;
All Discord, Harmony not understood;
All partial Evil, universal Good;
And, spite of Pride, in erring Reason's spite,
One truth is clear, WHATEVER IS, IS RIGHT.

Alexander Pope

From PROLOGUE TO THE SATIRES

Shut, shut the door, good John! fatigued I said,
Tye up the knocker, say I'm sick, I'm dead.

118

THE COMET AND THE STAR

The Dog-Star rages! nay, 'tis past a doubt,
All Bedlam, or Parnassus, is let out:
Fire in each eye, and papers in each hand,
They rave, recite, and madden round the land.

What walls can guard me, or what shades can hide?
They pierce my thickets, thro' my Grot they glide.
By land, by water, they renew the charge,
They stop the chariot, and they board the barge.
No place is sacred, not the Church is free,
Ev'n Sunday shines no Sabbath-day to me;
Then from the Mint walks forth the Man of rhyme,
Happy! to catch me, just at Dinner-time.

Is there a Parson, much bemused in beer,
A maudlin Poetess, a rhyming Peer,
A Clerk, foredoom'd his father's soul to cross,
Who pens a Stanza when he should engross?
Is there, who locked from ink and paper, scrawls
With desp'rate charcoal round his darken'd walls?
All fly to TWIT'NAM, and in humble strain
Apply to me, to keep them mad—or vain.
Arthur, whose giddy son neglects the laws,
Imputes to me and my damned works the cause;
Poor Cornus sees his frantic wife elope,
And curses Wit, and Poetry, and Pope.

Friend to my Life! (which did you not prolong,
The world had wanted many an idle song)
What drop or nostrum can this plague remove?
Or which must end me, a Fool's wrath or love?
A dire dilemma! either way I'm sped,
If foes, they write, if friends, they read me dead.
Seiz'd and ty'd down to judge, how wretched I
Who can't be silent, and who will not lye;
To laugh, were want of goodness and of grace,

And to be grave, exceeds all Pow'r of face.
I sit with sad civility, I read
With honest anguish, and an aching head;
And drop at last, but in unwilling ears,
This saving counsel, 'Keep your piece nine years.'

Nine years! cries he, who high in Drury-lane,
Lull'd by soft Zephyrs thro' the broken pane,
Rhymes 'ere he wakes, and prints before Term ends,
Oblig'd by hunger, and request of friends;
The piece, you think, is incorrect? why take it,
I'm all submission, what you'd have it, make it.
Three things another's modest wishes bound,
My Friendship, and a Prologue, and ten pound.

.   .   .   .

Why did I write? what sin to me unknown
Dipt me in ink, my parents', or my own?
As yet a child, nor yet a fool to fame,
I lisp'd in numbers, for the numbers came.
I left no calling for this idle trade,
No duty broke, no father disobey'd.
The Muse but served to ease some friend, not Wife,
To help me through this long disease, my Life,
To second, ARBUTHNOT! thy Art and Care,
And teach, the Being you preserv'd, to bear.
But why then publish? Granville the polite,
And knowing Walsh, would tell me I could write;
Well-natur'd Garth inflam'd with early praise,
And Congreve lov'd, and Swift endur'd my lays;
The courtly Talbot, Somers, Sheffield read,
Ev'n mitred Rochester would nod the head,
And St. John's self (great Dryden's friends before)
With open arms receiv'd one Poet more.
Happy my studies, when by these approv'd!
Happier their author, when by these belov'd!

On ADDISON

Peace to all such, but were there one whose fires
True Genius kindles, and fair Fame inspires;
Blest with each talent and each art to please,
And born to write, converse, and live with ease;
Should such a man, too fond to rule alone,
Bear, like the Turk, no brother near the throne,
View him with scornful, yet with jealous eyes,
And hate for arts that caused himself to rise;
Damn with faint praise, assent with civil leer,
And, without sneering, teach the rest to sneer;
Willing to wound, and yet afraid to strike,
Just hint a fault, and hesitate dislike;
Alike reserved to blame or to commend,
A timorous foe, and a suspicious friend,
Dreading e'en fools, by flatterers besieged,
And so obliging that he ne'er obliged;
(Who, if two wits on rival themes contest,
Approves of each, but likes the worst the best);
Like Cato, give his little senate laws,
And sit attentive to his own applause;
While Wits and Templars every sentence raise,
And wonder with a foolish face of praise,—
Who but must laugh if such a man there be?
Who would not weep if Atticus were he?

Alexander Pope

LETTER TO DR. SWIFT

Oct. 2, 1727

It is a perfect trouble to me to write to you: and your
kind letter left for me at Mr. Gay's affected me so much
that it made me like a girl. I cannot tell what to say to

you; I only feel that I wish you well in every circum-
stance of life: that it is almost as good to be hated as to
be loved, considering the pain it is to minds of any
tender turn, to find themselves so utterly impotent
to do any good, or give any ease to those who deserve
most from us.   I would very fain know as soon as you
recover your complaints, or any part of them. Would to
God I could ease any of them, or had been able even
to have alleviated any! I found I was not, and truly it
grieved me. I was sorry to find you could think yourself easier in any house than mine, though at the same
time I can allow for a tenderness in your way of thinking, even when it seemed to want that tenderness. I
cannot explain my meaning, perhaps you know it; but
the best way of convincing you of my indulgence, will
be, if I live, to visit you in Ireland, and act there as
much in my own way as you did here in yours. I will
not leave your roof if I am ill. To your bad health
I fear there was added some disagreeable news from
Ireland, which might occasion your sudden departure;
for the last time I saw you, you assured me you
would not leave us the whole winter, unless your
health grew better; and I do not find it did. I never
complied so unwillingly in my life with any friend as
with you, in staying so entirely from you; nor could I
have had the constancy to do it, if you had not promised that, before you went, we should meet, and you
would send to us all to come. I have given your re-
membrances to those you mention in yours: we are
quite sorry for you—I mean for ourselves. I hope, as
you do, that we shall meet in a more durable and more
satisfactory state; but the less sure I am of that, the
more I would indulge it in this. We are to believe we
shall have something better than even a friend there,
but certainly here we have nothing so good. Adieu, for
122

this time; may you find every friend you go to as pleased and happy as every friend you went from is sorry and troubled.

John Gay

SWEET WILLIAM'S FAREWELL TO BLACK-EYED SUSAN

I

All in the Downs the fleet was moor'd
    The streamers waving in the wind,
When black-eyed Susan came aboard,
    Oh! where shall I my true love find!
Tell me, ye jovial sailors, tell me true,
If my sweet William sails among the crew.

II

William, who high upon the yard
    Rock'd with the billow to and fro,
Soon as her well-known voice he heard,
    He sigh'd and cast his eyes below;
The cord slides swiftly through his glowing hands,
And (quick as lightning) on the deck he stands.

III

So the sweet lark, high-poised in air,
    Shuts close his pinions to his breast
(If, chance, his mate's shrill call he hear)
    And drops at once into her nest.
The noblest captain in the British fleet,
Might envy William's lip those kisses sweet.

IV

O Susan, Susan, lovely dear,
  My vows shall ever true remain;
Let me kiss off that falling tear,
  We only part to meet again.
Change, as ye list, ye winds; my heart shall be
The faithful compass that still points to thee.

V

Believe not what the landsmen say,
  Who tempt with doubts thy constant mind;
They'll tell thee, sailors, when away,
  In ev'ry port a mistress find.
Yes, yes, believe them when they tell thee so,
For thou art present wheresoe'er I go.

VI

If to far India's coast we sail,
  Thy eyes are seen in di'monds bright,
Thy breath is Africk's spicy gale,
  Thy skin is ivory, so white,
Thus ev'ry beauteous object that I view,
Wakes in my soul some charm of lovely Sue.

VII

Though battle call me from thy arms,
  Let not my pretty Susan mourn;
Though cannons roar, yet safe from harms,
  William shall to his dear return.
Love turns aside the balls that round me fly,
Lest precious tears should drop from Susan's eye.

VIII

The boatswain gave the dreadful word,
   The sails their swelling bosom spread,
No longer must she stay aboard;
     They kiss'd, she sigh'd, he hung his head;
Her less'ning boat unwilling rows to land;
Adieu! she cries; and waved her lily hand.

John Gay

From TRIVIA

Nor should it prove thy less important care
To chuse a proper coat for winter's wear.
Now in thy trunk thy D'Oily habit fold,
The silken drugget ill can fence the cold;
The frieze's spongy nap is sok'd with rain,
And show'rs soon drench the camlet's cockled grain,
True Witney broad cloth with its shag unshorn,
Unpierc'd is in the lasting tempest worn;
Be this the horseman's fence, for who would wear
Amid the town the spoils of Russia's bear?
With the Roquelaure's clasp thy hands are pent,
Hands, that stretch'd forth invading harms prevent.
Let the loop'd Bavaroy the sop embrace,
Or his deep cloak bespatter'd o'er with lace,
That garment best the winter's rage defends,
Whose ample form without one plait depends;
By various names in various counties known,
Yet held in all the true Surtout alone;
Be thine of Kersey firm, tho' small the cost,
Then brave unwet the rain, unchill'd the frost.

If the strong cane support thy walking hand,
Chairmen no longer shall the wall command;

Ev'n sturdy carmen shall thy nod obey,
And rattling coaches stop to make thee way;
This shall direct thy cautious tread aright,
Though not one glaring lamp enliven night.
Let beaus their canes with amber tipt produce,
Be theirs for empty show, but thine for use.
In gilded chariots while they loll at ease,
And lazily insure a life's disease;
While softer chairs the tawdry load convey
To Court, to White's, Assemblies, or the Play;
Rosy complexioned health thy steps attends,
And exercise thy lasting youth defends.
Imprudent men heaven's choicest gifts profane,
Thus some beneath their arm support the cane;
The dirty point oft checks the careless pace,
And miry spots thy clean cravat disgrace;
O! may I never such misfortune meet,
May no such vicious walkers croud the street,
May Providence o'er shade me with her wings,
While the bold Muse experienc'd danger sings.

Jonathan Swift

From GULLIVER'S TRAVELS

GULLIVER AMONG THE LILLIPUTIANS

And here it may perhaps divert the curious reader, .o
give some account of my domestics, and my manner of
living in this country, during a residence of nine
months and thirteen days. Having a head mechani-
cally turned, and being likewise forced by necessity, I
had made for myself a table and chair convenient
enough, out of the largest trees in the royal park. Two
hundred sempstresses were employed to make me shirts
and linen for my bed and table, all of the strongest

and coarsest kind they could get; which, however, they were forced to quilt together in several folds, for the thickest was some degrees finer than lawn. Their linen is usually three inches wide, and three feet make a piece. The sempstresses took my measure as I lay on the ground, one standing at my neck, and another at my mid-leg, with a strong cord extended, that each held by the end, while a third measured the length of the cord with a rule of an inch long. Then they measured my right thumb, and desired no more; for, by a mathematical computation, that twice round the thumb is once round the wrist, and so on to the neck and the waist, and by the help of my old shirt, which I displayed on the ground before them for a pattern, they fitted me exactly. . . .

I had three hundred cooks to dress my victuals, in little convenient huts, built about my house, where they and their families lived, and prepared me two dishes apiece. I took up twenty waiters in my hand, and placed them on the table; a hundred more attended below on the ground, some with dishes of meat, and some with barrels of wine, and other liquors, slung on their shoulders; all which the waiters above drew up, as I wanted, in a very ingenious manner, by certain cords, as we draw the bucket up a well in Europe. A dish of their meat was a good mouthful, and a barrel of their liquor a reasonable draught.

Jonathan Swift

From CADENUS AND VANESSA

Cadenus many things had writ:
Vanessa much esteemed his wit,
And called for his Poetic Works:

Meantime the boy in secret lurks;
And, while the book was in her hand,
The urchin from his private stand
Took aim, and shot with all his strength
A dart of such prodigious length,
It pierced the feeble volume through,
And deep transfixed her bosom too.
Some lines, more moving than the rest,
Stuck to the point that pierced her breast,
And, borne directly to her heart,
With pains unknown increased her smart.

Jonathan Swift

APHORISMS

I never wonder to see men wicked, but I often wonder to see them not ashamed.

Do we not see how easily we pardon our own actions and passions, and the very infirmities of our bodies; why should it be wonderful to find us pardon our own dulness?

There is no vice or folly that requires so much nicety and skill to manage, as vanity; nor any, which, by ill-management, makes so contemptible a figure.

Observation is an old man's memory.

Eloquence, smooth and cutting, is like a razor whetted with oil.

Imaginary evils soon become real ones, by indulging our reflections on them; as he, who in a melancholy fancy sees something like a face on the wall or the wainscot, can, by two or three touches with a lead pencil, make it look visible, and agreeing with what he fancied.

Men of great parts are often unfortunate in the management of public business, because they are apt to go

128

out of the common road by the quickness of their imagination. This I once said to my lord Bolingbroke, and desired he would observe, that the clerks in his office used a sort of ivory knife with a blunt edge to divide a sheet of paper, which never failed to cut it even, only requiring a steady hand; whereas if they should make use of a sharp pen-knife, the sharpness would make it often go out of the crease, and disfigure the paper.

THE COMET AND THE STAR

Swift (English Men of Letters)	Leslie Stephen
Swift, The Mystery of His Life and Love	J. Hay
Pope	R. Carruthers
The Reign of Queen Anne	Justin McCarthy
Eighteenth Century Vignettes	Austin Dobson
The English Humourists of the Eighteenth Century	W. M. Thackeray
Gay (Introductory Essay to Poems, Abbey Classics)	F. Bickley

CHAPTER SIX

NUMBER THIRTY, GREEN ARBOUR SQUARE

[1759]

AUGUST WAS ending its fourth week in heat and discomfort. George the Second, that 'dull little man of low tastes', who kept his sentimentalities for his Germans and his Queen and his courage for the battlefield, and who had neither dignity, learning, morals nor wit, had been for nearly a third of a century in more or less peaceful occupation of the throne of his father.

It had been a year and a month prodigal of excitement, and provided plenty of excuses for patriotic huzza-ing. On the first of August, Prince Ferdinand of Brunswick-Lunenburg, commanding an extremely mixed force in Westphalia, had met the French at Minden and administered a terrific drubbing. Some three weeks later—to be exact, on the 20th,—Admiral Boscawen had overhauled the French fleet off Cape St. Vincent, and there repeated the drubbing process with a loss of thirty-six of his own men killed and one hundred and ninety-six wounded. In England, a wretched usher named Eugene Aram (later to provide my Lord Lytton with the plot of a poor novel and Mr. Thomas Hood with material for some mediocre verses) was being tried at York for the murder of one Daniel Clark fourteen years earlier, while Southsea Castle, affected by the unlucky conjunction of nine barrels of cartridges in the cellar and sparks from a grate on an upper floor,

130

blew up with terrific and terrifying force, killing a number of unfortunate washerwomen. All of which facts one may find duly chronicled (together with a description of a patent chair, in which, by means of an elaborate incorporation of ear trumpets, a deaf person could be guaranteed to hear perfectly), in the *Gentleman's Magazine*.

A heavily-built man emerged from the gateway of Staple Inn, and stood with puckered, short-sighted eyes surveying Holborn's crowded footway.

The streets about him offered plenty in the way of diversions. The City proper, re-born since the Great Fire, had almost finished its day's work, the legal quarters, a warren stretching from Grays Inn to the Temple, were silent and deserted, but westward around Hyde Park the aristocratic world made merry, and north of the Strand were coffee-houses, taverns, theatres and a great market. Lower grades of society crowded Whitechapel and the south of the Thames, while a horrible huddle of slums surged about Westminster and the Houses of Parliament.

If, hating this feverish contact with humanity, he had been seized with a longing for open spaces, they were very near. Fifteen minutes brisk walking from any part of London would in those days have brought one beyond the chafing boundaries of bricks and mortar. North of Grays Inn were open fields; Islington, Camberwell and Denmark Hill were heavily-wooded villages; Lambeth Marsh and Rotherhithe were open spaces intersected with sluggish streams. Even at the back of Fetter Lane there were gardens, and there were other large gardens behind the great houses—Craven House, Powis House, Clarendon House, and others— which still stood, while Lincolns Inn Fields struck a rural note with its wooden palings, and St. James's and Soho Squares with their fountains and statues. (Golden Square alone boasted a lamp.) It was as if the invasion of the country by the city had been met by a counter-attack launched by the country at the very heart of the invader.

But the stoutly-built man had no passion for rural scenes. With an impatient thud of his stick on the pavement, he turned east and then south, and so came presently to Ludgate Hill. From there he proceeded by Seacoal Lane to a steep and worn ladder of flagstones named, not unfittingly, Breakneck Steps, to a dingy little rectangle called Green Arbour Square. (The 'Arbour', if ever such had existed, had long ago been sacrificed to poverty and neglect. The very Square itself, and the steps leading to it, are now among vanished traditions of the eighteenth century.) These steps the visitor climbed; discerned, in the gloom, a doorway numbered thirty and which might have led, as too many of such doorways in convenient proximity to the river did lead, to a den of robbers and cut-throats, rapped smartly with the head of his stick, and waited.

The door opened; a slatternly woman carrying a candle appeared. The man made brusque enquiries.

'I'll find out,' said the woman, and beckoning him into the passage, shuffled up the stairs.

The caller leant against the wall; then realizing the risks from grime and vermin, moved grimly to the centre of the rotting boards and waited. He heard a door open, and an impatient voice demand, with an unmistakable Irish accent, 'What is it?'

'There's a person to see you, Master Goldsmith. He waits below.'

'Granted that he be not merely gin-begotten from thine own brain—' every word came clearly to the visitor below—'he is welcome to wait, since I'll warrant that he's merely a drunken, out-at-elbows ruffian sent by some thievenous scoundrel of a tradesman to collect money which I cannot earn, borrow or beg! Tell him, if, again, he be substantial enough to hear thee and sober enough to understand, to go whence he came! No, on second thoughts, Mistress Puddle——'

'Poole, Master Goldsmith, is my name, as by now you should remember.'

'True. Well, since thou hast not *his* name, describe this individual, lest, perchance, I repel one of my regiment of wealthy friends.'

The man in the passage chuckled in anticipation, and strained his ears. But the slatternly woman appeared to find the task difficult, either because of an excess of alcohol or too limited a vocabulary.

'A—a solid man, Mr. Goldsmith.'

'Admirable news—I'll have no dealings with wraiths!'

'—With a heavy face, all crumpled into folds, a little grizzled, untidy wig, a brown coat stained with snuff and fingers stained with ink, and a monstrous heavy staff.'

133

'Grub Street, Madam, personified.'

'A voice as growling as a bear's, a manner——'

The man below had reached the limit of his patience. 'Noll!' he thundered, in tones that shook the crazy ceiling.

Hasty footsteps crossed the floor above; a pair of astonished blue eyes peered over the banisters.

'Come up, friend, come up, and receive my humble apologies.'

Samuel Johnson, now aged fifty,—the Great Cham of Literature; Master of Arts and of the most pungent and direct English; collector of books and fragments of orange-peel; by temperament an idler, by circumstances and the pressure of his own rough genius an over-driven slave; philosopher, tyrant; most violent and most charitable of men,—tramped obediently up the crazy stairs, past the slatternly Mrs. Poole, and into the wretched den occupied by Oliver Goldsmith.

Goldsmith himself, now in his thirty-first year, formed an almost grotesque contrast to his visitor. Lanky and awkward in figure, with a pale, pockmarked face, high forehead and retreating chin, he spoke and moved with the unrestrained impulsiveness of a child. And a child to the end of his all-too-short life he remained—innocently vain, naïvely envious of wiser though less talented men, as incapable of valuing money as he was of listening unmoved to another unfortunate's tale of distress, never without friends as he was never without debts; excitable, self-willed, most foolish of talkers in company, most pellucid of writers when he had given

134

his scatterbrain genius time to concentrate—thus he himself and those who knew and loved him best have drawn his portrait. Many purposeless wanderings, with sheer want for ever jogging his elbow, had brought him at last to London and this slum.

Though there were cracks in the walls and woodwork, and the window had a pane missing, the air seemed stagnant and stale. A bed, over the end of which had been flung three or four outdoor garments, stood against the wall. In the centre of the room was an unsteady little table, with a chair with half its back missing beside it. The only other furniture was the wooden box on which Goldsmith had been seated.

Johnson, stumbling into the chair, sent it crashing sideways, splintering a leg.

"'Tis of small account,' said Goldsmith. 'No man weighing more than half thy weight dare risk his body upon it. Try this—' He dragged forward the box.

'The bed will serve,' grunted Johnson, and sat down, puffing, upon the edge. 'And now tell me, since we have not met for a month or more, how the world wags in Green Arbour Square.'

Goldsmith shrugged his thin shoulders.

'There are many worlds, but only the dullest are seen here—save by the children.'

'Children?'

'Aye. Swarms of 'em. God only knows how they survive such surroundings, or what excuses for merriment they find.'

'Youth, Sir, if it be hardy enough, will thrive any-

135

where. And though half the deaths in London be those of babes, the rest, under Providence, live long enough to play their part in thrashing the French and establishing the next generation.'

'True. As for these innocents, sometimes I and my flute divert them, and we have childhood's own minuets and sarabands danced on the cobbles outside, with no payment to the musician beyond smiles and laughter. Shall I ask for a light?'

'No need; good talk needs no lamp. I'd as lief listen in the darkest night to a man who has something worth the saying.'

'I can offer you nothing worth listening to.'

'Tut, tut, where's thy vanity, Goldy!'

'Dead, friend, of starvation.'

'I cannot believe it—'twas too well-nourished. What keeps you captive in such a prison on such a night?'

'The prisoner's sternest and most frequent gaoler, debt, represented at present by the fair Poole, who did not know you.'

'I have never been further before than the door below.' Johnson's hand plunged into his pocket. 'How much will secure release?'

'Three guineas—nay, two—will convince her that I still have friends in London. . . . Believe me, I am grateful, though I do but exchange one debt for another.'

'Sir, a man who hath endured Poverty as a workmate and bedfellow for so long as I must needs be moved to mitigate her harshness where he can. . . . Let us take a walk.'

Goldsmith, clapping a hat on his head, went with his friend down the rickety stairs again. His landlady, the light of battle in her eyes, was awaiting them. At the sight of the money, avarice struggled with regret at being cheated out of an opportunity to deliver another lecture. Avarice won, and she let him go.

Outside, the darkness was now complete except for an occasional gleam of light from an unshuttered window. They groped their way down the steps, and thence into the comparative brilliance of Fleet Street. There Goldsmith stopped abruptly, and caught at one of the posts at the edge of the footway for support. Johnson for the first time saw his face clearly. It was colourless.

'I—I am ill.'

' "Famished" were a better word.' The big man grasped the younger one's arm, and half-supported, half-dragged him through the doorway of a nearby eating-house.

Through an atmosphere heavy with the smell of food and acrid with tobacco-smoke, they stumbled to a table. The seats were benches whose high backs shut off the occupants from their fellow-diners. A waiter came, and Johnson, who had himself eaten nothing since noon, ordered food. When it was brought, he devoured it with that strange concentrated voracity which was a legacy from the grinding poverty of his earlier days, and which remained to the end of his life. Now and again he glanced at his companion. Goldsmith, after the first hasty mouthfuls, was eating with pathetic deliberation, as though he feared to shorten the meal.

137

Once, when the eyes of the two men met, Goldsmith's filled with tears . . . Johnson's dropped quickly to his plate.

'And now, Sir,' said Johnson, when the meal was over, the bill paid, and the waiter tipped, and when the noisy stream of pedestrians outside had engulfed them again, 'what would you? Shall we take a stroll?'

'Aye,' assented Goldsmith absently. He glanced in the direction of the river, where the air, even if still, would at least be cooler, and where tubby little tilt-boats, provided with covers for wet weather, could be hired, waterman included, at half the hackney-coach's legalized shilling a mile. But Johnson had other plans.

'This way, then,' he said, and set off westward, past the candle-lit shops—Fleet Street was famous for its vendors of quack medicines and toys—with their swinging signs overhead. Oil lamps added a feeble light every hundred feet or so, link-boys with their torches made travelling, wavering patches of brilliance. Sedan chairs, private and public, stage-coaches, vast rumbling affairs covered with black leather and elaborately studded with heavy nails, chaises drawn by two horses and with the added glory of post-boys, crowded the road. Goldsmith was wearied and dazed by the time they reached Bow Street.

'Up here,' said Johnson, and led the way to Covent Garden, a place of strange shadows under a moon that was slowly disentangling itself from a ragged rampart of grey cloud.

There, in that open space, with a few curious porters

watching them, Johnson sat down on a box of fruit, and with a queer smile puckering his heavy lips, contemplated the scene. Goldsmith, puzzled but for once constrained to silence, lounged awkwardly beside him.

Johnson spoke.

'Seven years ago I sat here watching just such a moon. And I had to-night a mind to come again. For to repeat an experience is not of necessity to impair or to blur its memory.'

'There are few experiences in my own life which I would walk a mile to repeat,' said Goldsmith.

'Then, Sir, you are by inference accounting yourself a man to whom Providence has allocated more suffering than happiness and more pain than pleasure, and who must needs look upon Death as a welcome friend, instead of an enemy to be forgotten until, enfeebled by age or infirmity, we are at last overtaken by him. . . . 'Twas in '52, at three of the clock of a fine summer's morning, that I was aroused by the sound of footsteps outside my house in Gough Square. Suspecting that some villain might be breaking in, I left my bed, and went down.'

'Your wife—?' interrupted Goldsmith.

A shadow passed over Johnson's face. The elderly widow with the painted face and affected airs whom he had married when he was twenty-six, and loved devotedly, wrangled with, and served faithfully for so many years, was still a topic too sensitive for discussion.

'She had died, Sir, in the previous March. As I was saying, I went down, thrusting, in my haste, a wig upon my head in place of nightcap, and snatching up a poker—since I had neither sword nor blunderbuss—to defend my person. Before I could reach the street door, came a heavy beating on the panels. I flung it open, to discover upon the steps two youths. 'Twas Topham Beauclerk and Langton, who, having earlier wasted their substance in foolish gaieties, had had the temerity to call upon me, desiring that I should join them in further revels.'

'Did you bid the shameless rogues begone?'

'Sir, they were my friends. Moreover'—the tired eyes twinkled—'there are few things more cooling to a waked man's natural infirmity of temper than the breezes of early morning. So instead I cried, "What, is't you, you dogs?" And on learning their intent, "So be it; I'll have a frisk with you," and leaving them while I clothed myself reputably, presently came down again equipped with staff in place of my poker.

'Of Topham, that man of fashion—though by no means a fop—I would say that he commended himself to my notice firstly by reason of his likeness to his great-grandfather, Charles the Second, and secondly by his sly wit. No man was ever so free when he was going to say a good thing, from the look that expressed that it was coming, nor, when he had said it, from a look that expressed that it had come. As for Bennet Langton, he is so tall and slender that he reminds one of the stork in Raphael's cartoon of the "Miraculous Draught of Fishes". He is a man whose sluggishness of temperament is compensated for by his gentleness. With these
140

two, I say, I took the morning air. In Covent Garden, we essayed to assist the porters in their labours of hoisting and carrying bales of fruit and vegetables. But they, regarding us as mere roisterers, and rather an hindrance than a help, would have none of us. So we left them, and after calling at a tavern, and there brewing a bowl of bishop to slake our thirst, sought further diversions.'

'Where?'

'In Billingsgate, Sir, whither we proceeded by boat. There, after a while, Lanky deserted us, the dog preferring to take breakfast with a parcel of wretched un-idea'd girls of his acquaintance. Afterwards, Davy Garrick took me to task on the matter, swearing that he would have to bail his old friend out of the round-house, and that I should find myself in the *Chronicle* as a result of such a frolic. But I assured him that his wife would never permit it.'

'Besides which,' said Goldsmith impulsively,' a man of such literary distinction. . . . But the Dictionary was not then compiled.'

'A dictionary, Sir, may add to a man's reputation, but will not save him from prison, though the payment be ten times fifteen hundred guineas. Especially if such payment be spent in advance. Twice since it hath appeared have I been arrested for debt, and but for the good offices of Richardson, likely to spend unprofitable hours in a debtor's cell. While, but for the help of New-bery, a publisher but none the less an honest man, a natural idleness would have been enforced upon me for sheer lack of pens, ink and paper. Shall we be turning homeward?'

Goldsmith agreed. The moon was hidden, and a thin rain had begun to fall. Side by side they retraced their steps.

And as they walked, Samuel Johnson talked, with the strange, jerky gesticulations which went so oddly with the sonorous voice and careful, measured prose, of other friends. Of Dick Savage, his early companion in wretchedness, dead these sixteen years past, who had ended a short and bitter life in a debtors' prison at Bristol. Of Joshua Reynolds, who ranked greatest painter of his century, even as little Davy Garrick, Johnson's one-time pupil, ranked as its greatest comedian. Of Edmund Burke, orator and writer, twenty years Johnson's junior and a fellow-student with Goldsmith at Trinity College, Dublin.

'Why should not these friends of yours,' said Goldsmith suddenly, 'be gathered together, to dine, to talk, to listen, with yourself at the head of the table?'

'Where would you have us meet?'

'At a tavern, Sir, at a tavern. What was good enough for Shakespeare and his friends—'

'—Is good enough for Sam Johnson and his. There is no better rest for the soles of a man's foot than a sanded floor. Goldy, 'tis an inspiration! When the Club is born, I'll answer for it that you shall be among the first to be offered election.'

'And the first to accept, provided I have fitting garments.'

142

'The poorest need not buy ill-fitting ones. A man in homespun is more clubbable than he who wears a scarlet waistcoat lined with gold lace and a laced hat, as I did, when my play was produced—to discover that he cannot treat people with the same ease as he can in plain clothes.'

They reached the Square.

'I will make it my business to call upon you again before long,' said Johnson. 'Meanwhile, remember there is no evil which friendship may not mitigate. Farewell.'

With his cautious tread he went down the steps to the street. The rain had driven idle and sightseeing pedestrians into shelter. It had also filled the holes in the cobbled road with water, and set the gutter in the centre running noisily, with the filth of a City on its surface.

A line of wooden posts served in place of a kerb. Johnson, touching each in turn as he walked, missed one, and frowning, went back to complete the strange ceremony. He felt old, tired and lonely. To the loss of his wife, the beloved Tetty, had lately been added that of his mother. Even Frank, the black servant who had entered his service, had gone, enlisted as a sailor. The world seemed emptied of the warm, strenuous intimate humanity among which this man of letters loved to argue, to sharpen his wits. . . .

He stumbled over a foot projecting from a doorway. Peering, he could see the white face of a child, one arm flung protectingly about a smaller child. Both were asleep. He felt in his pockets, put some pennies in the grubby, outstretched palm, closed, with infinite gentleness, the lax fingers, and went on his way.

Samuel Johnson

From Boswell's Life of Johnson

He (Dr. Johnson) said, that for general improvement, a man should read whatever his immediate inclination prompts him to; though, to be sure, if a man has a science to learn, he must regularly and resolutely advance. He added, 'what we read with inclination makes a much stronger impression. If we read without inclination, half the mind is employed in fixing the attention; so there is but one half to be employed on what we read.' He told us, he read Fielding's 'Amelia' through without stopping. He said, 'If a man begins to read in the middle of a book, and feels an inclination to go on, let him not quit it, to go to the beginning. He may perhaps not feel again the inclination.'

Dr. Johnson advised me to-day, to have as many books about me as I could; that I might read upon any subject upon which I had a desire for instruction at the time. 'What you read *then* (said he) you will remember; but if you have not a book immediately ready, and the subject moulds in your mind, it is a chance if you again have a desire to study it.' He added, 'If a man never has an eager desire for instruction, he should prescribe a task for himself. But it is better when a man reads from immediate inclination.'

Another admonition of his was, never to go out without some little book or other in the pocket. 'Much time,' added he, 'is lost by waiting, by travelling, etc.,

144

and this may be prevented, by making use of every possible opportunity for improvement.'

Samuel Johnson

From THE VANITY OF HUMAN WISHES

On what foundation stands the warrior's pride,
How just his hopes, let Swedish Charles decide;
A frame of adamant, a soul of fire,
No dangers fright him, and no labours tire;
O'er love, o'er fear, extends his wide domain,
Unconquered lord of pleasure and of pain.
No joys to him pacific sceptres yield,
War sounds the trump, he rushes to the field;
Behold surrounding kings their powers combine,
And one capitulate, and one resign.
Peace courts his hand, but spreads her charms in vain;
'Think nothing gained,' he cries, 'till nought remain,
On Moscow's walls till Gothic standards fly,
And all be mine beneath the polar sky.'
The march begins in military state,
And nations on his eye suspended wait;
Stern Famine guards the solitary coast,
And Winter barricades the realms of Frost;
He comes, nor want nor cold his course delay:—
Hide, blushing glory, hide Pultowa's day!
The vanquished hero leaves his broken bands,
And shows his miseries in distant lands;
Condemned a needy supplicant to wait,
While ladies interpose, and slaves debate.
But did not Chance at length her error mend?
Did no subverted empire mark his end?
Did rival monarchs give the fatal wound?
Or hostile millions press him to the ground?

His fall was destined to a barren strand,
A petty fortress, and a dubious hand;
He left the name, at which the world grew pale,
To point a moral, or adorn a tale.

Samuel Johnson
From RASSELAS

THE BUSINESS AND QUALIFICATIONS OF A POET

To a poet nothing can be useless. Whatever is beautiful, and whatever is dreadful, must be familiar to his imagination; he must be conversant with all that is awfully vast, or elegantly little. The plants of the garden, the animals of the wood, the minerals of the earth, the meteors of the sky, must all concur to store his mind with inexhaustible variety; for every idea is useful for the enforcement or decoration of moral or religious truth; and he who knows most will have most power of diversifying his scenes, and of grati.ying his reader with remote allusions and unexpected instruction.

.   .   .   .

But the knowledge of nature is only half the task of a poet; he must be acquainted likewise with all the modes of life. His character requires that he estimate the happiness and misery of every condition, observe the power of all the passions in all their combinations, and trace the changes of the human mind as they are modified by various institutions, and accidental influences of climate or custom, from the sprightfulness of infancy to the despondence of decrepitude. He must divest himself of the prejudices of his age or country; he must consider right and wrong in their abstract and invariable
146

state; he must disregard present laws and opinions, and rise to general and transcendental truths, which will always be the same: he must therefore content himself with the slow progress of his name; contemn the applause of his own time, and commit his claims to the justice of posterity. He must write as the interpreter of nature, and the legislator of mankind, and consider himself as presiding over the thoughts and manner of future generations, as a being superior to time and place.

His labour is not yet at an end; he must know many languages and many sciences; and, that his style may be worthy of his thoughts, must, by incessant practice, familiarize to himself every delicacy of speech and grace of harmony.

Samuel Johnson

From THE RAMBLER

ON THE FOLLY OF ANGER

Pride is undoubtedly the origin of anger; but pride, like every other passion, if it once break loose from reason, counteracts its own purposes. A passionate man, upon the review of his day, will have very few gratifications to offer to his pride, when he has considered how his outrages were borne, and in what they are likely to end at last.

These sudden bursts of rage generally break out upon small occasions; for life, unhappy as it is, cannot supply great evils as frequently as the man of fire thinks it fit to to be enraged, therefore the first reflection upon his violence must show him that he is mean enough to be driven from his post by every petty incident, that he is the mere slave of casualty, and that his reason and virtue are in the power of the wind.

One motive there is of these loud extravagances, which a man is careful to conceal from others, and does not always discover to himself. He that finds his knowledge narrow and his arguments weak, is sometimes in hope of gaining that attention, by his clamours, which he cannot otherwise obtain, and is pleased with remembering, that at least he made himself heard, that he had the power to interrupt those whom he could not confute, and suspend the decision which he could not guide.

But it does not appear that a man can by uproar and tumult alter any one's opinion of his understanding, or gain influence, except over those whom fortune or nature has made his dependants. He may fright his children or harass his servants, but the rest of the world will look on and laugh; and he will at length perceive, that he lives only to raise contempt and hatred, and that he has given up the felicity of being loved, without gaining the honour of being reverenced.

When a man has once suffered his mind to be thus vitiated, he becomes one of the most hateful and unhappy of beings. He can give no security to himself that he shall not at the next interview alienate by some sudden transport, his dearest friend; or break out, upon some slight contradiction, into such terms of rudeness, as can never be perfectly forgotten. Whoever converses with him lives with the suspicion and solicitude of a man that plays with a tame tiger, always under a necessity of watching the moment in which the capricious savage shall begin to growl.

It is related by Prior, of the Duke of Dorset, that his servants used to put themselves in his way when he was angry, because he was sure to recompense them for any indignities which he made them suffer. This is the round of a passionate man's life; he contracts debts when he is furious, which his virtue, if he has any, obliges him to discharge at the return of reason. He spends his time in outrage and acknowledgment, in injury and reparation.

Nothing is more miserable or despicable than the old age of a passionate man; his rage sinks by decay of strength into habitual peevishness; the world falls off from around him, and he is left to prey upon his own heart in solitude and contempt.

Oliver Goldsmith

From THE VICAR OF WAKEFIELD

DR. PRIMROSE'S FAMILY FAIL TO REALIZE THEIR REDUCED CIRCUMSTANCES

The first Sunday in particular their behaviour served to mortify me. I had desired my girls the preceding night to be dressed early the next day, for I always loved to be at church a good while before the rest of the congregation. They punctually obeyed my directions; but when we were to assemble in the morning at breakfast, down came my wife and daughters dressed out in all their former splendour, their hair plastered up with pomatum, their faces patched to taste, their trains bundled up in a heap behind and rustling at every motion. I could not help smiling at their vanity, particularly that of my wife, from whom I expected more discretion. In this exigence, therefore, my only resource was to order my son, with an important air, to call our coach. The girls were amazed at the command, but I repeated it with more solemnity than before. 'Surely, my dear, you jest,' cried my wife; 'we can walk it perfectly well. We want no coach to carry us now.' 'You mistake, child,' returned I, 'we do want a coach; for if we walk to church in this trim, the very children in the parish will hoot after us.' 'Indeed,' replied my wife, 'I always imagined that my Charles was fond of seeing his children neat and handsome about him.' 'You may be as neat as you please,' interrupted I, 'and I shall love you the better for it; but all this is not neatness, but frippery. These rufflings and pinkings and patchings will only make us hated by all the wives of our neighbours. No, my children,' continued I more gravely, 'these gowns may be altered into something of a plainer cut, for finery is very unbecoming in us, who want the means of decency. I do not know whether such flouncing and shredding is becoming even in the rich, if we consider, upon a moderate calculation, that the nakedness of the indigent world might be clothed from the trimmings of the vain.'

This remonstrance had the proper effect. They went with great composure that very instant to change their dress, and the next day I had the satisfaction of finding my daughters, at their own request, employed in cutting up their trains into Sunday waistcoats for Dick and Bill, the two little ones; and what was still more satisfactory, the gowns seemed improved by this curtailing.

Oliver Goldsmith

From THE TRAVELLER

Ye glitt'ring towns, with wealth and splendour
  crown'd;
Ye fields, where summer spreads profusion round;
Ye lakes, whose vessels catch the busy gale;
Ye bending swains, that dress the flow'ry vale;
For me your tributary stores combine:
Creation's heir, the world, the world is mine.

As some lone miser, visiting his store,
Bends at his treasure, counts, recounts it o'er;
Hoards after hoards his rising raptures fill,
Yet still he sighs, for hoards are wanting still;
Thus to my breast alternate passions rise,
Pleas'd with each good that Heav'n to man supplies:
Yet oft a sigh prevails, and sorrows fall,
To see the hoard of human bliss so small;
And oft I wish amidst the scene to find
Some spot to real happiness consign'd,
Where my worn soul, each wand'ring hope at rest,
May gather bliss to see my fellows blest.

But where to find that happiest spot below
Who can direct, when all pretend to know?
The shudd'ring tenant of the frigid zone
Boldly proclaims that happiest spot his own;
Extols the treasures of his stormy seas,
And his long nights of revelry and ease;
The naked negro, panting at the line,
Boasts of his golden sands and palmy wine,
Basks in the glare, or stems the tepid wave,
And thanks his gods for all the good they gave.
Such is the patriot's boast where'er we roam;
His first, best country ever is at home.

Oliver Goldsmith

AN ELEGY ON THE DEATH OF A MAD DOG

Good people all, of every sort,
    Give ear unto my song,
And if you find it wond'rous short,
    It cannot hold you long.

In Islington there was a man,
    Of whom the world might say,
That still a godly race he ran,
    Whene'er he went to pray.

A kind and gentle heart he had,
    To comfort friends and foes;
The naked every day he clad,
    When he put on his clothes.

And in that town a dog was found,
    As many dogs there be,
Both mongrel, puppy, whelp, and hound,
    And curs of low degree.

This dog and man at first were friends;
    But when a pique began,
The dog, to gain some private ends,
    Went mad, and bit the man.

Around from all the neighbouring streets
    The wondering neighbours ran,
And swore the dog had lost his wits,
    To bite so good a man.

The wound it seemed both sore and sad
    To every Christian eye;
And while they swore the dog was mad,
    They swore the man would die.

But soon a wonder came to light,
    That showed the rogues they lied;
The man recover'd of the bite—
    The dog it was that died.

NUMBER 30, GREEN ARBOUR SQUARE

Life of Samuel Johnson, LL.D.	J. Boswell
Johnson (English Men of Letters)	Leslie Stephen
Samuel Johnson (Great Writers)	F. Grant
Johnson and His Circle	John Bailey
The Four Georges	W. M. Thackeray
London	Sir W. Besant
London in the Eighteenth Century	,, ,,

Chapter Seven

YOUNG OXFORD WAITS ON GENIUS

[1807]

OCTOBER HAD reached its end. Already the breath of winter was sending the brittle leaves whirling along the streets and alleys, and London was lighting its fires and oil lamps and doing its best to ignore the cold and darkness. But the countryside was still beautiful, and in the eyes of at least one of a party which was travelling northward by the pleasant, not to say exclusive, means of a post-chaise, filled with romantic interest.

The party consisted of five, an Oxford undergraduate and a lady with her three children—two boys aged nine and seven respectively, and a little girl of five. The undergraduate, a slightly-built youth with a sensitive face, would have claimed one's closest attention. His upbringing had been, to use his own expression, 'largely intellectual', and he had already packed an astonishing number of experiences into his twenty-two years. As a boy, one of an orphaned family of eight, he had run away from his school in Manchester, wandered about Wales subsisting on an allowance made by his mother, and from Wales gravitated to London, where he would have starved if a kindly attorney's clerk had not helped him. All his life he had been a dreamer; it was his dreams, presumably, which inspired him to invent an elaborate table of descent which included the addition of an aristocratic 'De' to the plain 'Quincey'

154

which had been good enough for his father, a prosperous Manchester tradesman, and the less imaginative members of the family. But not yet had those dreams received sinister reinforcement from opium. That was to begin when, during a visit to London, he was attacked by neuralgia and induced to take the drug to deaden the pain. (The climax was an incredible total of twelve thousand drops a day.)

In the meantime, bribed by his guardian with an allowance and the prospect of a University degree, he was studying at Oxford.

The lady in the chaise was the wife of a friend, one Samuel Taylor Coleridge—himself, by a coincidence, en route to becoming a drug-addict, even as young De Quincey was later to enslave himself with opium. He and De Quincey had first met in the previous summer.

'In height,' wrote De Quincey, recording, with his usual gusto, his first impressions of the author of "The Rime of the Ancient Mariner", 'he might seem to be about five feet eight, but he is in reality taller. His person is broad and tends to corpulency, his complexion is fair; though his hair is black, his eyes are large and soft. It was from the peculiar appearance of haze or dreaminess which mixed with their light that I recognized my object.' An exasperating but lovable genius who never reached the heights which that genius should have made possible, Coleridge possessed an extraordinary capacity for attracting friends who were swift and eager to offer the assistance which his erratic variations of temperament, to say nothing of his chronic ill-health, made inevitable.

If De Quincey's short life had been passed half in the land of fantasy and half among solid, not to say sordid realities, the older man's less ethereal career had, at any rate, been fantastically varied. From Christ's Hospital, where he had had Charles Lamb as a colleague, he went in 1791 to Cambridge. From there, under the double affliction of a tradesman's debt which he could not pay, and an affection for a damsel named Mary Evans which was not repaid, he fled to London. In London he sold several poems to the *Morning Chronicle*, and then enlisted in the 15th Dragoons under the name of Silas Tomkyn Comberback. He proved totally incapable of riding a horse, but he wrote letters for his less educated fellow-recruits, and a Latin inscription on a stable-door which led to his identity being discovered and to his being ultimately bought out by his brothers. He went back to Cambridge, but failed to take his degree; lectured, wrote poems and articles, decided to marry (but not Mary Evans) and emigrate; married without emigrating, collaborated with various distinguished men of letters, preached in Unitarian chapels, and finally—except that nothing Coleridge embarked upon had an authentic note of finality—became secretary to the Governor of Malta.

His secretaryship ended in the autumn of 1805. He lingered for some months in Rome, and was preparing to return, when he was warned that owing to certain articles he had written in the *Morning Post*, Napoleon had his eye on him. His family, anxiously awaiting him in England, seemed likely to wait in vain. Eventually, the Coleridge tradition being maintained and the incredible duly happening, he received a passport from the Pope himself, sailed from Leghorn in an American vessel, was chased by a French cruiser, and, after throwing all his papers overboard, escaped capture and arrived safely in August, 1806.

A year later, when he was staying with his family at Bridgwater, De Quincey, who had heard that the poet was there, made a special journey to meet him. It was a meeting in which youthful reverence for genius was combined with a practical offer of help. Coleridge, De Quincey discovered, had received an offer to lecture in London. On the other hand, Mrs. Coleridge and the children had, by some means or other, to be conveyed to their home in Keswick. One can visualize the puzzled distress in Coleridge's dreamy blue eyes and hear the fluent explanations of the dilemma with which he was confronted. De Quincey rose nobly and youthfully to the occasion. It would be his proud privilege, if permitted, to share the cost of the necessary equipage and at the same time escort the family to the end of its long journey.

A French philosopher of the eighteenth century once evolved a theory that, no matter how long a man lived, his life was invariably compounded of happiness and unhappiness in equal proportions. He might have used Samuel Coleridge as an example. Though he was sixty-two when he died, his finest poetry was written before

157

he was twenty-five; though for years he drugged and blunted his brain, he succeeded in escaping from the worst effects of laudanum, and developed into a literary critic of unique distinction; though constantly in the throes of some financial crisis or other, he never failed to possess friends eager to come to his rescue. Admiration and devotion were his to the end—but he proved the rule which has so astonishingly few exceptions, that if genius marries a commonplace wife it achieves something less than commonplace happiness. Sara Coleridge and her husband disagreed, drifted apart, and finally separated.

'A hundred horse-power engine—with the boiler burst'—so one critic summed up the author of the 'Ancient Mariner'.

.   .   .   .

Hartley, the elder of the two boys in the post-chaise, appeared destined to become as famous as his philosopher father. 'Precocious' seemed inadequate to describe his early mental strides. It is, for example, recorded that on February the 9th, 1801, being then four years, four months and twenty days old, he discussed with his father 'Life, Reality, Pictures and Thinking', pointing out, without difficulty (but not, one conceives, without a certain smug priggishness) that there might be five Hartleys—Real Hartley, Shadow Hartley, Picture Hartley, Looking-glass Hartley and Echo Hartley. He then explained in detail the differences between Shadow Hartley and Looking-

158

glass Hartley. After which, it is scarcely surprising to be told that he also discoursed on English history and metaphysics. He grew up; the infant prodigy developed into 'the strangest ghost of a human creature, with eyes that gleamed like two rainbows over a ruined world'. (So says Thomas Carlyle, who knew him.) He lived to no great age; studying the vague ineffectiveness of his career, one has the feeling that the Real Hartley was scarcely more substantial than Shadow Hartley, and that he left Life, with all its confusions and perplexities, with relief. He wrote some poetry lit by flashes akin to genius, and certain essays which possess a critical shrewdness of their own.

Derwent, his more commonplace younger brother, became a Protestant priest—'a smooth, sleek, sonorous fellow,' sneers Carlyle, 'who has the management of some High Church schools (St. Mark's) at Chelsea, and quacks away there.' As for Sara, the sunny-haired little sister named after her mother, she grew up to become an authoress, and to write a charming fairytale, *Phantasmion*, which deserves to be rescued from oblivion. She married her cousin Henry, who also wrote.

But the carriage waits.

. . . .

After a week's delay at Liverpool—one travelled with a superb and enviable disregard for time a hundred years ago, and a post-chaise has no fundamental connection with speed—the party reached Lancaster, dallied there another night, and by three o'clock on the following day had covered the thirty-six miles to Ambleside, and were mighty proud of it. At Ambleside they changed horses for the last time. An hour later found them at the foot of White Moss, a hill on the outskirts of Keswick. The vehicle slowed down.

'Here,' suggested Tom De Quincey, 'the lads and myself might alight and walk. It would make it easier for the horses.'

Mrs. Coleridge concurred. The three left the chaise, and walking rapidly, left it behind. From the top of the hill they looked down upon a scene to which the autumnal dusk added a fairy-like loveliness. But De Quincey's eyes were focussed upon a single white cottage beside which two yew trees grew.

They hurried down the slope. The emotional De Quincey's excitement and awe reached such a pitch that by the time Hartley Coleridge, running on ahead, turned in at a garden gate, he was half fainting. He followed the boy, the rest of the party forgotten. He heard a step, a voice—Wordsworth's step and Wordsworth's voice—and the poet emerged to welcome him. The chaise, luckily for what was left of De Quincey's reputation as an escort, drew up at the gate at the same time. The whole party went through a tiny vestibule into the living-room of the cottage. It was a pleasant, though rather dimly-lit room, made dimmer still by the jasmine growing about the casement window.

Two women came down from the upper storey to greet the visitors. The first was Mary Wordsworth, until she married, Mary Hutchinson. She was the poet's cousin, and they had known one another all their lives. Her fair complexion was her one real beauty, her deep and understanding placidity her chief charm. She spoke seldom—a spiteful acquaintance once insisted that 'God bless you' were the only three words she knew—being content to listen and appreciate without comment. But to the young and inexperienced she could be extraordinarily understanding and kind, and her friendliness set the embarrassed De Quincey at his ease almost at once.

If to be enshrined in an immortal poem is to achieve immortality, then the fame of Mary of the fair hair and blue eyes is secure. For it was of her that her husband was thinking when he wrote,

> 'She was a phantom of delight
> When first she gleamed upon my sight.'

(Coleridge wrote, too, a poem to Sara. But the effect was spoilt by three Saras claiming to be the original.)

The phantom of delight, who lived until her ninetieth year, possessed one physical defect which even De Quincey, anxious to idealize every detail of that tremendous visit, felt it his duty to record. 'Those eyes of vesper gentleness,' he wrote, 'had a considerable obliquity of vision, much beyond that slight obliquity which is supposed to be an attractive foible to the countenance.' Mary Wordsworth, in short, squinted.

The second woman was Dorothy Wordsworth—an angular, stooping brunette with a gaze which the same chronicler describes as 'wild and startling'. Her temperamental impulsiveness was continually being checked and rebuked by a sense of feminine propriety instilled in her youth by her uncle, the Reverend Doctor Cookson, 'Canon of Windsor and a personal friend of the Royal Family, especially of George III', the result being a jerky compromise which, when she was rather more excited than usual, manifested itself in a stammer. De Quincey, either from gallantry or sheer inexperience, recorded her age as about twenty-eight, whereas, in point of fact, she was thirty-six. How far Dorothy Wordsworth's fragile genius would have bloomed if it had not been overshadowed by her brother's towering personality, can only be guessed. She kept a journal, she wrote quite charming verse (some of which William incorporated, without even the acknowledgment of her initials, in a volume of his own, to Lamb's honest disapproval). A single-hearted and selfless help to her brother and Mary, and a devoted aunt to their two children, her life ended in mental twilight at the age of eighty-four. She retains her niche, small but secure, in the crowded gallery of literary figures of her generation.

.   .   .   .

And Wordsworth himself, the dominating figure in the little group assembled in that pleasant oak-panelled room. He was now thirty-seven, with a swarthy complexion, (so swarthy, in fact, that it suggested an Italian rather than an English origin,) which had not been coarsened by outdoor living. His face was long, with broad brows; the eyes under their drooping lids varied in colour as emotion moved him. His nose was prominent, while his mouth and chin bore an extraordinary resemblance to those of Milton. (The artist Haydon, that tragic mediocrity who killed himself because a dwarf proved a stronger box-office attraction than his own giant picture of 'Nero', introduced Wordsworth's portrait in the character of a disciple in his 'Last Supper', and underlined his admiration for British literary genius as distinct from French by painting Voltaire as Judas.)

A passion for walking—the meticulous De Quincey estimates that up to the date of the post-chaise visit his hero must have tramped about a hundred and eighty thousand miles on foot in England and abroad—had done nothing to improve that awkward and un-athletic figure. The narrow and drooping shoulders made him look less than his real height, which was five feet ten, while his legs were so badly shaped that an acid-tongued lady was moved to regret that he had not another pair for party wear.

'Is it possible—can *that* be William!' cried Dorothy, with sisterly candour, regarding the poet as he strode ahead one summer evening. 'How very mean he looks!'

William it indubitably was. Distance was incapable of lending enchantment to that large-boned, ungainly form.

An odd portrait, a portrait to move the ribald to laughter. Yet somehow one does not laugh much at

163

Wordsworth. Nor, for that matter, with him. With the Miltonic mouth and chin went a Miltonic deficiency. Though he was capable of laughter, Wordsworth's sense of humour was negligible. Did he not demonstrate the fact when, at an assembly of notables at which Milton's watch was exhibited, he produced his own watch for the same reverent inspection? The same lack of detachment—for humour implies detachment—allowed him to write verses whose childish bathos exasperated the reviewers, and did so much to delay the recognition of his real greatness. The country people, passing that swiftly striding figure and listening to the harsh voice holding communion with invisible companions, thought poor Mr. Wordsworth 'daft', and pitied his family. Their opinions probably remained unchanged when the fullness of time made him Poet Laureate. Carlyle, who met Wordsworth in his old age, summarized his character with a complete absence of illusion. (But the author of *Heroes and Hero-Worship* did very little hero-worshipping outside Germany, and his illusions were noticeably few.) 'Essentially a cold, hard, silent, practical man,' says Carlyle, 'with a habit of speaking whatever is in his mind at the time, with total indifference to the effect produced on his hearers. At our first meeting he persisted in discussing how far you could get out of London for 6d. Whether his hearers understood what he was talking about or not, Wordsworth maintained a stern composure and went his way.'

More disappointing still, 'when he spoke of poetry, he

harangued about metre, cadences and so forth, and one
could not be at the pains to listen to him. '

.   .   .   .

To return to the less critical De Quincey and Dove
Cottage.

A flight of narrow stairs—fourteen; he found time to
count them—led from the living-room to the one the
Poet used as a study. (But it needed the most inclement
weather to keep the owner indoors.) Though the accommodation of the cottage was limited, the entire party
were invited to break their journey to Keswick and
to stay at least for the night.

At eleven o'clock the guests went to their rooms.

The odour of cooking and the edifying sound of
Master Wordsworth, aged three, reciting the Creed as a
morning exercise, roused De Quincey from sleep. He
dressed and went downstairs, to find the kettle singing
on the fire and Mrs. Wordsworth getting breakfast in
true Dalesman fashion. Rain was falling heavily; nevertheless, when the meal was over Wordsworth suggested
that he and De Quincey should take a long ramble.
The day passed, and another. On the third morning of
the visitors' arrival, Wordsworth proposed that the
journey to Greta Hall, where Mrs. Coleridge was
joining her sister, Mrs. Southey, should be made by
the long and leisurely mountain route, instead of
direct.

The young man agreed enthusiastically. (One cannot
help feeling that, in the presence of his idol, he would

have agreed with the same enthusiasm to travelling by balloon!) And the next day they started.

Part of the distance—forty-three miles of every type of country except level highway—they walked, part rode, part traversed in a farm-cart, De Quincey discovering fresh objects for admiration and wonder with every mile, including the smiling affability of the country-folk, the condescension of Miss Wordsworth, and even the startling habit of the buxom lady who drove the cart, which habit consisted of taking a flying leap from the vehicle and perching on the shafts.

At the foot of Lake Ewsmere, rather more than half-way to Greta Hall, they halted for the night. The next morning, the day being Sunday and the month now November, Wordsworth made for ever memorable a ramble with his young disciple by reciting 'The White Doe of Rylstone' to him. One smiles a little at the naïve gusto with which the great poets of the past read their effusions and the equally naïve awe with which their listeners listened and admired. Nowadays, such a passion for self-expression would receive less encouragement. We are bored too soon, we jeer too readily, we are too difficult to impress. Wordsworth with his harsh recitative, the deep-toned and melodious Tennyson, or even the polished and incomprehensible Browning might find it difficult to appeal to impatient twenty-two to-day.

Leaving the other members of the party to follow, the two men continued the journey together, Wordsworth still discoursing, De Quincey still the rapt listener. At
166

Penrith, seventeen miles from Keswick, Wordsworth effaced himself, possibly to commune direct with Nature as an alternative to communing with one of Nature's oddest productions, an Oxford undergraduate in a permanent condition of humility. De Quincey was left to finish the trip on foot, which, still overcome—one might almost say doped—by the honours which had been showered upon him, the youth proceeded to do. And at seven o'clock in the evening, having walked for seven hours in the dark, he arrived at Greta Hall, where the Coleridge family had already joined their co-tenants, the Southeys.

He records that his arrival 'created little sensation'—which, in view of the fact that he was expected, seems hardly remarkable; also that Southey himself, with his black hair and hazel eyes, opened the door.

It has been said of Robert Southey that he was both greater and better than any of his writings. It is certain that, though he was a gifted and conscientious man of letters, little of what he wrote is read or remembered now, while as Poet Laureate—he held the office for forty years—he ranks incomparably below Wordsworth, who succeeded him, or Tennyson, who succeeded Wordsworth. An aloof and reserved idealist, his circle of intimate friends was never large. But he could be charmingly courteous and hospitable, and in the case of the casual Coleridge, generous beyond all accepted canons of friendship. Between Southey and Wordsworth there was esteem, but nothing warmer; their temperaments differed too sharply. Sorrow was to darken the younger

167

man's life as it never darkened the long sunset of Wordsworth's. Southey's only son, who gave every promise of an intellectual genius even greater than his father's, developed an organic disease of the heart, and died while a mere boy. And with him died Southey's brightest dreams.

.   .   .   .

The ménage at Greta Hall was an odd one. Part of the house was occupied by the Coleridges, part by the Southeys, the feminine heads of the household being sisters. With the Southey family also lived a third sister, Mrs. Lowell, widow of a minor poet whose only claim to recognition appears to lie in the fact that he and Southey once collaborated in a volume of verse. The families did not meet at breakfast, but shared a communal dinner-table. To Southey, as the senior and less intermittent tenant, a study had been allotted, with a window commanding noble views of Derwentwater in one direction and Bassenthwaite in the other. Like Milton's study, it contained an organ; unlike Milton's (or, for that matter, any other poet's) it was always available for family use when greater space was required. And while Wordsworth was satisfied with a tattered, ill-kept collection of two or three hundred volumes, housed in 'little homely bookcases' on either side of the fireplace, Southey possessed not only a library of over seven thousand finely-bound volumes in English, Spanish and Portuguese, but many rare manuscripts. There the visionary who had seen so many of
168

his visions fade, who had turned his back on politics and refused a title, lived and worked amid the placid silences of the Lakes.

And there young De Quincey's journey ended.

.   .   .   .

He himself became, for a time, a member of that little colony of poets. But only for a time; Destiny had decreed a less tranquil career for him. It included the editorship of a local paper, marriage with a farmer's daughter, and many aimless wanderings, with opium always as his companion and tyrant. He lived to be acknowledged one of the masters of English prose, and to die, at the age of seventy, a shabby old man, separated from his family and drifting from one dingy lodging to another.

But that was a story which ended in 1859. And the De Quincey of 1807 still burned with youthful faith in his fellow-creatures and youthful hopes for the triumph of noble principles. Wordsworth, Coleridge, Southey—had he not been the guest and friend of them all?

Thomas De Quincey

From CONFESSIONS OF AN ENGLISH OPIUM EATER

I thought that it was a Sunday morning in May, that it was Easter Sunday, and as yet very early in the morning. I was standing, as it seemed to me, at the door of my own cottage. Right before me lay the very scene which could really be commanded from that situation, but exalted, as was usual, and solemnized by the power of dreams. There were the same mountains, and the same lovely valley at their feet; but the mountains were raised to more than Alpine height, and there was inter-space far larger between them of meadows and forest lawns; the hedges were rich with white roses; and no living creature was to be seen, excepting that in the green churchyard there were cattle tranquilly reposing upon the verdant graves, and particularly round about the grave of a child whom I had tenderly loved, just as I had really beheld them, a little before sunrise in the same summer, when that child died. I gazed upon the well-known scene, and I said aloud (as I thought) to myself: 'It yet wants much of sun-rise; and it is Easter Sunday; and that is the day on which they celebrate the first-fruits of resurrection. I will walk abroad; old griefs shall be forgotten to-day; for the air is cool and still, and the hills are high, and stretch away to heaven; and the forest glades are as quiet as the churchyard; and with the dew I can wash the fever from my fore-head, and then I shall be unhappy no longer.' I turned as if to open my garden gate; and immediately I saw upon the left a scene far different; but which yet the power of dreams had reconciled into harmony with the other. The scene was an Oriental one; and there also it was Easter Sunday, and very early in the morn-ing. And at a vast distance were visible, as a stain upon the horizon, the domes and cupolas of a great city—an image or faint abstraction, caught perhaps in childhood from some picture of Jerusalem. And not a bow-shot from me, upon a stone, and shaded by Judean palms, there sat a woman; and I looked; and it was—Ann! She fixed her eyes upon me earnestly; and I said to her at length: 'So then I have found you at last.' I waited; but she answered me not a word. Her face was the

same as when I saw it last, and yet again how different!
Seventeen years ago, when the lamplight fell upon her
face, as for the last time I kissed her lips (lips, Ann, that
to me were not polluted), her eyes were streaming with
tears; the tears were not wiped away; she seemed more
beautiful than she was at that time, but in all other
points the same, and not older. Her looks were tranquil,
but with unusual solemnity of expression; and I now
gazed upon her with some awe; but suddenly her
countenance grew dim, and, turning to the mountains,
I perceived vapours rolling between us; in a moment,
all had vanished; thick darkness came on, and in the
twinkling of an eye, I was far away from mountains,
and by lamplight in Oxford Street, walking again with
Ann—just as we had walked seventeen years before,
when we were both children.

S. T. Coleridge

YE ICE-FALLS! SILENT CATARACTS!

Who made you glorious as the gates of Heaven
Beneath the keen full Moon? Who bade the Sun
Clothe you with rainbows? Who, with living flowers
Of loveliest blue, spread garlands at your feet?

'God!' Let the torrents, like a shout of nations,
Answer! and let the ice-plains echo, 'God!'
'God!' sing ye meadow-streams with gladsome voices!
Ye pine-groves, with your soft and soul-like sounds!
And they, too, have a voice, yon piles of snow,
And in their perilous fall shall thunder 'God'!

171

S. T. Coleridge

KUBLA KHAN

In Xanadu did Kubla Khan
A stately pleasure-dome decree:
Where Alph, the sacred river, ran
Through caverns measureless to man
Down to a sunless sea.

So twice five miles of fertile ground
With walls and towers were girdled round;
And here were gardens bright with sinuous rills
Where blossomed many an incense-bearing tree;
And here were forests ancient as the hills,
Enfolding sunny spots of greenery.

But oh! that deep romantic chasm which slanted
Down the green hill athwart a cedarn cover!
A savage place! as holy and enchanted
As e'er beneath a waning moon was haunted
By woman wailing for her demon-lover!
And from this chasm, with ceaseless turmoil seething,
As if this earth in fast thick pants were breathing,
A mighty fountain momently was forced;
Amid whose swift half-intermitted burst
Huge fragments vaulted like rebounding hail,
Or chaffy grain beneath the thresher's flail;
And 'mid those dancing rocks at once and ever
It flung up momently the sacred river.
Five miles meandering with a mazy motion
Through wood and dale the sacred river ran,
Then reached the caverns measureless to man,
And sank in tumult to a lifeless ocean;
And 'mid this tumult Kubla heard from far
Ancestral voices prophesying war!

The shadow of the dome of pleasure
Floated midway on the waves;
Where was heard the mingled measure
From the fountain and the caves.
It was a miracle of rare device,
A sunny pleasure-dome with caves of ice!

A damsel with a dulcimer
In a vision once I saw:
It was an Abyssinian maid,
And on her dulcimer she played,
Singing of Mount Abora.
Could I revive within me
Her symphony and song,
To such a deep delight 't would win me,
That with music loud and long,
I would build that dome in air,
That sunny dome! those caves of ice!
And all who heard should see them there,
And all should cry, Beware, beware!
His flashing eyes, his floating hair!
Weave a circle round him thrice,
And close your eyes with holy dread,
For he on honey-dew hath fed,
And drunk the milk of Paradise.

Hartley Coleridge

From BIOGRAPHIA BOREALIS: WILLIAM ROSCOE

Books, no less than their authors, are liable to get
ragged, and to experience that neglect and contempt
which generally follows the outward and visible signs

173

of poverty. We do therefore most heartily commend the man, who bestows on a tattered and shivering volume such decent and comely apparel as may protect it from the insults of the vulgar, and the more cutting slights of the fair. But if it be a rare book, 'the lone survivor of a numerous race', the one of its family that has escaped the trunk-makers and pastry-cooks, we would counsel a little extravagance in arranging it. Let no book perish, unless it be such an one as it is your duty to throw into the fire. There is no such thing as a worthless book, though there are some far worse than worthless; no book which is not worth preserving, if its existence may be tolerated; as there are some men whom it may be proper to hang, but none who should be suffered to starve.

The binding of a book should always suit its complexion. Pages, venerably yellow, should not be cased in military morocco, but in sober brown russia. Glossy hot-pressed paper looks best in vellum. We have sometimes seen a collection of old whitey-brown black-letter ballads etc., so gorgeously tricked out, that they remind us of the pious liberality of the Catholics, who dress in silk and gold the images of saints, part of whose saintship consisted in wearing rags and haircloth. The costume of a volume should also be in keeping with its subject, and with the character of its author. How absurd to see the works of William Penn in flaming scarlet, and George Fox's Journal in Bishop's purple! Theology should be solemnly gorgeous. History should be ornamented after the antique or Gothic fashion. Works of science, as plain as is consistent with dignity. Poetry, *simplex munditiis*.

Hartley Coleridge

EARLY DEATH

She pass'd away like morning dew
　　Before the sun was high;
So brief her time, she scarcely knew
　　The meaning of a sigh.

As round the rose its soft perfume,
　　Sweet love around her floated;
Admired she grew—while mortal doom
　　Crept on, unfear'd, unnoted.

Love was her guardian Angel here,
　　But Love to Death resign'd her;
Tho' Love was kind, why should we fear
　　But holy Death is kinder?

William Wordsworth

SHE WAS A PHANTOM OF DELIGHT

She was a phantom of delight
When first she gleamed upon my sight;
A lovely apparition, sent
To be a moment's ornament;
Her eyes as stars of twilight fair,
Like twilight's, too, her dusky hair;
But all things else about her drawn
From May-time and the cheerful dawn;
A dancing shape, an image gay,
To haunt, to startle, and waylay.

I saw her upon nearer view,
A spirit, yet a woman too!
Her household motions light and free,
And steps of virgin liberty;
A countenance in which did meet
Sweet records, promises as sweet;
A creature not too bright or good
For human nature's daily food,
For transient sorrows, simple wiles,
Praise, blame, love, kisses, tears, and smiles.

And now I see with eye serene
The very pulse of the machine;
A being breathing thoughtful breath,
A traveller betwixt life and death;
The reason firm, the temperate will,
Endurance, foresight, strength and skill;
A perfect woman, nobly planned,
To warn, to comfort, and command;
And yet a spirit still, and bright
With something of an angel light.

William Wordsworth

THE SOLITARY REAPER

Behold her, single in the field,
Yon solitary Highland lass!
Reaping and singing by herself;
Stop here, or gently pass!
Alone she cuts, and binds the grain,
And sings a melancholy strain;
Oh listen! for the vale profound
Is overflowing with the sound.

No nightingale did ever chant
So sweetly to reposing bands
Of travellers in some shady haunt
Among Arabian sands;
A voice so thrilling ne'er was heard
In spring-time from the cuckoo-bird,
Breaking the silence of the seas
Among the farthest Hebrides.

Will no one tell me what she sings?
Perhaps the plaintive numbers flow
For old, unhappy, far-off things,
And battles long ago:
Or is it some more humble lay,
Familiar matter of to-day,
Some natural sorrow, loss, or pain,
That has been, and may be again?

Whate'er the theme, the maiden sang
As if her song could have no ending;
I saw her singing at her work,
And o'er the sickle bending;—
I listened till I had my fill,
And when I mounted up the hill,
The music in my heart I bore
Long after it was heard no more.

William Wordsworth

LONDON 1802

Milton! thou shouldst be living at this hour;
England hath need of thee; she is a fen
Of stagnant waters: altar, sword, and pen,
Fireside, the heroic wealth of hall and bower,
Have forfeited their ancient English dower

177

Of inward happiness. We are selfish men;
Oh! raise us up, return to us again;
And give us manners, virtue, freedom, power.
Thy soul was like a Star, and dwelt apart:
Thou hadst a voice whose sound was like the sea:
Pure as the naked heavens, majestic, free,
So didst thou travel on life's common way,
In cheerful godliness; and yet thy heart
The lowliest duties on itself did lay.

William Wordsworth

UPON WESTMINSTER BRIDGE

Earth has not anything to show more fair;
Dull would he be of soul who could pass by
A sight so touching in its majesty;
This city now doth like a garment wear
The beauty of the morning; silent, bare,
Ships, towers, domes, theatres, and temples lie
Open unto the fields and to the sky,
All bright and glittering in the smokeless air.
Never did sun more beautifully steep
In his first splendour valley, rock, or hill;
Ne'er saw I, never felt, a calm so deep!
The river glideth at his own sweet will:
Dear God! the very houses seem asleep;
And all that mighty heart is lying still.

Dorothy Wordsworth

LOVING AND LIKING

Say not you *love* a roasted fowl,
But you may love a screaming owl,
And, if you can, the unwieldy toad

That crawls from his secure abode,
Within the grassy garden wall,
When evening dews begin to fall.
Oh! mark the beauty of his eye,
What wonders in that circle lie!
So clear, so bright, our fathers said
He wears a jewel in his head!
And when, upon some showery day,
Into a path or public way,
A frog leaps out from bordering grass
Startling the timid as they pass,
Do you observe him, and endeavour
To take the intruder into favour;
Learning from him to find a reason
For a light heart in a dull season.
And you may love the strawberry flower,
And love the strawberry in its bower;
But when the fruit, so often praised
For beauty, to your lip is raised,
Say not you *love* the delicate treat,
But *like* it, enjoy it, and thankfully eat.

Robert Southey

PIZARRO

Pizarro here was born; a greater name
The list of glory boasts not. Toil and pain,
Famine, and hostile elements, and hosts
Embattled, failed to check him in his course;
Not to be wearied, not to be deterred,
Not to be overcome. A mighty realm
He overran, and with relentless arms
Slew or enslaved its unoffending sons,
And wealth, and power, and fame, were his rewards.

There is another world, beyond the grave,
According to their deeds where men are judged,
O Reader! if thy daily bread be earned
By daily labour,—yea, however low,
However wretched be thy lot assigned,
Thank thou, with deepest gratitude, the God
Who made thee, that thou art not such as he.

Robert Southey

To a Lark

O Thou sweet lark, who in the heaven so high
Twinkling thy wings, dost sing so joyfully,
    I watch thee soaring with a deep delight
And when at last I turn mine aching eye
    That lags below thee in the infinite,
Still in my heart receive thy melody.
O thou sweet lark, that I had wings like thee!
    Not for the joy it were in yon blue light
    Upward to mount, and from my heavenly height
Gaze on the creeping multitude below;
    But that I soon would wing my eager flight
To that loved home, where Fancy even now
    Hath fled, and Hope looks onward through a tear,
    Counting the weary hours that hold her here!

Robert Southey

From a Letter to S. T. COLERIDGE

... Talk of the happiness of getting a great prize in the
lottery! What is that to the opening a box of books! The
joy upon lifting up the cover must be something like
what we shall feel when Peter the Porter opens the door
upstairs, and says, 'Please to walk in, sir.' That I shall

never be paid for my labour according to the current value of time and labour, is tolerably certain; but if any one should offer me £10,000 to forgo that labour, I should bid him and his money go to the devil, for twice the sum could not purchase me half the enjoyment. It will be a great delight to me in the next world, to take a fly and visit these old worthies, who are my only society here, and to tell them what excellent company I found them here at the lakes of Cumberland, two centuries after they had been dead and turned to dust. In plain truth, I exist more among the dead than the living, and think more about them, and, perhaps, feel more about them.

YOUNG OXFORD WAITS ON GENIUS

Wordsworth   R. Masson

     ,,   (*English Men of Letters*)   F. W. H. Myers

Wordsworth, and Wordsworth and Southey (*Autobiographic Sketches*)

                                                     T. de Quincey

William Wordsworth, His Life, Works and Influence

                                                     G. McL. Harper

CHAPTER EIGHT

TO SUP WITH MR. LAMB

[1812]

IT WAS SIX O'CLOCK on the evening of Wednesday, October the 14th, and dusk was already falling. London was its usual noisy but humorously imperturbable self —a fact which to patriotic Britons who regarded their capital as the hub of the universe might have brought a thrill of pride. For the rest of the world was rotating very dizzily and dangerously indeed. The year had seen Ciudad Rodrigo taken by Lord Wellington, to be followed by even stronger hints that the French were more popular out of the Iberian Peninsula than in it. Napoleon had not merely declared war on Russia, but begun that campaign which had culminated in the burning of Moscow and, incidentally, of the invader's own fingers. The Senate in Paris had conscripted another 137,000 men; America had declared war on Great Britain, and Great Britain had made Lord Liverpool Prime Minister.

In London itself, the peace was kept by venial and grossly incompetent watchmen who were the butt of every practical joker—it was an age of practical joking —and drunken reveller. But if the Law was not administered efficiently, there was no question as to its vindictiveness, since nearly a hundred and thirty offences were still punishable by death. Duelling still survived, while prize-fighting was at its zenith. Bear-baiting

182

and cock-fighting were both among an Englishman's legitimate amusements. 'The King's indisposition' had become an accepted phrase; his shattered mind was incapable even of the small demands tradition made upon it, and in his place ruled the Prince Regent, otherwise 'Prinny', a contemptible profligate whose taste in architecture is exemplified by the Royal Pavilion at Brighton, and whose idea of wit was to creep behind fully-dressed members of his court and push them into one of the Royal fountains. Mr. John Constable was painting his incomparably English landscapes, and Sir Thomas Lawrence his portraits; as for Science, the age of steam was still to dawn, and while Mr. William Murdoch had succeeded in lighting his Soho factory with coal gas, the streets were still illuminated, where they were illuminated at all, with oil.

And while all these things were happening to stimulate the imagination of the lethargic Englishman, and while far beyond the straits of Dover a short, plump Corsican general with a Grecian profile was pitting his strategy against a tall, thin English general with a nose like a vulture's beak, certain literary-minded gentlemen were writing delicious essays on tea-kettles, on the art of Shakespeare, on getting up on cold mornings, on walking-sticks, on anything and everything. Writing essays that were to achieve immortality.

A small man in black, with a head that seemed over heavy for the frail body; dark curling hair, brown eyes that held in their depths the queerest blend of humour and sorrow, and a mobile mouth capable of a sudden, extraordinarily attractive smile, stood at the window of an upper room in the Temple, staring absently through the darkness and drizzle at the three shivering plane trees and the old pump in the courtyard below.

From Fleet Street the sounds of traffic—the humble market wagon, the democratic coach, the aristocratic chaise—came faint and muffled. London's roar was capable of being softened a century ago, as it is to-day, by the intervention of London's brick and mortar.

Flint scraped on tinder-box, and to the flicker of the fire two candles added their light. A woman spoke.

'Charles.'

Charles Lamb turned, and moved towards his sister with the jerky step that was characteristic. 'Yes, Mary?'

'There's likely to be convivial company this evening. You'll remember not to—'

'To indulge in high s-s-spirits on my own account?' He stuttered a little, as he had stuttered all his life. 'Yes, I'll remember. B-b-but you must not seek to impose too heavy a burden on me, my dear.' His tones were half-soothing, half-remonstrative.

She looked up at him. Tears tingled in her eyes. They came easily to this odd little woman with the big mob-cap, where her adored brother was concerned.

'I don't mind your being smoky, Charles. But not drinky. Is the room to your liking?'

It had been to his liking since they had first come there, three years ago. It was, if he had realized it (perhaps he did) the room in which the happiest years of his life were to be passed; and its very charms were

184

ultimately to drive him to other lodgings in Covent Garden, to Islington, to Edmonton. To the 'friendly harpies' who came too often and stayed too long Lamb could never turn a cold and unwelcoming face. He loved contact with humanity, he loved to flash the light of his own whimsical, modest genius upon each facet of his friends' characters. Nevertheless, he was already becoming uneasily, almost guiltily, conscious that these jolly days at Number 4, Inner Temple Court were a heavy handicap upon serious work. There were too many demands upon his energy, too much tobacco, and—for one so highly-strung—too many potations.

The room in which they stood was low and dingy. Old books and prints lined the walls; in the centre the mahogany card-table had been arranged for whist, with the snuff-box set hospitably in its centre. Cold beef and porter stood on the sideboard: the guests helped themselves to food and drink, as part of the ritual.

Steps sounded outside, a knock.

'Come in,' cried brother and sister together, and the door was flung open and a tall, shabby figure with a wild thatch of hair and brilliant, restless eyes stood on the threshold. It was William Hazlitt, who, destined for the church, had abandoned portrait-painting for lecturing, and lecturing in turn, thanks to the kindly offices of Lamb, for the position of parliamentary reporter on the *Morning Chronicle*.

'Am I too early?' he asked.

'Say, rather, t-too late. Confiscate his cloak, Mary,

and constrain him to dry his damp footgear at the blaze.'

'You would have had further to come a year ago,' observed Mary.

'My house in York Street,' agreed Hazlitt, with his cynical smile, 'is indisputably nearer to the Temple than Winterslow is. And if association count for aught,' he added, 'a higher source of inspiration, since the first belonged to Milton, and the second to my wife.'

'I hear Mr. Hunt outside,' Mary interrupted.

Entered Leigh Hunt—his full baptismal endowment was James Henry Leigh—with his short, crisp step and general air of breathless buoyancy. He was now twenty-eight. Nine years younger than Lamb, his early education, too, had been in the uncompromising hands of the Reverend James Boyer, the upper grammar-school master whose stumpy figure dominated Christ's Hospital for so many years. Afterwards there had been miscellaneous journalism, and with his brother, John Hunt, the editorship of the *Examiner*. (In a recent issue of that pungently-conducted journal he had referred to the Prince Regent as 'a fat Adonis of fifty'—a character-sketch which, had he known it, was later to result in two years' imprisonment and a fine of £200.) Married, even as Hazlitt was married, to an unattractive wife who had already discovered the penalties of a permanent partnership with a genius, he was to live long enough to appreciate Tennyson's Victorian muse, to enjoy the financial security of a Civil List pension,

186

and to furnish Dickens with the original of Harold Skimpole.

Followed the Reverend William Godwin, the strangest tangle of human contradictions that ever joined that unconventional circle. Minister of religion incapable of practising what he preached, revolutionary who abhorred violence, philosopher, historian, novelist, bookseller, publisher, and finally, under the patronage of Lord Grey, a 'yeoman usher of the Exchequer', his long life was crowded with ambitions that never materialized and failures that merely created fresh ambitions. He was now fifty-eight, a little man with the head of a giant and the finicky voice and manner of a dreamy aristocrat; a firm friend of the Lambs, as well as the publisher of their *Tales from Shakespeare*.

Later still came George Dyer, gaunt and awkward, wearing, as usual, a rusty coat that was far too large and trousers far too short; with straggling grey hair and innocent grey eyes that were perpetually round with wonder at the preposterous stories that Lamb's puckish spirit was moved to invent. A born butt, credulously making his way at dawn to the top of Primrose Hill, because he had been told that he would see the Persian ambassador worshipping the sun there; dashing to inform Leigh Hunt—again Lamb was the inventor of the statement—that Lord Castlereagh was the true author of the Waverley Novels; worried by the fears (excited by Lamb) that the Government might make him a peer without his knowledge or consent.

The hours passed. The haze of tobacco-smoke grew thicker; laughter, begotten of assured friendship, made the low-ceilinged room noisy as the scene of a children's party. A dozen topics were discussed—the financial and domestic misfortunes of Coleridge—(to the end they hoped, but hoped vainly, that he might appear), the new Regents Canal, the strange case of John Williams, a ruffian who, having cheated the gallows by committing suicide, had lately been placed on a platform 'having a clean white shirt, very neatly frilled', conveyed in solemn procession from one scene of his crimes to another, to be finally 'cast into a hole, amid the acclamations of thousands of spectators'.

Was there not, too, the new Theatre Royal in Drury Lane, risen magnificent from the ashes of the old, and opened on the previous Saturday with a performance of *Hamlet*? Lamb's stammer increased as he dealt with its glories—the immense group of sphinxes in bronze with their brazen tripods of hydrostatic lights, 'the invention of Mr. Barton', and the tastefulness of the management's box, surmounted, as it was, by a magnificent cornice above which, in turn, was the statue of 'a Muse, all finely picturesque'. There was, furthermore, a second Muse, visible above the overpowering brightness of the stage, and 'standing in all the grace of chaste, lonely Greek simplicity'. While to guard against the risk of any future fires, had not Colonel Congreve designed, free of charge, 'an arrangement by which from the hand of Apollo in the centre of the ceiling a heavy shower may be spread over every part of

188

the pit and boxes, to the extent of two hundred hogs-head'?

'I have more than half a m-mind to write another play myself and submit it to the management,' Lamb concluded.

'My dear Charles,' murmured Hazlitt, 'half a mind is more than most plays demand nowadays. Your previous comedy, if I remember correctly, was entitled "Mr. H.", the initial standing for "Hogsflesh", concerning which name your hero was abnormally sensitive.'

'Charles hath ever had a passion for pork,' commented Godwin.

Lamb nodded seriously. 'S-some day I may be moved to write an essay on the origin of roast-pig.'

'Charles,' said Hunt, 'hath a passion for many things beginning with "p". For pork, porter, poetry, prints—'

'I would ask nothing b-better than that my last b-b-breath might be inhaled through a pipe and expelled in a pun,' said Lamb.

So, in turn, they held the stage, these good companions. There was only one who was content to remain a member of the audience all the time. Mary Lamb, detached and demure, listened, but she kept her thoughts to herself. This dingy, jolly room in the Temple was part, and the best part, of her normal world. And there Charles, whose own over-sensitive brain had once, for a little time, become unbalanced, presided as her god and her child. But there was another world, in which those whom Providence has touched with madness are condemned to wander help-lessly. (The tragedy that bound brother and sister so closely had happened while she was there. Only once in her letters afterwards was Mary Lamb able to refer to her mother.)

 .   .   .   .

The evening ended; the guests left; only Charles and she remained.

Charles dropped, with a sigh of weariness, into a chair.

'Those others,' said Mary abruptly. 'Do you envy them?'

'Why should I? They will achieve greatness, all of them. While I'—he smiled whimiscally—'I shall never be more than an obscure clerk of the Honourable East India Company, eternally beset by a weakness for bad jokes, tobacco and strong drink.'

She shook her head fiercely. 'Charles, Charles, you speak wrongly. You will hold a place that none of them will fill; you will live and be loved when they are little more than an empty name.'

'Mary, Mary,' he mimicked. 'You are foolish!'

'I am wise. Oh, if I could be articulate, if I could make you understand! But it is late, and you——'

'I am still, in this year of grace, a scribbler with bread and butter to earn for two.'

'Far, far more than that, dearest brother. . . . Good night.'

'Good night, Mary.'

190

She passed to her room. Charles snuffed a guttering candle, and then walked absently to the window, and stood drumming with idle fingers upon the pane. The rain had ceased; all the stars in the Heavens seemed to be twinkling. His thoughts drifted back to the days when, as a small, delicate boy, hatless and yellow-stockinged, he had trudged to the old school in New-gate Street, to his queer, delightful father, to Aunt Hetty . . . to the holidays spent in lovely Hertfordshire with his grandmother. And then, with pitiless clarity, he had a vision of that frightful day, when he had found himself confronting Mary, frenzied and distraught, with the mother she had killed lying between them. With the dedication of his life to her care had come the end of many, many dreams.

Outside the voice of a passing watchman chanted his monotonous 'All's well!'

Charles Lamb

From OLD CHINA

Do you remember the brown suit, which you made to hang upon you, till all your friends cried shame upon you, it grew so threadbare—and all because of that folio Beaumont and Fletcher, which you dragged home late at night from Barker's in Covent Garden? Do you remember how we eyed it for weeks before we made up our minds to the purchase, and had not come to a determination till it was near ten o'clock of the Satur-day night, when you set off from Islington, fearing you should be too late—and when the old book-seller with some grumbling opened his shop, and by the twinkling

191

taper (for he was setting bedwards) lighted out the relic from his dusty treasures—and when you lugged it home, wishing it were twice as cumbersome—and when you presented it to me—and when we were exploring the perfectness of it ('collating' you called it) —and while I was repairing some of the loose leaves with paste, which your impatience would not suffer to be left till daybreak—was there no pleasure in being a poor man? Or can those neat black clothes, which you wear now, and are so careful to keep brushed, since we have become rich and finical, give you half the honest vanity, with which you flaunted it about in that over-worn suit—your old corbeau—for four or five weeks longer than you should have done, to pacify your conscience for the mighty sum of fifteen—or sixteen shillings was it?—a great affair we thought it then— which you had lavished on the old folio. Now you can afford to buy any book that pleases you, but I do not see that you ever bring home any nice old purchases now.

Charles Lamb

From Dream-Children: a Reverie

Children love to listen to stories about their elders, when *they* were children; to stretch their imagination to the conception of a traditionary great-uncle or gran-dame, whom they never saw. It was in this spirit that my little ones crept about me the other evening to hear about their great-grandmother Field, who lived in a great house in Norfolk (a hundred times bigger than that in which they and Papa live) which had been the scene—so at least it was generally believed in that part of the country—of the tragic incidents which they

192

had lately become familiar with from the ballad of The Children in the Wood. Certain it is that the whole story of the children and·their cruel uncle was to be seen fairly carved out in wood upon the chimney-piece of the great hall, the whole story down to the Robin Red-breasts, till a foolish rich person pulled it down to set up a marble one of modern invention in its stead, with no story upon it. Here Alice put out one of her dear mother's looks, too tender to be called upbraiding. Then I went on to say, how religious and how good their great-grandmother Field was, how beloved and respected by everybody, though she was not indeed the mistress of the great house, but had only the charge of it (and yet in some respects she might be said to be the mistress of it too) committed to her by the owner, who preferred living in a newer and more fashionable mansion which he had purchased somewhere in an adjoining county; but still she lived in it in a manner as if it had been her own, and kept up the dignity of the great house in a sort while she lived, which afterwards came to decay and was nearly pulled down, and all its old ornaments stripped and carried away to the owner's other house, where they were set up, and looked as awkward as if someone were to carry away the old tombs they had lately seen at the Abbey, and stick them up in Lady C's tawdry gilt drawing-room. Here John smiled, as much as to say, 'That would be foolish indeed'. And then I told how, when she came to die, her funeral was attended by a concourse of all the poor, and some of the gentry too, of the neighbourhood for many miles round, to show their respect for her memory, because she had been such a good and religious woman; so good, indeed, that she knew all the Psaltery by heart, ay, and a great part of the Testament besides. Here little Alice spread her hands. Then I told what a tall, upright, graceful person their great-grandmother Field once was, and how in her youth she was esteemed the best dancer—here Alice's little right foot played an involuntary movement, till upon my looking grave, it desisted. . . . I told how she used to sleep by herself in a lone chamber of the great lone house; and how she believed that an apparition of two infants was to be seen at midnight gliding up and down the great staircase near where she slept, but she said, 'Those innocents would do her no harm'; and how frightened I used to be. . . . Here John expanded all his eyebrows and tried to look courageous.

Then I told how good she was to all her grand-children, having us to the great-house in the holydays, where I in particular used to spend many hours by my-self, in gazing upon the old busts of the Twelve Cæsars, that had been Emperors of Rome, till the old marble heads would seem to live again, or I to be turned into marble with them. . . . Or in watching the dace that darted to and fro in the fish-pond, at the bottom of the garden, with here and there a great sulky pike hanging midway down the water in silent state, as if it mocked at their impertinent friskings,—I had more pleasure in these busy-idle diversions than in all the sweet flavours of peaches, nectarines, oranges, and such-like common baits of children. Here John slyly deposited back upon the plate a bunch of grapes, which, not unobserved by Alice, he had meditated dividing with her, and both seemed willing to relinquish them for the present as irrelevant. Then in somewhat a more heightened tone, I told how, though their great-grandmother Field loved all her grandchildren, yet in a special manner she might be said to have loved their uncle, John L——, because he was so handsome and spirited a youth and a king to the rest of us . . . and how he used to carry me upon his back when I was a lame-footed boy, and how in after life he became lame-footed too, and I did not always (I fear) make allowances enough for him when he was impatient or in pain; and how when he died, though he had not been dead an hour, it seemed as if he had died a great while ago, such a distance there is betwixt life and death; and how I bore his death as I thought pretty well at first, but afterwards it haunted and haunted me, and knew not till then how much I had loved him. . . . Here the children fell a-crying, and asked if their little mourning which they had on was not for Uncle John, and they looked up, and prayed me not to go on about their uncle, but to tell them some stories about their pretty dead mother. Then I told how for seven long years, in hope sometimes, sometimes in despair, yet persisting ever, I courted the fair Alice W——n; and, as much as children could understand, I explained to them what coyness, and difficulty, and denial meant in maidens—when suddenly, turning to Alice, the soul of the first Alice looked out at her eyes with such a reality of representment, that I became in doubt which of them stood there before me, or whose that bright hair was; and while I stood gazing, both children gradually grew fainter to my view, receding, and still receding, till nothing at last but two mournful features was seen in the uttermost distance, which, without speech, strangely impressed upon me the effects of speech; 'We are not of Alice, nor of thee, nor are we children at all. The children of Alice call Bartrum father. We are nothing; less than nothing, and dreams. We are only what might have been, and must wait from the tedious shores of Lethe million of ages before we have existence, and a name.'—And immediately awaking, I found myself quietly seated in my bachelor arm-chair, where I had fallen asleep, with the faithful Bridget unchanged by my side.

Charles Lamb

Letter to John Dyer Collier
1812

Dear Sir,

Mrs. Collier has been kind enough to say that you would endeavour to procure a reporter's situation for William Hazlitt. I went to consult him upon it last night and he acceded very eagerly to the proposal and requests me to say how very much obliged he feels to your kindness and how glad he should be for its success. He is, indeed at his wits' end for a livelihood, and I should think, especially qualified for such an employment, from his singular facility in retaining all conversations at which he has been ever present. I think you may recommend him with confidence. I am sure I shall *myself* be obliged to you for your exertions, having a great regard for him.

Yours truly,

C. Lamb.

Mary Lamb

The Mock-Hero

Horatio, of ideal courage vain,
Was flourishing in air his father's cane,
And, as the fumes of valour swelled his pate,
Now thought himself this hero, and now that;
'And now,' he cried, 'I will Achilles be;
My sword I brandish; mark! the Trojans flee!
Now I'll be Hector, when his angry blade
A lane through heaps of slaughtered Grecians made!
And now my deeds, still braver, I'll evince,

196

I am no less than Edward the Black Prince—
Give way, ye coward French!' As thus he spoke,
And aimed in fancy a sufficient stroke
To fix the fate of Crecy or Poictiers—
Heroically spurning trivial fears—
His milk-white hand he strikes against a nail,
Sees his own blood, and feels his courage fail—
Ah! where is now that boasted valour flown,
That in the tented field so late was shown?
Achilles weeps, great Hector hangs his head,
And the Black Prince goes whimpering to bed.

William Hazlitt

From SHAKESPEARE AND MILTON

The four greatest names in English poetry are almost
the four first we come to: Chaucer, Spenser, Shakespeare and Milton. There are no others that can really
be put in competition with these. The two last have had
justice done them by the voice of common fame. Their
names are blazoned in the very firmament of reputation; while the two first (though 'the fault has been
more in their stars than in themselves that they are
underlings') either never emerged far above the horizon
or were too soon involved in the obscurity of time.

In comparing these four writers together, it might be
said that Chaucer excels as the poet of manners, or of
real life; Spenser, as the poet of romance; Shakespeare
as the poet of nature (in the largest use of the term);
and Milton, as the poet of morality. Chaucer most
frequently describes things as they are; Spenser, as we
wish them to be; Shakespeare, as they would be; and
Milton, as they ought to be. As poets, and as great
poets, imagination, that is, the power of feigning things

according to nature, was common to them all; but the principle or moving power to which this faculty was most subservient in Chaucer was habit or inveterate prejudice; in Spenser, novelty and the love of the marvellous; in Shakespeare, it was the force of passion, combined with every variety of possible circumstances; and in Milton only with the highest. The characteristic of Chaucer is intensity; of Spenser, remoteness; of Milton, elevation; of Shakespeare, everything.

.   .   .   .

The striking peculiarity of Shakespeare's mind was its generic quality, its power of communication with all other minds, so that it contained a universe of thought and feeling within itself, and had no one peculiar bias or exclusive excellence more than another. He was just like any other man, but that he was like all other men. He was the least of an egotist that it was possible to be. He was nothing in himself; but he was all that others were, or that they could become. He not only had in himself the germs of every faculty and feeling, but he could follow them by anticipation, intuitively, into all their conceivable ramifications, through every change of fortune or conflict of passion, or turn of thought. He had 'a mind reflecting ages past' and present; all the people that ever lived are there. There was no respect of persons with him. His genius shone equally on the evil and on the good, on the wise and the foolish, the monarch and the beggar. 'All corners of the earth, kings, queens, and states, maids, matrons, nay, the secrets of the grave', are hardly hid from his searching glance. He was like the genius of humanity, changing places with all of us at pleasure, and playing with our purposes as with his own. He turned the globe round for his amusement, and surveyed the generations of men,

198

and the individuals as they passed, with their different concerns, passions, follies, vices, virtues, actions, and motives—as well those that they knew as those which they did not know, or acknowledge to themselves. The dreams of childhood, the ravings of despair, were the toys of his fancy. Airy beings waited at his call and came at his bidding. Harmless fairies 'nodded to him, and did him courtesies'; and the night-hag bestrode the blast at the command of 'his so potent art'. The world of spirits lay open to him, like the world of real men and women; and there is the same truth in his delineations of the one as of the other; for if the preternatural characters he describes could be supposed to exist, they would speak, and feel, and act as he makes them. He had only to think of anything in order to become that thing, with all the circumstances belonging to it.

Leigh Hunt

From COACHES

The stage-coach is a great and unpretending accommodation. It is a cheap substitute, notwithstanding all its eighteenpenny and two-and-sixpenny temptations, for keeping a carriage or a horse; and we really think, in spite of its gossipping, is no mean help to village liberality; for its passengers are so mixed, so often varied, so little yet so much together, so compelled to accommodate, so willing to pass a short time pleasantly, and so liable to the criticism of strangers that it is hard if they do not get a habit of speaking, or even thinking more kindly of one another than if they mingled less often, or under other circumstances. The old and infirm are treated with reverence; the ailing sympathized with; the healthy congratulated; the rich not distinguished; the poor well met, the young, with their faces conscious of pride, patronized, and allowed to be extra. Even the fiery, nay the fat, learn to bear with each other; and if some high-thoughted persons will talk now and then of their great acquaintances, or their preference of a carriage, there is an instinct which tells the rest that they would not make such appeals to their good opinion if they valued it so little as might be supposed. Stoppings and dust are not pleasant, but the latter may be had on grander occasions; and if anyone is so unlucky as never to keep another stopping himself, he must be content with the superiority of his virtue.

The mail or stage coachman, upon the whole, is no inhuman mass of great-coat, gruffness, civility, and old boots. The latter is the politer, from the smaller range of acquaintance, and his necessity for preserving them. His face is red, and his voice rough, by the same process of drink and catarrh. He has a silver watch with a steel-chain, and plenty of loose silver in his pocket, mixed with halfpence. He serves the houses he goes by for a clock. He takes a glass at every alehouse; for thirst, when it is dry, and for warmth when it is wet. He likes to show the judicious reach of his whip, by twigging a dog or a goose on the road, or children that get in the way. His tenderness to descending old ladies is particular. He touches his hat to Mr. Smith. He gives 'the young woman' a ride, and lends her his box-coat in the rain. His liberality in imparting his knowledge to any one that has the good fortune to ride on the box with him is a happy mixture of deference, conscious possession, and familiarity. His information chiefly lies in the occupancy of houses on the road, prize-fighters, Bow Street runners, and accidents. He concludes that you know Dick Sams, or Old Joey, and proceeds to relate some of the stories that relish his pot and tobacco in the

200

evening. If any of the four-in-hand gentry go by, he shakes his head, and thinks they might find something better to do. His contempt for them is founded on modesty. He tells you that his off-hand horse is as pretty a goer as ever was, but that Kitty—'Yeah, now there, Kitty, can't you be still? Kitty's a devil, Sir, for all you wouldn't think it.' He knows that the boys on the road admire him, and gives the horses an indifferent lash with his whip as they go by. If you wish to know what rain and dust can do, you should look at his old hat. There is an indescribably placid and paternal look in the position of his corduroy knees and old top-boots on the foot-board, with their pointed toes and never-cleaned soles. His beau-ideal of appearance is a frock-coat, with mother-o'-pearl buttons, a striped yellow waistcoat, and a flower in his mouth.

Leigh Hunt

A LIBRARY OF ONE

Were I to name, out of the times gone by,
The poets dearest to me, I should say,
Pulci for spirits, and a fine, free way;
Chaucer for manners, and close, silent eye;
Milton for classic taste, and harp strung high;
Spenser for luxury, and sweet, sylvan play;
Horace for chatting with, from day to day;
Shakespeare for all, but most, society.

But which take with me, could I take but one?
Shakespeare—as long as I was unoppressed
With the world's weight, making sad thoughts intenser;
But did I wish, out of the common sun
To lay a wounded heart in leafy rest,
And dream of things far off and healing—Spenser.

William Godwin

From THE ENQUIRER

ON THE COMMUNICATION OF KNOWLEDGE

The Schoolmaster

Nothing can be more happily adapted to remove the difficulties of instruction than that the pupil should first be excited to desire knowledge, and next that his difficulties should be solved for him, and his path cleared, as often and as soon as he thinks proper to desire it.

This plan is calculated entirely to change the face of education. The whole formidable apparatus which has hitherto attended it is swept away. Strictly speaking, no such characters are left upon the scene as either preceptor or pupil. The boy, like the man, studies, because he desires it. He proceeds upon a plan of his own invention, or which, by adopting, he has made his own. Everything bespeaks independence and equality. The man, as well as the boy, would be glad in cases of difficulty to consult a person more informed than himself. That the boy is accustomed almost always to consult the man, and not the man the boy, is to be regarded rather as an accident, than anything essential. Much even of this would be removed, if we remembered that the most inferior judge may often, by the varieties of his apprehension, give valuable information to the most enlightened.

The boy, however, should be consulted by the man unaffectedly, not according to any preconcerted scheme, or for the purpose of persuading him that he is what he is not.

There are three considerable advantages which would attend upon this species of education.

First, liberty. Three-fourths of the slavery and restraint that are now imposed upon young persons would be annihilated at a stroke.

Secondly, the judgment would be strengthened by continual exercise. Boys would no longer learn their lessons after the manner of parrots. No one would learn without a reason, satisfactory to himself, why he learned; and it would perhaps be well, if he were frequently prompted to assign his reasons. Boys would then consider for themselves, whether they understood what they read. To know when and how to ask a question is no contemptible part of learning. Sometimes they would pass over difficulties, and neglect essential preliminaries; but then the nature of the thing would speedily recall them, and induce them to return to examine the tracts which before had been overlooked. For this purpose it would be well that the subjects of their juvenile studies should often be discussed, and that one boy should compare his progress and his competence to decide in certain points with those of another. There is nothing that more strongly excites our inquiries than this mode of detecting our ignorance.

Thirdly, to study for ourselves is the true method of acquiring habits of activity. The horse that goes round in a mill, and the boy that is anticipated and led by the hand in all his acquirements, are not active. I do not call a wheel that turns round fifty times in a minute, active. Activity is a mental quality. If therefore you would generate habits of activity, turn the boy loose in the fields of science. Let him explore the path for himself. Without increasing his difficulties, you may venture to leave him for a moment, and suffer him to ask himself the questions before he asks you, or, in other words, to ask the question before he receives the information. Far be it from the system here laid down, to increase the difficulties of youth. No, it diminishes them a hundred fold. Its office is to produce information; and a willing temper makes every burthen light.

Lastly, it is the tendency of this system to produce in the young, when they are grown up to the stature of men, a love of literature. The established modes of education produce the opposite effect, unless in a fortunate few, who, by the celerity of their progress, and the distinctions they obtain, perhaps escape from the general influence. But, in the majority of cases, the memory of our slavery becomes associated with the studies we pursued, and it is not till after repeated struggles, that those things can be rendered the objects of our choice, which were for so long a time the themes of compulsion. This is particularly unfortunate, that we should conquer with much labour and application the difficulties that beset the entrance of literature, and then should quit it when perhaps, but for this unfortunate association, the obstacles were all smoothed, and the improvement to be made was attended through all its steps with unequivocal delight.

TO SUP WITH MR. LAMB

Chapter Nine

THE SPLENDID EXILES

[1822]

IT WAS JUNE. The tideless waters of the Mediterranean, intolerably sparkling, rippled in blue and violet waves against the shores of the Bay of Spezzia. But though only Naples could claim to be lovelier, the Bay was almost deserted. The hand of Austria rested heavily upon Northern Italy, and the pulse of national life beat fitfully and feebly. Only a few wretched fishing-villages dotted the sandy beach.

Near the centre, with San Tirinzo on one side and Lerici on the other, stood a white building, lonely and abandoned. It was the Casa Magni, once a Jesuit convent. The ground floor was unpaved, and since the waves washed in through the high arched entrance, in any case unfit for human habitation. The fishing-tackle and gear stored there heightened the general resemblance of the place to a boat-house. Above was a single storey divided into a hall and four small rooms. There was one chimney, for cooking. The only architectural charm of the place was a veranda that faced and almost overhung the sea.

The view was worth some discomfort. On the right and behind the building rose noble mountains. Walnut and ilex trees, whose dark loveliness was to haunt one of the tenants to the end of her long life, grew on the lower slopes. Eastward a winding footpath led over

205

precipitous rocks to Lerici, with its cluster of flat-roofed houses. Little black huts belonging to the fishermen clung to the cliffs for shelter like swallows' nests, while over all brooded the hot Southern sky. But sometimes the sunshine would vanish abruptly, and a vicious wind, the dreaded 'pomente', would spring up, lashing the waters of the Bay into yeasty foam.

It was a primitive spot, peopled by natives who were equally primitive. 'They are,' wrote Mary Shelley, that same tenant of the Casa Magni, 'wilder than the place—more like savages than any people I ever before lived among. Many a night they pass on the beach singing, or rather howling, the women dancing among the waves that break at their feet, the men leaning against the rocks and joining in their wild chorus. . . . Had we been wrecked on an island of the South Seas, we could scarcely have found ourselves further from civilization!'

Hither, in the sweltering summer weather, came Shelley and his family from Pisa, where they had been lodging, with Byron as a near neighbour. He and Shelley were both exiles. England might condone the moral lapses of George and his Court, but it refused to tolerate the attitude of Lord Byron to his wife, or of Mr. Shelley to his Creator. When the first entered a ballroom, every lady walked out; when the second asked for the custody of his children, he was told that as an infidel he was unworthy. Hence—Pisa.

England herself was recuperating after long years of war. Waterloo was seven years past; the little Corsican, whose genius could make and unmake kings, but who

could not make even a gentleman of himself, was piti-
ably dead and buried in St. Helena. Lord Castlereagh,
his life-long opponent, trembled on the brink of a
mental collapse which was to culminate in the tragedy
of a penknife overlooked by a valet. . . . The exiles
were not wholly uninterested in the rise of this general
or statesman or the fall of that. Had not Shelley himself
written,

> 'I met murder on the way
> Very smooth he looked and grim
> He had a face like Castlereagh
> Seven bloodhounds followed him.'

and did not Byron issue fiery challenges to enemies in
distant England? But their interest had, inevitably, a
certain ironic detachment.

With the Shelleys had come, as fellow-tenants at the
Casa Magni, their friends the Williams'. The whole
business of moving there had been a series of frustra-
tions, softened by unexpected mercies. It had been, in
fact, oddly typical of Shelley's life (one might almost
add, of his death). The furniture had been sent on from
Pisa before the house had been definitely leased, and
difficulties had arisen about landing it, until the good-
natured harbour-master came to the rescue. The in-
clusion of a second family into that crowded upper floor
was owing to the fact that at the last moment it was
discovered that no other lodgings were available in the
neighbourhood for the Williams'.

Shelley himself (the surname alone was used by his

wife when she spoke of him, and his letters, even to intimate friends, were signed with a simple 'S') stands out with stereoscopic detachment against all backgrounds, human or otherwise. He did not dominate them, as Byron did; even when most passionately moved, there was an aloofness. . . . That tall, stooping, boyish figure, with the clear blue eyes, curling brown hair, and high-pitched voice, drifted through life absorbed in ethical abstractions, while the petty problems born of poverty and his eager, uncalculating generosity gathered, were dispersed—and gathered again. Forget them he could—and did—in concrete, everyday pleasures; in bathing, shooting, and riding; in reading, in friendly talk. And when these pleasures wearied, was there not always that other world awaiting him, the intangible, invisible world of poetry?

Of the women who had come into his life three, at least, loved him greatly, though one of them, Claire, his sister-in-law, kept her secret until more than half a century after his death. Then, an old, wrinkled woman, she confessed. Harriet, the golden-haired schoolgirl with whom he had made a runaway match, had tired of him even sooner than he had tired of her, and leaving him, trodden a pilgrimage of tragic loneliness and shame which ended in the waters of the Serpentine. (Even his name had not remained with her; the inquest was held upon 'Harriet Smith'.) Of her he had now nothing left but memories. The children she had borne him had been taken from his charge; Lord

Chancellor Eldon had forbidden him even to see them except in the presence of their legal guardian.

Mary, his second wife, witty, social, with fair hair and calm grey eyes, not merely loved but understood him at least as much as Shelley's genius made understanding possible. But there heredity spoke. Harriet Westbrook's father had been a tavern-keeper; Mary's father was William Godwin, the brilliant, despicable, illogical philosopher, whose theories upon education were a hundred years in advance of his time, and who lived and died a failure who only just missed greatness. Mary herself was the author of a novel. *Frankenstein*, written and published before she was twenty-one, still survives, a typical product of immaturity, precocity, and the age of sham romance and delicious melancholy. She lived to write many other books, but that story of the semi-human monster was her best.

She was five years younger than Shelley.

The Shelleys were migrating to the sea. Byron, too, took another and cooler domicile, the Villa Rossa, at Monte Nero, on the outskirts of Leghorn. But he still retained his tenancy of the Palazzo Lanfranchi, a noble feudal building in Pisa. The local authorities were far from happy about Milord, regarding him with an uncomfortable blend of suspicion, admiration, dislike and amusement. The suspicion had its origin in his companions—the Count Gamba; his son, Count Pietro Gamba, and his daughter, the exquisite Countess Guicciolo, all of whom had come on from Pisa with Byron to the Villa Rossa. Both Italians were regarded as dangerous by the Government, and were more or less under sentence of expulsion. The admiration for Milord was a reluctant tribute to one who was aristocratic, brilliant, wealthy and, despite a slight lameness and the ravages of dissipation, conspicuously handsome. In short, the possessor of personality. Dislike? Well, there had been incidents, which certainly did not make for popularity. The affair of Sergeant-of-Dragoons Masi, for example, whose sole offence was that he had galloped, with perhaps regrettable roughness, through a party of riders which included Byron and Shelley. Milord, affronted, had dashed after in pursuit. Masi had drawn his sabre in defence—what were sabres for?—but little harm would have been done if a servant of Byron's had not attacked with a gardening-fork, dangerously wounding the sergeant. An unpleasant and sinister business from beginning to end.

Lastly, amusement. That had been provided by the manner of the English nobleman's arrival. Servants one would expect; hangers-on, male and female, would not have been surprising; dogs and horses—why not? But when a visitor appears accompanied by a parrot, monkeys, fowls and geese, what can one do but shrug?

However they regarded him, Byron was utterly uninterested. Local gossip might accuse him, as indeed it did, of the most fantastic crimes and follies; he ignored it contemptuously. He was entirely content to be the head of his own small circle of literary companions and admirers. Trelawney, big, bluff, travelled (you may see him, as he looked in his old age, painted to the life in Millais' 'The North-West Passage'); Lieutenant Edward Williams, and Jane, his attractive and sympathetic wife; Captain Medwin, cousin to Shelley; Claire Clermont, half-sister to Shelley's wife; one Taffe, a genial Irishman who was consumed by an unquenchable conviction that he had accomplished the one perfect translation of Dante, and was continually pestering the long-suffering Byron to find a publisher for what was an extraordinarily dull piece of work. And finally, Shelley himself, whom Byron both attracted and repelled. Clear-sighted and generous enough to recognize Byron's genius and charm, Shelley had a healthy hatred of the brutal egotism of the older man. Once, at least, he had left the Villa Rossa in a state of fury which only just stopped short of physical violence.

'I had difficulty in restraining myself from knocking him down!' blazed Shelley, describing the visit to a friend; and then added bitterly, 'But he can no more help being what he is than that door can help being a door!'

Said the friend shrewdly, 'You are wrong in your fatalism. If I were to horsewhip that door, it would still remain a door. But if Lord Byron were well horsewhipped, my opinion is that he would become as humane as he is now inhumane. It is the subserviency of his friends that makes him the insolent tyrant that he is.'

It may have been true. But no one tried the experiment.

It was one of these periodical revolts, as well as the

stifling summer weather, which impelled the Shelleys to leave Pisa for the Casa Magni.

But the separation could scarcely be more than brief. Established amid that lovely desolation, with Genoa to the north-west and Leghorn to the south-east, Shelley was still bound by chains of his own forging to Milord. Yet another exile and his family were on their way to Italy. In the previous autumn James Leigh Hunt, financially foundering as usual, had written distracted letters to Shelley; Shelley, himself in financial straits (for the insatiable Godwin, his father-in-law, was a permanent drain on his small income) had had an inspiration. Hunt should migrate to the Mediterranean coast, where living was far cheaper than in England. There he and Byron and Shelley himself would found a periodical whose unconventional brilliance would bring, not merely a fortune, but added fame to them all. Byron had been approached. His interest, tepid at first, had eventually been heated up to the point of consenting to assist Hunt with the magazine. Hunt was triumphantly notified. He was also supplied with money. The voyage to Italy, begun in November, had suffered a series of comic-opera delays, involving calls at Ramsgate, Dartmouth and Plymouth. (If they were lucky, observed one caustic commentator, they might spend the following Christmas at Falmouth!) By the end of January they were still in England, and again short of money. The indefatigable Shelley contrived by some means to remit another £150. Byron, in a further burst of generosity, agreed to surrender the ground floor of his own house, the Palazzo Lanfranchi, to the exiles when they did arrive.

On June the 19th Shelley received a letter saying that the Hunts, leaving Plymouth a month earlier, had at last reached Genoa. The whole Micawber-ish family of nine were well and in excellent spirits. On their way to Leghorn, they would pass Lerici; would it be possible from the steamer's deck to distinguish the low white house at the water's edge?

It might have been possible. But Shelley's impetuous spirit could not wait for that distant glimpse of his friend. Since May he had possessed a boat of his own, an exquisite thing, twenty-eight feet long by eight feet wide. Schooner-rigged and without a deck, she had been built upon a model brought from the Royal Dockyards in England. Her crew comprised Williams, a boy of eighteen named Vivian, and Shelley himself. Trelawney had wisely suggested the addition of some Genoese sailor who knew the coast and the currents, but Williams' nautical pride revolted, and Shelley, who boasted that he could read a book and control the boat at the same time, saw no reason for an extra hand. For Byron a duplicate vessel, save that it possessed a deck, had been supplied by the same builders.

The *Ariel*—she would have been the 'Don Juan', and did, under Byron's malicious instructions, arrive with that name painted on her sails, until Shelley cut out the offending canvas and rechristened her—was a perpetual inspiration and delight to her owner. In her, with all sail spread, he would have hastened to Genoa to greet the Hunts on their arrival. But the letter had been delayed; commonsense suggested that the family might by now have actually reached Leghorn.

Thither, therefore, in the *Ariel* he went, with Williams and the boy. The Hunts had arrived; whether they had their glimpse of Casa Magni from the ship's deck remains unknown. Shelley's immediate task was to shepherd the family to the Palazzo that awaited them at Pisa, seven miles inland. He left the *Ariel* in harbour with her crew on board, under instructions to await his return.

Byron's greeting to the newcomers was cordial enough. Unfortunately the friendliness rapidly evaporated. Hunt himself Byron liked, but his wife, with her impertinence and tactlessness, he detested, and the horde of children, 'dirtier and more mischievous than Yahoos', disgusted him. Shelley, instead of returning at once as he had planned, loyally lingered in a desperate effort to put matters on a pleasanter basis. Williams, waiting with the boat in Leghorn harbour, grew more and more impatient.

.   .   .   .

July the eighth arrived. Shelley had at last returned. By noon he and the others were already upon the schooner. Trelawney suddenly decided to accompany them on Byron's *Bolivar*. But he had no clearance-papers, and the health authorities, unexpectedly vigilant, intervened. Trelawney tried bluff, was brusquely threatened with fourteen days' quarantine, and eventually agreed to obtain the necessary documents. Two hours were frittered away, and at last Williams, losing patience, refused to delay any longer. Shelley supported him. There was so little wind that in any case the *Ariel* would have difficulty in reaching home before night.

Half-an-hour later she left harbour. Trelawney resignedly anchored afresh and refurled the *Bolivar's* sails. With a ship's glass he watched the little boat edging seawards, in company with two feluccas.

. . . .

The air grew suffocating. The sea, lead-like in colour and texture, was covered with an oily scum. Gusts of wind swept over, but did not ruffle it. When, from a sky filled with ragged clouds, heavy rain fell, the drops seemed to rebound from the water without penetrating.

Shelley was entirely unperturbed. His face, when he raised it from the volume of Keats he had borrowed from Hunt, and studied the horizon, was pale, but calm. Whatever Gods, if Gods there were, held his destiny in their hands, he was unafraid.

The boy Vivian was at the masthead, Williams steering. The sail had been furled, the topmast prudently lowered. The moan of the wind rose to a shriek, the rain became a torrent. Shelley thrust the book into his pocket; reading was impossible. His thoughts drifted to another exile, dead now over a year; to Keats, a mere boy of twenty-five, gasping out his life on that grey

215

February morning in Rome with only the faithful Severn for company; Keats, whom passion for a commonplace woman had ravaged so intolerably that the end had come as a boon, and who had asked that *'Here lies one whose name was writ in water'* should be inscribed upon his grave. But Shelley himself had given the humble-minded stableman's son a nobler—and truer—epitaph than that.

Happy, thrice happy Adonais!

As the storm reached its climax, a swift and shattering blow smote the *Ariel*, sending both masts crashing overboard and carrying away the bowsprit. The mortally stricken schooner leapt up and forward under the impact; then, with the waters foaming through her splintered timbers, she lurched back into the sea. In that one wild moment the calm eyes of Shelley met Williams'. The sailor's lips formed the word 'swim'.

Shelley shook his head and smiled. He recognized the inevitable and accepted it with a soul as serene as it was steadfast. The end—or was it the beginning?—had come.

The *Ariel* plunged . . . down, down.

· · · · · · · ·

More than forty years passed. The ill-starred periodical which had brought Hunt to Italy was long forgotten. It had survived only four numbers. Byron himself was dead, the intolerable battle between body and spirit ended in the fever-infested marshes of Missolonghi. Heroic legends had already begun to cluster about a name once infamous.

Hunt, too, was dead, after a stormy life ending in the placid security of a civil list pension and the suburban trivialities of Putney. Always he was forgiven much because of his intellectual honesty.

Mary Shelley lived until 1851. Trelawney would have married her, but Mary refused; the name she already bore was 'so pretty' that she wished to have it upon her tombstone. But Jane Williams had no such scruples, perhaps because, as she confessed to a new suitor of her own, her marriage to the Lieutenant had never been a valid one. Claire, Mary's half-sister, lived longest of any of them. Migrating to Russia, she became a governess there, until an inheritance of twelve thousand pounds brought her freedom.

.   .   .   .

An old fisherman lay dying. He belonged to the village of Sarzana. A priest stood at the bedside listening with trained immobility to a halting and broken confession.

There were two boats, one belonging to the mad English lord, the other to the mad English poet. So alike that it was difficult to know which was which. Especially in a storm. There had been a bitter storm one afternoon in July, long, long ago. He and four companions had been in a felucca. They had seen the English boat in difficulties. They had believed it to be the *Bolivar*, with Milord Byron, the reckless, the wealthy, on board. They had planned—all in a moment, for so such temptations come to poor fishermen— to run her down while yet darkness and rain screened

217

their crime; to sink the boat, or, (this as an alternative) to board her, and overcome the crew—and seize the gold. But the Devil, Father of Evil, had lured them unavailingly. Too late, in the very moment of the crash, they had realized that the boat was the *Ariel*. She had gone down like a stone, and her passengers with her. One of the men had swum for a little. They dare not try to rescue him. The boy and the tall Englishman with the womanish face had hardly struggled. . . . What the crew of the felucca had sworn afterwards at the inquiry was a fabric of lies. But what else was possible?

There was no answer; no answer was needed, for the man was dead.

The priest, breaking the oath of the confessional, made the pitiful story public.

But how little it mattered.

P. B. Shelley

From ADONAIS

Peace, peace! he is not dead, he doth not sleep—
He hath awakened from the dream of life—
'Tis we, who, lost in stormy visions, keep
With phantoms an unprofitable strife,
And in mad trance, strike with our spirit's knife
Invulnerable nothings.—We decay
Like corpses in a charnel; fear and grief
Convulse us and consume us day by day,
And cold hopes swarm like worms within our living clay.

He has outsoared the shadow of our night;
Envy and calumny and hate and pain,

And that unrest which men miscall delight,
Can touch him not and torture not again;
From the contagion of the world's slow stain
He is secure, and now can never mourn
A heart grown cold, a head grown grey in vain;
Nor, when the spirit's self has ceased to burn,
With sparkless ashes load an unlamented urn.

.   .   .   .

The One remains, the many change and pass;
Heaven's light for ever shines, earth's shadows fly;
Life, like a dome of many-coloured glass,
Stains the white radiance of eternity,
Until death tramples it to fragments. Die,
If thou wouldst be with that which thou dost seek!
Follow where all is fled—Rome's azure sky,
Flowers, ruins, statues, music, words are weak
The glory they transfuse with fitting truth to speak.

P. B. Shelley

MUSIC, WHEN SOFT VOICES DIE

Music, when soft voices die,
Vibrates in the memory;
Odours, when sweet violets sicken,
Live within the sense they quicken.

Rose leaves, when the rose is dead,
Are heap'd for the beloved's bed;
And so thy thoughts, when thou are gone,
Love itself shall slumber on.

219

P. B. Shelley

TIME

Unfathomable sea! whose waves are years,
Ocean of Time, whose waters of deep woe
Are brackish with the salt of human tears!
    Thou shoreless flood, which in thy ebb and flow
Claspest the limits of mortality!
And sick of prey, yet howling on for more,
Vomitest thy wrecks on its inhospitable shore;
Treacherous in calm, and terrible in storm,
              Who shall put forth on thee,
              Unfathomable sea?

P. B. Shelley

To TRELAWNEY AND WILLIAMS

Mine is a life of failures. Peacock says my poetry is composed of day-dreams and nightmares, and Leigh Hunt does not think it good enough for the *Examiner*. Jefferson Hogg says all poetry is inverted sense, and consequently nonsense. . . . I wrote, and the critics denounced me as a foolish visionary, and my friends said that I had mistaken my vocation, that my poetry was mere rhapsody of words.

Mary Shelley

From a Preface to FRANKENSTEIN

HOW FRANKENSTEIN CAME INTO BEING

During a conversation between Lord Byron and Shelley various philosophical doctrines were discussed, and among others, the nature of the principle of life, and whether there was any probability of its ever being discovered and communicated. . . . Night waned upon this talk, and even the witching hour had gone by before we retired to rest. When I placed my head upon my pillow I did not sleep, nor could I be said to think. My imagination, unbidden, possessed and guided me, gifting the successive images that arose in my mind with a vividness far beyond the usual bounds of reverie. I saw—with shut eyes but acute mental vision—I saw the pale student of unhallowed arts kneeling beside the thing he had put together—I saw the hideous phantasm of a man stretched out, and then, on the working of some powerful engine, show signs of life, and stir with an uneasy half-vital motion. Frightful it must be; for supremely frightful would be the effect of any human endeavour to mock the stupendous mechanism of the Creator of the world. His success would terrify the artist,—he would rush away from his odious handi-work, horror-stricken. He would hope, that, left to itself, the slight spark which he had communicated would fade; that this thing, which had received such imperfect animation, would subside into dead matter; that he might sleep in the belief that the silence of the grave would quench for ever the transient existence of the hideous corpse which he had looked upon as the cradle of Life. He sleeps; but he is awaked; he opens his eyes; behold, the horrid thing standing at his bedside, opening his curtains and looking on him with yellow, watery but speculative eyes.

I opened mine in terror. . . . Swift as light and as cheering was the idea that broke in upon me. 'I have found it! What terrified me will terrify others; and I need only describe the spectre which haunted my midnight pillow.' On the morrow I announced that I had thought of a story. I began that day with the words, *It was a dreary night of November*, making only a transcript of the grim terrors of my waking dream.

Lord Byron

NIGHT IN ROME

The stars are forth, the moon above the tops
Of the snow-shining mountains. Beautiful!
I linger yet with Nature, for the Night
Hath been to me a more familiar face
Than that of man; and in her starry shade
Of dim and solitary loveliness,
I learned the language of another world.
I do remember me, that in my youth,
When I was wandering upon such a night
I stood within the Coliseum's wall,
'Midst the chief relics of almighty Rome;
The trees which grew along the broken arches
Waved dark in the blue midnight, and the stars
Shone through the rents of ruin; from afar
The watch-dog bayed beyond the Tiber; and
More near from out the Cæsar's palace came
The owl's long cry, and, interruptedly,
Of distant sentinels the fitful song
Begun and died upon the gentle wind.
Some cypresses beyond the time-worn breach
Appeared to skirt the horizon, yet they stood
Within a bowshot. Where the Cæsars dwelt,
And dwell the tuneless birds of night, amidst
A grove which springs through levelled battlements,
And twines its roots with the imperial hearths,
Ivy usurps the laurel's place of growth;
But the gladiator's bloody Circus stands,
A noble wreck in ruinous perfection,

222

While Cæsar's chambers, and the Augustan halls,
Grovel on earth in indistinct decay.
And thou didst shine, thou rolling moon, upon
All this, and cast a wide and tender light,
Which softened down the hoar austerity
Of rugged desolation, and filled up,
As 'twere anew, the gaps of centuries;
Leaving that beautiful which still was so,
And making that which was not, till the place
Became religion, and the heart ran o'er
With silent worship of the great of old—
The dead but sceptred sovereigns, who still rule
Our spirits from their urns.

Lord Byron

There be None of Beauty's Daughters

There be none of Beauty's daughters
    With a magic like thee;
And like music on the waters
    Is thy sweet voice to me;
When, as if its sound were causing
The charmèd ocean's pausing,
The waves lie still and gleaming,
And the lulled winds seem dreaming:

And the midnight moon is weaving
    Her bright chain o'er the deep;
Whose breast is gently heaving,
    As an infant's asleep;
So the spirit bows before thee,
To listen and adore thee;
With a full but soft emotion,
Like the swell of Summer's ocean.

223

Lord Byron
SHE WALKS IN BEAUTY

She walks in beauty, like the night
    Of cloudless climes and starry skies;
And all that's best of dark and bright
    Meet in her aspect and her eyes;
Thus mellow'd to that tender light
    Which heaven to gaudy day denies.

One shade the more, one ray the less,
    Had half impair'd the nameless grace
Which waves in every raven tress,
    Or softly lightens o'er her face;
Where thoughts serenely sweet express
    How pure, how dear their dwelling-place.

And on that cheek, and o'er that brow,
    So soft, so calm, yet eloquent,
The smiles that win, the tints that glow,
    But tell of days in goodness spent,
A mind at peace with all below,
    A heart whose love is innocent!

John Keats

ODE ON A GRECIAN URN

Thou still unravish'd bride of quietness,
    Thou foster-child of Silence and slow Time,
Sylvan historian, who canst thus express
    A flowery tale more sweetly than our rhyme;

What leaf-fringed legend haunts about thy shape
    Of deities or mortals, or of both,
        In Tempe or the dales of Arcady?
What men or gods are these? What maidens loth?
What mad pursuit? What struggle to escape?
        What pipes and timbrels? What wild ectasy?

Heard melodies are sweet, but those unheard
    Are sweeter; therefore, ye soft pipes, play on;
Not to the sensual ear, but, more endear'd,
    Pipe to the spirit ditties of no tone;
Fair youth, beneath the trees, thou canst not leave
    Thy song, nor ever can those trees be bare;
        Bold Lover, never, never canst thou kiss,
Though winning near the goal—yet, do not grieve;
    She cannot fade, though thou hast not thy bliss,
        For ever wilt thou love, and she be fair!

Ah, happy, happy boughs! that cannot shed
    Your leaves, nor ever bid the Spring adieu;
And, happy melodist, unwearièd,
    For ever piping songs for ever new;
More happy love! more happy, happy love!
    For ever warm and still to be enjoy'd,
        For ever panting, and for ever young;
All breathing human passion far above,
    That leaves a heart high-sorrowful and cloy'd,
        A burning forehead, and a parching tongue.

Who are these coming to the sacrifice?
    To what green altar, O mysterious priest,
Lead'st thou that heifer lowing at the skies,
    And all her silken flanks with garlands drest?

What little town by river or sea-shore,
 Or mountain-built with peaceful citadel,
  Is emptied of its folk, this pious morn?
And, little town, thy streets for evermore
 Will silent be; and not a soul, to tell
  Why thou art desolate, can e'er return.

O Attic shape! fair attitude! with brede
 Of marble men and maidens overwrought,
With forest branches and the trodden weed;
 Thou, silent form! dost tease us out of thought
As doth eternity. Cold Pastoral!
 When old age shall this generation waste,
  Thou shalt remain, in midst of other woe
Than ours, a friend to man, to whom thou say'st,
 'Beauty is truth, truth beauty'—that is all
  Ye know on earth, and all ye need to know.

John Keats
LA BELLE DAME SANS MERCI

 Ah! what can ail thee, wretched wight,
  Alone and palely loitering?
 The sedge is withered from the lake,
  And no birds sing.

 Ah! what can ail thee, wretched wight,
  So haggard and so woe-begone?
 The squirrel's granary is full,
  And the harvest's done.

 I see a lily on thy brow,
  With anguish moist and fever-dew;
 And on thy cheek a fading rose
  Fast withereth too.

226

I met a lady in the meads,
 Full beautiful—a fairy's child;
Her hair was long, her foot was light,
 And her eyes were wild.

I set her on my pacing steed,
 And nothing else saw all day long;
For sideways would she lean and sing
 A fairy's song.

I made a garland for her head,
 And bracelets too, and fragrant zone;
She looked at me as she did love,
 And made sweet moan.

She found me roots of relish sweet,
 And honey wild, and manna-dew;
And sure in language strange she said,
 I love thee true.

She took me to her elfin grot,
 And there she gazed and sighèd deep;
And there I shut her wild sad eyes—
 So kissed to sleep.

And there we slumbered on the moss,
 And there I dreamed, ah! woe betide,
The latest dream I ever dreamed,
 On the cold hill-side.

I saw pale kings and princes too,
 Pale warriors—death-pale were they all;
Who cried, 'La Belle Dame Sans Merci
 Hath thee in thrall!'

I saw their starved lips in the gloom,
    With horrid warning gapèd wide;
And I awoke, and found me here
    On the cold hillside.

And this is why I sojourn here,
    Alone and palely loitering;
Though the sedge is withered from the lake,
    And no birds sing.

THE SPLENDID EXILES

Byron (English Men of Letters) — John Nichol

Glorious Apollo — E. Barrington

Ariel — André Maurois

Life of Shelley — Ed. Dowden

Records of Shelley, Byron, etc, — E. J. Trelawney

Shelley, Godwin, and their Circle — H. N. Brailsford

Keats (Introductory Sketch to Canterbury Poets Edition) — J. Hogben

Literary History of England (Vol. III.) — Mrs. Oliphant

CHAPTER TEN

THE BLUDGEONINGS OF FATE

[1835]

THE MONTH WAS MARCH, the scene London. Upon the throne, his short reign already nearing its end, sat that fussy amiable old gentleman known as William the Fourth. Flatterers referred to him as 'our Sailor King', though the admiralty were doing their best to forget the last years of his career in the Senior Service. To those for whom divinity did not hedge a king he was 'Silly Billy'. What else could one label one who greeted a returned North Pole explorer with the remark that he looked as brown as if he had been to the South Pole! Mr. Charles Greville has recorded in his *Journal* the undeniable fact that His Majesty's head was shaped like a pineapple, that his manners in public were worse than those of George the Fourth, and that he twaddled over politics and bored the Duke of Wellington to death. Sir Robert Peel's premiership had come to an end, and Lord Melbourne, with an unstable majority of ten behind him, had taken his place. It was not, either physically or morally, a comfortable place, since the Houses of Parliament had been burnt down on the previous October, and five years were to pass before the new buildings were even begun.

A mile or so from the ruins the eldest son of a Scotch peasant-farmer had lately taken up his residence. He had saved a little money, though not much; he had a few friends in London, but was not the type whose friendships formed easily. Robbie Burns, dead a generation ago, and Walter Scott, killed by overwork these two years past, had both their devotees and hero-worshippers. But Thomas Carlyle of Ecclefechan wove no spells and cast no charms, either rustic or romantic, over those with whom he came into contact.

He was thirty-seven, and already a confirmed dyspeptic. Ruggedly honest and aggressively independent, he stood like a rough-hewn fragment of Scotch granite among London's more gracious stone. However bleak his own prospects, help to other members of his family was never withheld. A man of prejudices which rarely warped his judgment, of grievances which seldom destroyed his sense of proportion, and of hatreds that never affected his innate generosity of spirit, Carlyle found Life a battleground and the battle worth fighting.

He was a married man. And the story of his courtship and marriage is in its own way as remarkable as that of the sturdy old philosopher, critic, and historian with whom he had so many points in common. One is tempted, indeed, into elaborate comparisons between Samuel Johnson and Thomas Carlyle. Nearly a century separated their births, and each was a typical product of his century. One was English of the English, the other Scotch to the tips of his unexpectedly delicate and artistic fingers. Each came to London to make his fortune, and made it. Their moral qualities were extraordinarily alike, and included kindliness, intellectual honesty, intolerance, and a dogged patience that

230

battled with the twin enemies of poverty and persistent ill-health. In both cases the ill-health remained after the poverty was vanquished—though never forgotten.

There was, too, a Mrs. Johnson and a Mrs. Carlyle. Both accorded their husbands devotion, and received it.

Jane Baillie Welsh was nearly six years Thomas Carlyle's junior, and came of a family which had definite, though rather slender, claims to gentility, the patriot Wallace being included in the family tree. Thomas never claimed to be anything greater than a peasant; he would probably have been ashamed of possessing aristocratic forebears. Jane, in the days of her wooing, had been pretty enough to earn the title of the Rose of Haddington. Perhaps 'piquant' is the better word to describe her early portraits, which show her as possessing alert, amused eyes, a straight little nose, lips which might enchant a lover but in which a colder-blooded physiognomist might discover a capacity for uttering devastating truths, a slender neck, and soft, demurely-parted hair. Thomas himself, square-jawed and with eyes deep-set under a brooding forehead, laid no claim to distinction, let alone good looks. Jane of the early days was a bit of a flirt; one boggles hopelessly at the mere thought of Thomas flirting. Jane was by way of being an heiress on a small scale; Thomas inherited nothing beyond the family characteristics. Jane's genius—for she had genius—was like a rippling brook which the sunshine of admiration set flashing. Thomas' genius was a Niagara which obscured and obliterated

231

the lesser stream. His courtship had been slow, a prolonged comedy (but never a farce) in its plodding
assaults and its strategical retreats. He had triumphed
in the end, after a sufficiently candid exhibition of
traits which, had Jane not loved as well as esteemed
him, would have ended the whole business. They had
been married over six years now, and she had had time
to grow used to his 'strange, dark humours'. It proved
a partnership in which she was to be audience, critic
and adviser, while he struggled to reduce his turgid
Scotch philosophy to plain English. Particularly he
struggled with *Sartor Resartus*—surely the oddest serial
ever published in a monthly paper.

Sartor was his first original work which involved sustained effort. It deserved recognition as the work of an
original genius. But it did not achieve even financial
success. The book was sneered at because it was not
understood; its author 'impracticable, impersuadable,
unmalleable, as wilful as if he were the eldest son and
heir to a peerage'—the summary springs from the pen
of a friend, not an enemy—was left to go his own per-
verse and obstinate way. And Jane, the gently nur-
tured, attractive, volatile Jane, was constrained to go
with him.

One is impelled to pause here and discuss, lightly
and reverently, the reaction of the Carlyles upon one
another. Well-meaning Froude spilt quantities of un-
necessary ink in mysterious hints; correspondence
intended for no eyes but the recipients' was exhibited to
a distressed and bewildered public; Carlyle's nephew

became vocal when silence would have been the better part. But when all was said and written, no one studying the accumulated facts with a reasonably unprejudiced mind could doubt the deep, unshakable affection which existed beneath the petty irritations and exasperations inevitable in the linked lives of two geniuses, one of whom happened to be a dyspeptic male and the other a neurotic female. Jane, furthermore, was a spoilt child. She was accustomed to be the focus of attraction, and in her own home had filled that position with complete success. Like so many highly-strung women, she had a natural instinct for dramatization; her letters paint exaggerated pictures of an anguish which was as ephemeral as a thunderstorm. Carlyle, who understood even as he loved her, exaggerated in turn his own boorish character, listened with complete good humour to her exposure of his foibles before their circle of friends, and roared with laughter when the exposure was completed. Both had their moments of black depression—but neither would have chosen another companion to share them. And when they were apart, each was frantic if there was delay in the arrival of the daily letter. They had no children; the legend has arisen that while Jane was left to eat her heart out in lonely bitterness, Carlyle went his way, indifferent, if not antagonistic to childhood. Antagonistic! Read, as you still may, the notes sent with gifts he made to his childish friends. There could be no more touching testimony to his innate tenderness.

During their brief married life the Carlyles' homes

had been many. From their first lodging in Edinburgh they had emigrated to the farm owned by Jane's mother at Craigenputtock. From there they went to London, came back to the farm, left it again for Edinburgh, and finally decided that London offered the best prospects to a Scotsman of revolutionary tendencies and limitless literary ambitions. For a short time they lodged in the Grays Inn Road—the same rooms in that uninspiring thoroughfare had sheltered them on a previous visit—and eventually, thanks to the kindly activities of Leigh Hunt, took a lease of Number 5, Cheyne Row, Chelsea, the rental being thirty-five pounds a year and the date June the 4th, 1834.

Leigh Hunt, that strange figure which seems to drift like a feckless, restless ghost among the literary giants of the early nineteenth century, was one of Carlyle's little circle of London friends. (His 'Jenny Kiss'd Me', a delicious little classic, was written apropos of Mrs. Carlyle, the 'Jenny' being herself.) His age was now fifty; his circumstances, as usual, deplorable. Carlyle himself gives a picture of Hunt's home in Upper Cheyne Row, in which figure 'four or five strange, beautiful, gipsy-looking children, a sickly, large wife, rickety chairs, ragged carpets, books, paper, eggshells and scissors', and of how Hunt received him with imperturbable dignity in the loose-flowing muslin nightgown in which he always wrote. Hunt it was who discovered Number 5, after prolonged house-hunting on the part of the Carlyles themselves. The number has now been changed to 24. But little else is changed.

Carlyle, not frequently moved to enthusiasm, described it as 'a right old strong, roomy brick house,'
eminent, antique, wainscoted to the very ceiling'. It
had a narrow frontage, being one of a terrace, with the
door on the right. Southward was Cheyne Walk and
the River. The front room on the ground floor was for
twenty years the parlour, then, when increasing pros-
perity justified it, the Carlyles used it as a dining-room,
and the one above as a drawing-room. Folding doors
open into a second room whose window overlooks the
prim, arid little garden. Near the end wall, which dates
from Tudor days, is erected a memorial stone to
Jane's little dog. The whole house now is a Carlyle
memorial, crowded with little intimate domesticities
which stir the imagination and touch the heartstrings.
Here is one of the 'churchwarden' pipes which Carlyle
used to smoke, and when he had done with them, fill
with tobacco and leave on the doorstep, for poorer men
to discover and take away. Here is the leather case
which invariably accompanied him on his journeys,
with its neatly docketed paper packets of pens and
buttons and bootlaces, the equipment of a thrifty and
experienced traveller. Here is his inkpot, the very quill
which wrote the last pages of *Sartor*, and some of the
cups and saucers in everyday use. ('All the others,'
an American tourist recently assured his wife, 'are
smashed because he threw them at her!')

And Jane? There is the screen her nimble fingers
ornamented with scraps, her special weakness being
for famous men. There is a corner bracket, similarly

235

pictorial. There is the bed reading-lamp that burnt so many candles for them both. There, beside one of his, is a lock of her hair. There is scarcely any difference in the colour of the two.

These things exist to-day as silent, infinitely pathetic survivals. Ninety-eight years ago their owners were a married couple, neither in their first youth, and living dangerously, almost desperately near to destitution. A couple who had brought their possessions all the way from Scotland to that terraced house whose one indisputable beauty was its carved and twisted banisters.

Many years were to pass before that tenancy came to an end. (To the last the tenant never paid more than the original thirty-five pounds a year.)

.   .   .   .

The Carlyles' friends in the Metropolis were few. But they were worth knowing and worth keeping. Leigh Hunt, their near neighbour, has been mentioned. Edward Irving, the fellow-student to whom Carlyle owed his introduction to Jane, and to whom Jane herself was originally engaged, had long preceded him to London, and there developed into a spectacularly brilliant preacher. But it was one of the lesser tragedies of Carlyle's life that Irving had left London to return to his native Scotland a year or two before the house in Cheyne Row was occupied. Jeffrey, the critic whose sledge-hammer reviews were a feature of the *Edinburgh Review*, was another friend. Ralph Waldo Emerson, the

American critic and essayist, who had lately visited England, was another. A fifth was John Stuart Mill.

.   .   .   .

Among the fantastic, almost incredible characters which startle the student of nineteenth-century literature, Mill deserves more prominence than he receives, if only on account of his education. Before he was three, he had learnt lists of Greek words with their English meanings; by his eighth year he had read many Greek authors in the original, to say nothing of lighter literary fare such as the works of Gibbon, Robertson and Hume; Plutarch's Lives, Mosheim's Ecclesiastical History, Latin and philosophy followed. The infant prodigy survived to develop into a lank youth with auburn hair, a ruddy complexion, and 'a gentle, pathetic expression'.

In 1830, being then twenty-four, he made the acquaintance of a Mrs. Taylor. The lady, two years Mill's junior, was a vivacious semi-invalid with a marked taste for coquetry. Her health precluded her living entirely in London with her husband, an estimable drysalter and druggist, but not from coming up from the country at least twice a week. She took complete possession of the enchanted John Stuart. Mr. Taylor protested, but was assured that the friendship was absolutely platonic and that 'he might blow up the house before she would abandon it'—i.e., the friendship. Whereupon the house remained *in situ* and the friendship remained also. Mill and she not only met frequently in the country, but dined together twice a week in Town, upon which occasions the chastened and tactful Mr. Taylor absented himself from the feasts of reason and the flow of soul until 1851, when his absence become involuntary and permanent, and the now middle-aged philosopher, with fewer auburn locks but much brilliant writing to his credit, duly married his charmer. Jane Carlyle did not care for her, and thought her affected and empty-headed. Mill himself never spoke of her to his family or his friends, perhaps because he winced at their possible comments. Posterity, however, has his word for it that the lady's 'excellencies of heart and mind were unparalleled in any human being I have ever known or heard of', and that 'her influence upon my intellectual and moral development was of the highest importance'. And who should perceive the truth if a philosopher cannot? The fact that ribald observers remarked that her excellencies consisted chiefly in echoing his own views merely exhibits the pettiness of Human Nature.

Financially, as well as in a domestic sense, Mill was a lucky man. From a junior clerkship in the Examiner's Department at the India House under his father, he rose steadily until, by the age of sixty, he was chief of his office and drawing a salary of two thousand pounds a year. His introduction to Carlyle dated from 1831, in which year he had written a series of papers which had attracted the Scotsman's attention. The intimacy of their friendship increased with the Carlyles' migration to London.

238

Those early months of arrival and settling down had passed. Already it had become increasingly doubtful whether London's paving-stones were any more golden than those of Edinburgh, and how long his slender capital could hold out. For, to quote a candid biographer, 'in Cheyne Row he was more neglected than he had been in Scotland. No one seemed to want his services, no one applied to him for contributions. When visiting such friends as he had, he was stared at as if he were a strange wild animal. Silent unless addressed, his opinions, if asked, were given contemptuously. He was considered "sarcastic for so young a man".' Month after month passed; his savings continued to dwindle. The management of a review, which he hoped might be offered him, went elsewhere. An introduction to the editor of *The Times* led to nothing because, desperately poor though Carlyle was, he refused to express any opinion which was not genuinely his own.

'I can reverence no existing man,' he wrote scornfully about this time (1834). . . 'I could write a better book than has been written here in this generation.'

He planned to write it. The book was to be a history of the French Revolution, in those days a mere generation distant. The subject possessed an immense appeal to one whose whole life was a revolt against the dead incubus of tradition. But it demanded more than enthusiasms and a temperamental affinity. Books—works of reference—were essential. Mill, to whom the project was confided, not merely approved, but offered

239

to lend from his own library as many volumes as might be helpful. Under which stimulus the task was begun.

Throughout the autumn and winter of 1834 Thomas Carlyle laboured. The piles of paper covered with that neat, vertical script grew in number. If self-expression be happiness, then this Scotch dyspeptic, his tall figure swathed in a buff-coloured dressing-gown, his pen travelling tirelessly over the quarto sheets, had little to ask of the Gods in those days. Jane shared that happiness—so, at least, one likes to believe. The chapters were read to her; her comments listened to. If, when her shaggy Genius withdrew to commune with himself again, she suffered from loneliness, and, as a lonely and clever woman will, exaggerated the miseries of her lot, one need not blame her. Having paid for one's happiness, what harm in occasionally exhibiting the receipts? In practical details she never showed anything but the completest devotion and loyalty.

It was Jane, for example, who grappled with the problem of the fowls in the garden next door; they crowed and clucked, and clucked and crowed, until Genius averred itself goaded to the borderline of insanity. Jane bought up the fowls and disposed of them. For a time there was peace, and Genius recovered. Then new tenants arrived, and brought with them a new colony for the chicken-run! Jane was distracted—until she discovered, after waiting in anguish, that Thomas was not. The new epidemic of crowing had not impinged itself upon his consciousness. His fury was now concentrated upon the insistent shrilling of distant railway-whistles.

The New Year saw Carlyle still struggling in a bog of ill-luck and depression. Edward Irving was dead of consumption at forty-two. 'I am friendless—or as good as that'—groaned Carlyle, and the world was 'a noisy inanity'. Jane was in bed, 'very unhappily ill of a foot which a puddle of a maid scalded three weeks ago'. His writing, though he stuck to it like a burr, refused to make progress.

Nevertheless, the beginning of February saw the completion of the first book—or, to be more exact, the first volume—of the *History of the French Revolution*.

The fact brought no sense of triumph to the author. 'Soul and body both very sick,' he recorded. 'It is now some three-and-twenty months since I have earnt one penny by the craft of literature.' And then, with an unexpected lapse into the second person, 'To ask editors to employ you will not improve, but worsen matters. You are like a spinster waiting to get married.'

Emerson, whose friendship remained unshaken throughout their long lives, wrote suggesting a lecturing tour in the States. Carlyle thanked him, but declined. 'Thanks to thrift and my good Scotch wife, we can hold out many months yet,' he replied, with a touch of defiance. Later in the same month he made the acquaintance of Southey, the Poet Laureate, 'A lean, grey, white-headed man of dusky complexion, unexpectedly tall when he rises, and still leaner then; a man with the shallowest chin, prominent snubbed

Roman nose, small care-lined brow, huge bush of white-grey hair on high crown, and the most vehement pair of faint hazel eyes I have ever seen. A well-read, honest, limited (strait-laced, even) kindly-hearted, most irritable man.' (What a superb reporter Thomas would have made!)

Mill's interest in the new book increased rather than diminished. He borrowed each section of the manuscript as it was written, with the object of making notes and suggestions. So, by degrees, the whole of the first volume passed into his possession.

On the fifth of March he went to dine with his goddess. He took the manuscript with him, and left it at the Taylors' house.

Twenty-four hours passed. Carlyle, after a day of steady, exhausting work, was sitting with Jane upstairs. They heard a rap at the front door, heard it opened, heard hurried footsteps ascending the stairs. Mill appeared, breathless, his face ghastly. Mrs. Carlyle exclaimed involuntarily, 'Gracious Providence, he has gone off with Mrs. Taylor!' Carlyle leapt to his feet, crying, 'Why, Mill, what ails ye, man! What is it?' and as his visitor staggered, caught him by the arm.

'Go down—speak to someone—waiting in a carriage —outside,' gasped Mill.

Jane, torn between apprehension and curiosity, fled downstairs. Carlyle, still supporting the half-fainting man, could only suppose that whatever the reason, Mill had come to take a final leave of him. But Jane, returning swiftly, brought the truth.

The 'someone waiting in the carriage' was Mrs. Taylor. She had driven with Mill to Cheyne Row to support him in breaking the news that Carlyle's manuscript had been left forgotten on her dining-room table, and that a housemaid, descending in the early morning, had found the pages scattered over the floor by errant breezes and used them to light the fire. A few charred wisps were all that were left.

Carlyle listened without wincing to the story of the tragedy. For tragedy it was. There was no second copy; even the rough notes he made from time to time had been destroyed as the work progressed. For five months he had laboured at white heat; now the fires of inspiration had died down into a grey ash of lethargy. . . . But the soul is greater than the intellect, and all that was noblest in the soul of Thomas Carlyle rose majestically then.

His first instinct was to comfort his friend.

Mill, having broken the news, should have gone. But he did not go. For two interminable hours he lingered, explaining, protesting, apologizing. . . . At last husband and wife were alone again. Carlyle closed the door, and came back to Jane's chair.

'Mill, poor fellow,' he said, 'is terribly cut up. We must try to hide from him how serious this business is for us.'

And her answer?

'My dear wife'—so he wrote in his journal—'has been very kind, and has become dearer to me. . . . This morning I have determined that I can still write a

THE HUMAN APPROACH TO LITERATURE

book on the French Revolution, and will do it. Oh, that I had faith! Cry silently in thy inmost heart to God for it. It is as though my Invisible Schoolmaster had torn my copybook when I showed it, and said, "No, boy. Thou must write it better." '

[APRIL 1866]

The 'copy' was re-written, Mill's insistence on financial compensation robbing the delay of its most sordid terrors. The final volume appeared in 1837. The French Revolution found its most eloquent historian, and Carlyle at last found recognition among his countrymen. The years rolled on. The house with the twisted banisters had many visitors now; 'friendless' was the last word one would have used in connection with its tenants. To the little circle of friends belonging to those early years in London long ago there had been added Lord Houghton, John Stirling (whose father had offered Carlyle a position on *The Times*), Mazzini, Froude the historian, Ruskin, Tennyson, the Ashburtons, and a host of humbler admirers. Age touched the brown, tousled hair and etched lines about the dogged mouth; a beard hid the chin. But the eyes still retained their clear and childlike blue.

And Jane—what of Jane?

She had passed through troubled waters. As the spectre of poverty receded—Carlyle had achieved independence by the time he was forty-five—other spectres took its place. Her health was uncertain; her nerves ran away with her, and Thomas, more self-absorbed than ever and more than ever tormented by dyspepsia—'the rat gnawing in the pit of his stomach' —was sustaining his reputation of being 'gey ill to live wi'.' They still loved one another, but there were moments when Jane forgot it. There were ugly flashes of jealousy. Lady Ashburton, clever, handsome in her plump aristocratic way, and with a social standing which made the Rose of Haddington's claims merely provincial, smiled upon Thomas, and Thomas, grim but not contemptuous, smiled back. Jane's only weapons were her tongue and her pen, both of which retained their gay and biting vivacity. One sees her, a little faded, mid-Victorian figure in stiff black gown and a cap, sometimes invading the attic room, with its double walls that persistently failed to keep out heat or draughts or noises, in which her gaunt and distrait Genius worked and smoked. But more often Jane was alone.

Carlyle himself the world refused to leave alone. The Ecclefechan burr might still be heard in intimate conversation, but clear and comprehensible English now took its place in the lecture-room, and as a lecturer he was 'popular' in the best and most literal sense.

As long ago as 1854 he had been nominated for the Lord Rectorship of Glasgow University. He was not elected; his religious and social views, harshly and openly expressed, jarred too uncomfortably on the authorities' ears. But a few years later his *Life of Frederick the Great* gave him new eminence, and in 1865 Edinburgh offered him the honour which Glasgow had refused. In the April of the following year he went down to deliver the Rectorial Address which his election demanded. His subject was 'On the Choice of Books'.

The lecture was a triumphant and magnificent success.

Did he recall, as he faced those ranks of eager youth, his own early days in the Capital, when he and Jane were so young, so defiant, so ignorant, so poor in everything but one another? Perhaps. Certainly he thought of her; demonstrably she thought of him. By his favourite window-seat in Cheyne Row, overlooking the garden, there still hangs the crude oil-painting of Frederick the Great which she bought, after a certain amount of shrewd Scotch haggling, and concerning which she wrote during that ceremonial visit.

He went on to Scotsbrig, sprained an ankle, and—being Carlyle—probably grumbled enormously. But in his heart was content. And he wrote to Jane, waiting for him nearly four hundred miles away. And Jane wrote to him.

Her letters reached him. He opened them with steady fingers, but with a broken heart. They had been overtaken by a telegram.

Jane, his companion for forty years, who had shared every grim defeat and every hard-won triumph, was dead.

She had been unwell, and then better, though still troubled by a pain below her heart and worried by the loss of her little dog. She had been taking her customary afternoon drive, alone, as usual. At Hyde Park Corner

246

the coachman turned to ask for directions. Jane did not answer. Jane would answer no questions this side of eternity. . . .

Thomas Carlyle left the scenes of his triumphs to finish his long pilgrimage alone in the narrow house of memories in Cheyne Row.

Thomas Carlyle

From THE FRENCH REVOLUTION (Volume One)

THE SIEGE OF THE BASTILLE

All morning, since nine, there has been a cry every-where: To the Bastille! Repeated 'deputations of citizens' have been here, passionate for arms; whom De Launay has got dismissed by soft speeches through portholes. Towards noon, Elector Thuriot de la Rosière gains admittance; finds De Launay indisposed for sur-render; nay, disposed for blowing up the place rather. Thuriot mounts with him to the battlements; heaps of paving-stones, old iron and missiles lie piled; cannon all duly levelled; in every embrasure a cannon—only drawn back a little!

. . . .

Wo to thee, De Launay, in such an hour, if thou canst not, taking some one firm decision, *rule* circumstances! Soft speeches will not serve; hard grapeshot is question-able; but hovering between the two is *un*questionable. Ever wilder swells the tide of men; their infinite hum waxing ever louder, into imprecations, perhaps into crackle of stray musketry,—which latter, on walls nine feet thick, cannot do execution. The Outer Drawbridge has been lowered for Thuriot; new deputation of citizens (it is the third, and noisiest of all) penetrates that way into the Outer Court; soft speeches producing no clearance of these, De Launay gives fire; pulls up his Drawbridge. A slight sputter;—which has *kindled* the too combustible chaos; made it a roaring fire-chaos! Bursts forth Insurrection, at sight of its own blood (for there were deaths by that sputter of fire), into endless rolling explosion of musketry, distraction, execration; —and over head, from the Fortress, let one great gun, with its grapeshot, go booming, to show what we *could* do. The Bastille is besieged!

. . . .

Let conflagration rage; of whatsoever is combustible! Guardrooms are burnt, Invalides mess-rooms. A distracted 'Peruke-maker with two fiery torches' is for burning 'the saltpetres of the Arsenal'; had not a woman run screaming; had not a Patriot, with some tincture of Natural Philosophy, instantly struck the wind out of him (butt of musket on pit of stomach), overturned barrels, and stayed the devouring element. A young beautiful lady, seized escaping in these Outer Courts, and thought falsely to be De Launay's daughter, shall be burnt in De Launay's sight; she lies swooned on a paillasse; but again a Patriot, it is brave Aubin Bonnemere the old soldier, dashes in, and rescues her. Straw is burnt; three cartloads of it, hauled thither, go up in white smoke; almost to the choking of Patriotism itself; so that Elie had, with singed brows, to drag back one cart; and Reole the 'gigantic haberdasher' another. Smoke as of Tophet; confusion as of Babel; noise as of the Crack of Doom!

Blood flows; the aliment of new madness. The wounded are carried into houses of the Rue Cerisaie;

248

the dying leave their last mandate not to yield till the accursed Stronghold fall. And yet, alas, how fall? The walls are so thick! Deputations, three in number, arrive from the Hotel-de-Ville; Abbe Fauchet (who was of one) can say, with what almost superhuman courage of benevolence. These wave their Townflag in the arched Gateway; and stand, rolling their drum; but to no purpose. In such Crack of Doom, De Launay cannot hear them, dare not believe them; they return, with justified rage, the whew of lead still singing in their ears. What to do. The Firemen are here, squirting with their fire pumps on the Invalides cannon, to wet the touchholes; they unfortunately cannot squirt so high; but produce only clouds of spray. Individuals of classical knowledge propose *catapults*. Santerre, the sonorous Brewer of the Suburb Saint-Antoine, advises rather that the place be fired, by a 'mixture of phosphorus and oil-of-turpentine spouted up through forcing pumps'; O Spinola-Santerre, hast thou the mixture *ready*? Every man his own engineer! And still the fire-deluge abates not: even women are firing, and Turks; at least one woman (with her sweetheart) and one Turk. Gardes Francaises have come; real cannon, real cannoneers. Usher Maillard is busy; half-pay Elie, half-pay Hulin rage in the midst of thousands.

How the great Bastille Clock ticks (inaudible) in its Inner Court there, at its ease, hour after hour; as if nothing special, for it or for the world, were passing! It tolled One when the firing began; and is now pointing towards Five, and still the firing slakes not.—Far down, in their vaults, the seven Prisoners hear muffled dins as of earthquakes; their Turnkeys answer vaguely.

Wo to thee, De Launay, with thy poor hundred Invalides! Broglie is distant, and his ears heavy: Besenval hears, but can send no help. One poor troop of Hussars has crept, reconnoitering, cautiously along the Quais, as far as the Pont Neuf. 'We are come to join you,' said the Captain; for the crowd seems shoreless. A large-headed dwarfish individual of smoke-bleared aspect, shambles forward, opening his blue lips, for there is sense in him; and croaks: 'Alight then, and give up your arms!' The Hussar-Captain is too happy to be escorted to the Barriers, and dismissed on parole. Who the squat individual was? Men answer, It is M. Marat, author of the excellent pacific *Avis au Peuple*! Great truly, O thou remarkable Dogleech, is this thy day of emergence and new-birth; and yet this same day come four years—! But let the curtains of the Future hang.

Thomas Carlyle

From his Inaugural Address at Edinburgh University

April 2nd 1866

Gentlemen,

When this office was first proposed to me, some of you know I was not very ambitious to accept it, but had my doubts rather. I was taught to believe that there were certain more or less important duties which would lie in my power. This, I confess, was my chief motive in going into it and overcoming this objection I felt to such things; if I could do anything to serve my dear old Alma Mater and you, why should not I? (Loud cheers.) Well, but on practically looking into the matter when the office actually came into my hands, I find it grows more and more uncertain and abstruse to me whether there is much real duty I can do at all. I live four hundred miles away from you, in an entirely different

250

scene of things, and with the burden of weak health now accumulating on me, and my total unacquaintance with such subjects as concern your affairs here— All this fills me with apprehension that there is nothing worth the least consideration that I can do on that score. You may depend on it, however, that if any such duty arise in any form, I will use my most faithful endeavour to do in it whatever is right and proper according to the best of my judgment. (Cheers.)

Advices, I believe, to young men, as to all men, are very seldom much valued. There is a great deal of advising and very little faithful performing, and talk that does not end in any kind of action is better suppressed altogether. I would not, therefore, go much into advising; but there is one advice I must give you. In fact, it is the summary of all advice, and doubtless you have heard it a thousand times, but I must nevertheless let you hear it the thousandth and first time, whether you will believe it at present or not—namely, that above all things the interest of your whole life depends on your being *diligent*, now, while it is called to-day, in this place where you have come to get education. Diligent; that includes all the virtues that a student can have; I mean it to include all those qualities of conduct that lead to the acquirement of real instruction and improvement in such a place.

Leigh Hunt

JENNY KISS'D ME

Jenny kiss'd me when we met,
    Jumping from the chair she sat in;
Time, you thief, who love to get
    Sweets into your list, put that in!

Say I'm weary, say I'm sad,
  Say that health and wealth have miss'd me,
Say I'm growing old, but add,
  Jenny kiss'd me.

R. W. Emerson

Days

Daughters of Time, the hypocritic Days,
Muffled and dumb like barefoot dervishes
And marching single in an endless file,
Bring diadems and faggots in their hands.
To each they offer gifts after his will—
Bread, kingdoms, stars, and sky that holds them all.
I, in my pleachèd garden, watch'd the pomp,
Forgot my morning wishes, hastily
Took a few herbs and apples, and the day
Turn'd and departed silent. I, too late,
Under her solemn fillet saw the scorn.

John Stuart Mill

From On the Subjection of Women

  All causes, social and natural, combine to make it un-
likely that women should be collectively rebellious to
the power of man. They are so far in a position different
from all other subject classes that their masters require
something more from them than actual service. Men do
not want solely the obedience of women, they want
their sentiments. All men, except the most brutish,
desire to have in the woman most nearly connected
with them, not a forced slave, but a willing one; not a

slave merely, but a favourite. The master of other slaves rely, for maintaining obedience, on fear; either fear of themselves, or religious fears. The masters of women wanted more than simple obedience, and they turned the whole force of education to effect their purpose. All women are brought up from their earliest years in the belief that their ideal of character is the very opposite of that of men; not self-will, and government by self-control, but submission and yielding to the control of others. . . . We are continually told that civilization and Christianity have restored to woman her just rights. Meanwhile the wife is the actual bondservant of her husband; no less so, so far as legal obligation goes, than slaves commonly so-called. She vows a lifelong obedience to him at the altar, and is held to it all through her life by law. She can do no act whatever but by his permission, at least tacit. She can acquire no property but for him; the instant it becomes hers, even by inheritance, it becomes *ipso facto* his. In every grade of the descending scale are men to whom are committed all the legal powers of a husband. The vilest malefactor has some wretched woman tied to him, against whom he can commit any atrocity except killing her, and, if tolerably cautious, can do that without much danger of the legal penalty.

When it is suggested that women's executive capacities and prudent counsels might sometimes be found valuable in affairs of state, lovers of fun hold up to the ridicule of the world, as sitting in Parliament or in the Cabinet, girls in their teens, or young wives of two or three and twenty, transported bodily, exactly as they are, from the drawing-room to the House of Commons. Commonsense would tell them that if such trusts were confided to women, it would be to such as have no special vocation for married life, or prefer another

253

employment of their faculties (as many women even now prefer to marriage some of the few honourable occupations within their reach).

THE BLUDGEONINGS OF FATE

CHAPTER ELEVEN

THE SMALLEST THEATRE IN THE WORLD

[1855]

THE CENTURY WAS GROWING a trifle blasé for its age—
though the prim chroniclers of those remote days would
not have admitted it, even if they had known the meaning of the word. Too many events had crowded themselves into the four short years which had passed since
Sir Joseph Paxton had wrought his glazed and glittering miracle upon the unoffending turf in Hyde Park
and the Prince Consort had inaugurated an era of
Universal Peace by a Universal Exhibition which
exhibited everything except a change in human nature.
The war in the Crimea was still running its confused
and apparently endless course. The Lady with the
Lamp had, within five months, succeeded in lowering
the death-rate among the wounded at Scutari from
forty-two per cent. to two, to the natural exasperation of
Dr. Hall, a chief medical officer and champion of red-
tape-and-hang-the-consequences. (Later, his outraged
feelings were solaced by promotion and a K.C.B.) The
electric telegraph was being used for the first time in
warfare; as the harassed commander-in-chief complained, 'it upset everything'. Native India was sullen
and restless, but John Company still ruled, and two
years were still to pass before the Mutiny materialized.
The ninth—and last—of the Royal babies was old
enough to walk. The Emperor and Empress of the

255

French had paid a visit to England and charmed the Queen and her Consort; the Consort himself had charmed an economically-minded Cabinet by voluntarily resigning not merely the rank but the salary of a field-marshal. The Press waxed caustic over the unseemly scuffles and struggles which had become a feature of Royal levees and drawing-rooms, where crinolines of maximum size were exhibited with a minimum of good manners. It had also something to say about the official snobbery which erected a brass railing between Her Majesty and the returned warriors to whom she presented medals.

.   .   .   .

Hampstead was basking in the clear if uncertain sunshine proper to a morning in mid-April when two friends met, by the sheerest chance, on the Heath. One was broad and bluff, with a jolly boyish laugh. He was Mark Lemon, dramatist, critic, and first editor of *Punch*; known to every child of his acquaintance as 'Uncle Mark'. The other was of a different type, being slightly built, with a thin face and fine forehead. The mouth, partly hidden by a heavy moustache, was large and mobile, the wavy hair and slight, pointed beard were light brown. But the deepset eyes were his most extraordinary feature. Normally dark blue, they changed, chameleon-fashion, with each emotion, from light blue to hazel, hazel to grey, grey to blue-grey, and thence to a blue so dark that it was almost black.

His clothes, even for those days of sartorial latitude,

256

were startlingly bright. An emerald-green waistcoat was buttoned over an equally vivid scarlet cravat, and, with a velvet coat, suggested a compromise between the sporting and the theatrical. He wore a gay nosegay in his buttonhole and carried a stick. His full baptismal name was Charles John Huffham, (the 'John Huffham' was abandoned early) and his surname Dickens. Now, at the age of forty-three, he was unassailably the most popular of living novelists. Nearly fifteen years had passed since *The Posthumous Papers of the Pickwick Club* finished their triumphal issue; since then, *Oliver Twist, Nicholas Nickleby, Martin Chuzzlewit, Dombey and Son, David Copperfield, Bleak House* and *Hard Times* had added to his reputation with almost mathematical regularity.

Conversation, drifting from one topic to another, revealed the reasons for that morning stroll. Dickens had wandered there to think out his forthcoming speech at the Theatrical Fund dinner which was to be held in a few days time. Lemon was on his way to visit Clarkson Stanfield, marine artist and friend of both, who had been lying seriously ill at his house, 'Green Hill'.

The two walked there together. They found Stanfield on the way to recovery, but depressed and restless. Times, he complained bitterly, were hard for ageing artists—'Stanny' was then in his sixty-second year. He could no longer paint large pictures; they were too much for him. In future, if there was any future, which was problematical, he would have to confine himself to little pictures, trivialities which might bring in a casual guinea or two. And so on.

257

'Nonsense!' cried Dickens, clapping him on the shoulder. 'You must paint larger pictures than ever. To turn out pot-boilers at your age would be demnition and unforgivable treachery to your art. And that, as fellow-artists, we can't permit. Hey, Mark?'

Lemon agreed. But a trifle uneasily: Dickens' suddenly improvised plans were apt to be disconcerting.

'I have in mind,' Dickens continued, 'a certain theatre which, in the language of the estate-agents, is known and situate in Tavistock House, Tavistock Square. A poor thing, but mine own.' He was striding up and down the room now, his eyes shining. 'For that theatre, which, I may add, is the smallest in the world, a new act-drop is required. You know what an act-drop is, Stanny?'

'I do. But, Heavens above, you're not suggesting——!'

'That the brush that has painted a thousand scenes should paint scenery? I am. Think, think of the audiences!'

'Spectators, Charles, spectators,' Lemon interrupted.

'I said "audiences", and audiences I meant. This picture is going to be a speaking one. Even Herr Winterhalter's newest portrait of Her Majesty won't hold a roomful of people entranced for a couple of hours, as your work will. There'll be dozens turned away nightly. Children with mothers in arms not admitted—I mean, t'other way about—and all royalties received devoted to works of national importance, as all Royalties ought to be.'

The listeners glanced at one another helplessly.

258

'Wherefore,' concluded the irrepressible Dickens, 'Mr. Clarkson Stanfield, Royal Academician, is hereby definitely commanded, instructed, commissioned, requested and implored to paint a new and original act-drop, the exact dimensions of which shall be scheduled in due course, for the next drama produced at the Tavistock House Theatre already mentioned. Is that commission accepted?'

Stanfield broke into a roar of laughter and held out his hand.

. . . .

Wrote Charles Dickens to Clarkson Stanfield, on Sunday, May the twentieth, 'Collins has done a regular old-style melodrama in which there is a very good notion. . . . There is only one scene in the piece, and that, my tarry lad, is the inside of a lighthouse . . . a mere wall, of course, but Mark and I have sworn that you must do it. Write me a line in reply. We mean to burst upon an astonished world with the melodrama without any note of preparation.'

When Stanfield, recalling the fantastic interview of the previous month, had duly replied, the enthusiastic commissioner of act-drops dispatched the following:

'Tuesday afternoon, six o'clock, May 22, 1855. Your note came while I was out walking. Unless I hear from you to the contrary, I shall expect you here sometime to-morrow, and will remain at home. I only wait your instructions to get the little canvases made. Oh, what a pity it is not the outside of the light'us, with the sea a-rowling agin' it! Never mind, we'll get an effect out of

259

the inside, and there's a storm and a shipwreck "off", and the great ambition of my life will be achieved at last, in the wearing of a pair of very corse petticoat trousers. So hoorar for the salt sea, mate, and bouse up!

'Ever affectionately,

'DICKY'

To Mark Lemon he wrote, a day later, 'Stanny says he is only sorry it is not the outside of the lighthouse with a raging sea, and a transparent light. He enters into the project with the greatest delight, and I think we shall make a capital thing of it.

'It now occurs to me that we may as well do a farce too. It ought to be broad, as a relief to the melodrama, unless we could find something funny with a story in it too. I rather incline myself to "Animal Magnetism". Will you come round and deliver your sentiments?'

Other letters followed from that ever-active pen. For the time being everything was subordinated to drama. The novelist left his desk to step into the world of the stage which in his youth had so nearly claimed him, and on the borderlands of which he dwelt in spirit to the end of his life. To Frank Stone, another artist friend, he wrote, on May the twenty-fourth:

'Great projects are afoot here for a grown-up play in about three weeks time. Former schoolroom arrangements are to be reversed—large stage and small audience. Stanfield is bent on desperate effects, and all day long with his coat off, up to his eyes in distemper colours.

'Will you appear in your celebrated character of Mr. Nightingale? I want to wind up with that popular farce, we all playing our old parts.'

And again, later in the same day, when Stone apparently demurred:

'You will find the words come back very quickly. Why *of course* your people are to come, and if Stanfield don't astonish 'em, I'm a Dutchman. O Heaven, if you could hear the ideas he proposes to me, making even *my* hair stand on end!'

On that same Thursday he sent a note to Wilkie Collins, who, by something of a coincidence, had been born in that same Tavistock Square some thirty-one years before. Collins had several claims on Dickens' friendship. He was not yet famous: *The Woman in White*, with its entirely original villain in the person of the bland and bird-loving Count Fosco, had not yet been written. But he was already recognized as one of 'Household Words'' most promising recruits—and 'Household Words' had been founded and was edited by the creator of 'Pickwick'. The two men had temperamental resemblances. Collins, like Dickens, had an ineradicable tendency to regard the novel as a series of dramatic episodes of varying emotional intensity. Dramatist or novelist, the writer's business was to interest, to thrill, to enthrall. He had written the play, he was a member of the cast. And Dickens was not the man to belittle the services of a loyal colleague.

'I shall expect you to-morrow evening at "Household Words". I have written a little ballad for Mary, "The

261

Story of the Ship's Carpenter and the Little Boy, in the Shipwreck".

'Let us close up with "Mr. Nightingale's Diary". All other matters and things hereunto belonging when we meet.'

.   .   .   .

It was the evening of Tuesday, the 19th of June.

A tall brick house, with a slated mansard roof and an imposing porch, whose columns supported a stone balcony, was ablaze with light. Carriage after carriage clattered up the drive and deposited privileged and distinguished visitors at the entrance. Within, the air was tense with excitement. At 'the smallest theatre in the world' 'The Lighthouse' was about to be presented for the first time on any stage, by Mr. Vincent Crummles, lessee and manager, producer, stage-manager and stage sailorman. 'Mr. Crummles', otherwise Mr. Dickens, was the most, though not the only, distinguished member of a cast which included, besides Collins, Mark Lemon, and Egg, painter of historical subjects and an A.R.A. Dickens' sister-in-law and daughter supplied the feminine talent. Two farces, 'Mr. Nightingale's Diary' and 'Animal Magnetism', already established successes, were to follow. For the melodrama itself, Dickens had composed 'The Song of the Wreck', sung to the tune of a favourite ballad called 'Little Nell'. The whole thing had been kept an elaborate secret until the night of the performance. Dickens, who to the end of his life took a boyish delight in surprises, refused to let even

262

the burly Forster know what was going to happen. And Forster had been his close friend ever since the day, nearly twenty years before, when Harrison Ainsworth had introduced him.

'The smallest theatre in the world' was packed long before the curtain rose. Dickens had spoken to Stanfield of 'our family and yours' being the sole audience. But the room would at a pinch hold ninety. Friends, as well as the families, filled the seats.

The curtain rose, revealing 'The Lighthouse'. There was a burst of spontaneous applause. Stanfield had spent only a couple of mornings at it, but he had produced an extraordinarily effective drop-scene in the time. (Later, it was framed and placed in the hall at Gads Hill; later still, sold for a thousand guineas when death scattered the owner's possessions.) The 'new and original melodrama' began. From the first there was no question of its success. When the curtain was finally allowed to fall, Mr. Crummles had promised that he and his gifted fellow-actors should give at least two further performances.

.   .   .   .

The long table was crowded. All literary London would have been there if it could, with all theatrical and legal and artistic London to keep it company. The third and last performance of 'The Lighthouse' had been given. This was the supper which, as usual, followed.

A Pickwickian meal in its fare and jollity, with Pickwick's own creator as host! Did not Lord Campbell,

263

sitting there, admit that he would rather have written such a book than be Lord Chief Justice of England and a peer of Parliament? Did not Mr. Thomas Carlyle, that Scotch volcano, hurl forth the statement—which no one else present had the temerity or learning to deny —that Dickens' wild picturesqueness as the old light-house-keeper was reminiscent of the famous figure in Poussin's 'Bacchanalian Dance' at the National Gallery? Did not the entire assembly cheer itself hoarse when at length, humorously protesting, their host rose to speak? Erect and dapper, with twinkling eyes, he smiled down upon his guests. The modulated voice, the carefully finished syllables, the slightly exaggerated sibilants— all emphasized the fact, which needed no emphasis, that Charles Dickens was a born actor. The chance acceptance of a casual contribution had set his feet on the literary highway, but there could never be any question of what the alternative profession might have been.

'Ladies and gentlemen,' he began, 'to-night has witnessed the final performance of a drama so powerful that even the box-office was overcome, and incapable of receiving further pecuniary emoluments, while the eyes of the programme-sellers and cloak-room attenddants were so suffused with happy tears that they were unable to distinguish between a florin and half-a-crown. (Laughter.) Our little company has achieved— if one may be permitted to revert, even metaphorically, to the raging main—the high watermark of success. (Loud applause.) To-night has recalled, perhaps because of the contrast, a performance which I and some of my distinguished colleagues gave three years ago in Sunderland, the native town of our gifted scene-painter, unfortunately absent to-night. The play was entitled, fittingly enough, "Not so Bad as We Seem", and was followed, as to-night, by "Mr. Nightingale's Diary". The performance was given in a hall built like a theatre with pit, boxes and gallery, into which twelve hundred people contrived, by some miracle of compression, to squeeze. Applause as vociferous as I have been vouch-safed to hear to-night began from the moment the conductor's white waistcoat was discerned in the orchestra, and continued until the fall of the curtain.

'Believe me, ladies and gentlemen, the stimulus of that applause was needed. For to begin with, the hall was a new one, so new that it had only had its slates put on by torchlight on the previous night, while the plaster on the dressing-room walls was still oozing water. Furthermore, the hall had been constructed on a new principle, with an arched iron roof that had no brackets or pillars. The proprietors of certain oppo-sition rooms had, I discovered, been loudly proclaiming that our buildings were unsafe, with the result that already panic-stricken subscribers were demanding the return of their money. The whole ghastly responsibility for any possible accident rested upon myself, for I had only to announce that we wouldn't act, and all danger would have been averted. I asked Wilkie what *he* thought about it; he retorted that his digestion was so bad that death had no terrors for him. (Loud and prolonged laughter.) Ladies and gentlemen, it was no occasion for mirth. My sole source of consolation was a builder, a practical northcountryman, who swore that there wasn't a stronger building in the world, and added that it had already given shelter to an audience of several thousand working people. I still, however, remained in such dread of disaster that when the curtain rose, I thought I perceived the gallery out of the perpendicular and the ceiling lights crooked. And each round of applause terrified me because of the possible effect upon the building. The slightest stumble on the dressing-room stairs set my heart palpitating, and in one scene, where the villain has to be startled, I had a bell rung, instead of the usual piece of wood flung down, lest it should create sudden apprehension. In short, the anxiety was so intense and the relief when all passed off successfully so great, that I was half dead all next day. Even the fact that one of the vans at Newcastle railway station was upset by a couple of runaway horses, and our entire stock of scenery overturned, seemed by comparison a minor misfortune. I left Sunderland with the feeling that I should never be able to bear the smell of new deal and fresh mortar again as long as I lived.

'Ladies and gentlemen, I have perhaps wearied you: (No, no, go on.) but can only plead in extenuation that, encouraged by the favour you have shown to "The Lighthouse", I have been tempted to illuminate certain tempestuous and distressful scenes which would otherwise be hidden in merciful oblivion. (Loud and prolonged applause.) In conclusion, ladies and gentle-men, I raise my glass to our absent scene-painter, Mr. Clarkson Stanfield, R.A.'

The run of 'The Lighthouse' was finished. Mr. Vincent Crummles' occupation had come to an end too. But although the actor might for a space have left the stage, and the smallest theatre in the world be empty and desolate, the indefatigable pen was busy.

'Last night was perfectly wonderful! ! ! !' wrote Dickens to Stanfield on the following morning. 'Such an audience! Such a brilliant success from first to last. Lemon and I did every conceivable absurdity, I think, in the farce; and they never left off laughing. At supper I proposed your health, which was drunk with nine times nine and three cheers over. We then turned to at Scotch reels (having had no exercise) and danced in the maddest way until five this morning. . . .'

Charles Dickens

From NICHOLAS NICKLEBY

MR. CRUMMLES RECOMMENDS A THEATRICAL CAREER

'The stage!' cried Nicholas.

'The theatrical profession,' said Mr. Vincent Crummles. 'I am in the theatrical profession myself, my wife is in the theatrical profession, my children are in the theatrical profession. I had a dog that lived and died in it from a puppy; and my chaise-pony goes on in "Timour the Tartar". I'll bring you out, and your friend too. Say the word. I want a novelty.'

267

'I don't know anything about it,' rejoined Nicholas, whose breath had been almost taken away by this sudden proposal. 'I never acted a part in my life, except at school.'

'There's genteel comedy in your walk and manner, juvenile tragedy in your eye, and touch-and-go farce in your laugh,' said Mr. Vincent Crummles. 'You'll do as well as if you had thought of nothing else but the lamps from your birth downwards.'

Nicholas thought of the small amount of small change that would remain in his pocket after paying the tavern bill, and he hesitated.

'You can be useful to us in a hundred ways,' said Crummles. 'Think what capital bills a man of your education could write for the shop windows.'

'Well, I think I could manage that department,' said Nicholas.

'To be sure you could,' replied Mr. Crummles. ' "For further particulars see small handbills"—we might have half a volume in every one of 'em. Pieces, too; why, you could write us a piece to bring out the whole strength of the company, whenever we wanted one.'

'I am not quite so confident about that,' said Nicholas. 'But I dare say I could scribble something now and then that would suit you.'

'We'll have a new show-piece out directly,' said the manager. 'Let me see—peculiar resources of this establishment—new and splendid scenery—you must manage to introduce a real pump and two washing-tubs.'

'Into the piece?' said Nicholas.

'Yes,' replied the manager. 'I bought 'em cheap, at a sale the other day, and they'll come in admirably. That's the London plan. They look up some dresses and properties, and have a piece written to fit them. Most of the theatres keep an author on purpose.'

'Indeed!' cried Nicholas.

'Oh, yes,' said the manager, 'a common thing. It'll look very well in the bills in separate lines—Real pump!—Splendid tubs!—Great attraction! You don't happen to be anything of an artist, do you?'

'That is not one of my accomplishments,' rejoined Nicholas.

'Ah! Then it can't be helped,' said the manager. 'If you had been, we might have had a large woodcut of the last scene for the posters, showing the whole depth of the stage, with the pump and tubs in the middle; but however, if you're not, it can't be helped.'

'What should I get for all this?' inquired Nicholas, after a few moments reflection. 'Could I live by it?'

'Live by it!' said the manager. 'Like a prince! With your own salary, and your friend's, and your writings, you'd make a pound a week!'

·   ·   ·   ·   ·   ·   ·   ·

As Mr. Crummles had a strange four-legged animal in the inn stables which he called a pony, and a vehicle of unknown design on which he bestowed the appellation of a four-wheeled phaeton, Nicholas proceeded on his journey next morning with greater ease than he had expected; the manager and himself occupying the front seat; and the Masters Crummles and Smike being packed together behind, in company with a wicker basket defended from wet by a stout oilskin, in which were the broadswords, pistols, pigtails, nautical costumes, and other professional necessaries of the aforesaid young gentlemen.

The pony took his time upon the road, and—possibly in consequence of his theatrical education—evinced, every now and then, a strong inclination to lie down. However, Mr. Vincent Crummles kept him up pretty well by jerking the rein and plying the whip; and when these means failed, and the animal came to a stand, the elder Master Crummles got out and kicked him. By dint of these encouragements, he was persuaded to move from time to time, and they jogged on (as Mr. Crummles truly observed) very comfortably for all parties.

'He's a good pony at bottom,' said Mr. Crummles, turning to Nicholas.

He might have been at bottom, but he certainly was not at top, seeing that his coat was of the roughest and most ill-favoured kind. So Nicholas merely observed that he shouldn't wonder if he was.

'Many and many is the circuit this pony has gone,' said Mr. Crummles, flicking him skilfully on the eyelid for old acquaintance's sake. 'He is quite one of us. His mother was on the stage.'

'Was she?' rejoined Nicholas.

'She ate apple-pie at a circus for upwards of fourteen years,' said the manager; 'fired pistols, and went to bed in a nightcap; and, in short, took the low comedy entirely. His father was a dancer.'

'Was he at all distinguished?'

'Not very,' said the manager. 'He was rather a low sort of pony. The fact is, he had been originally jobbed out by the day, and he never quite got over his old habits. He was clever in melodrama, too, but too broad —too broad. When the mother died, he took the port wine business.'

'The port wine business!' cried Nicholas.

'Drinking port wine with the clown,' said the manager; 'but he was greedy, and one night bit off the bowl of the glass, and choked himself, so his vulgarity was the death of him at last.'

The descendant of this ill-starred animal requiring

increased attention from Mr. Crummles as he progressed in his day's work, that gentleman had very little time for conversation. Nicholas was thus left at leisure to entertain himself with his own thoughts, until they arrived at the drawbridge at Portsmouth, when Mr. Crummles pulled up.

'We'll get down here,' said the manager, 'and the boys will take him round to the stable, and call at my lodgings with the luggage. You had better let yours be taken there for the present.'

Thanking Mr. Vincent Crummles for his obliging offer, Nicholas jumped out, and, giving Smike his arm, accompanied the manager up High Street on their way to the theatre, feeling nervous and uncomfortable enough at the prospect of an immediate introduction to a scene so new to him.

.   .   .   .

At half-past five there was a rush of four people to the gallery door; at a quarter before six there were at least a dozen; at six o'clock the kicks were terrific; and when the elder Master Crummles opened the door, he was obliged to run behind it for his life. Fifteen shillings were taken by Mrs. Grudden in the first ten minutes.

Behind the scenes the same unwonted excitement prevailed. Miss Snevellicci was in such a perspiration that the paint would scarcely stay on her face. Mrs. Crummles was so nervous that she could hardly remember her part. Miss Bravassa's ringlets came out of curl with the heat and anxiety; even Mr. Crummles himself kept peeping through the hole in the curtain, and running back every now and then to announce that another man had come into the pit.

At last the orchestra left off, and the curtain rose upon the new piece. The first scene, in which there was

271

nobody in particular, passed off calmly enough, but when Miss Snevellicci went on in the second, accompanied by the phenomenon as child, what a roar of applause broke out! The people in the Borum box rose as one man, waving their hats and handkerchiefs, and uttering shouts of 'Bravo!' Mrs. Borum and the governess cast wreaths upon the stage, of which, some fluttered into the lamps, and one crowned the temples of a fat gentleman in the pit, who, looking eagerly towards the scene, remained unconscious of the honour; the tailor and his family kicked at the panels of the upper boxes till they threatened to come out altogether; the very ginger-beer boy remained transfixed in the centre of the house; a young officer, supposed to entertain a passion for Miss Snevellicci, stuck his glass in his eye as though to hide a tear. Again and again Miss Snevellicci curtsied lower and lower, and again and again the applause came down louder and louder. At length, when the phenomenon picked up one of the smoking wreaths and put it on, sideways, over Miss Snevellicci's eye, it reached its climax, and the play proceeded.

But when Nicholas came on for his crack scene with Mrs. Crummles, what a clapping of hands there was! When Mrs. Crummles (who was his unworthy mother) sneered, and called him 'presumptuous boy', and he defied her, what a tumult of applause came on! When he quarrelled with the other gentleman about the young lady, and producing a case of pistols, said, that if he *was* a gentleman, he would fight him in that drawing-room, until the furniture was sprinkled with the blood of one, not of two—how boxes, pit and gallery joined in one most vigorous cheer! When he called his mother names, because she wouldn't give up the young lady's property, and she relenting caused him to relent likewise, and fall down on one knee and ask her blessing, how the ladies in the audience sobbed! When he was hid behind the curtain in the dark, and the wicked relation poked a sharp sword in every direction, save where his legs were plainly visible, what a thrill of anxious fear ran through the house! His air, his figure, his walk, his look, everything he said or did, was the subject of commendation. There was a round of applause every time he spoke. And when at last, in the pump-and-tub scene, Mrs. Grudden lighted the blue fire, and all the unemployed members of the company came in, and tumbled down in various directions—not because that had anything to do with the plot, but in order to finish off with a tableau—the audience (who had by this time increased considerably) gave vent to such a shout of enthusiasm as had not been heard in those walls for many and many a day.

In short, the success of both new piece and new actor was complete, and when Miss Snevellicci was called for at the end of the play, Nicholas led her on, and divided the applause.

Charles Dickens

From DAVID COPPERFIELD

MEMORIES

There comes out of the cloud, our house—not new to me, but quite familiar, in its earliest remembrance. On the ground-floor is Peggotty's kitchen, opening into a back yard; with a pigeon-house on a pole, in the centre, without any pigeons in it; a great dog-kennel in a corner, without any dog; and a quantity of fowls that look terribly tall to me, walking about in a menacing

273

and ferocious manner. There is one cock who gets upon a post to crow, and seems to take particular notice of me as I look at him through the kitchen window, who makes me shiver, he is so fierce. Of the geese outside the side-gate who come waddling after me with their long necks stretched out when I go that way, I dream at night; as a man environed by wild beasts might dream of lions.

Here is a long passage—what an enormous perspective I make of it!—leading from Peggotty's kitchen to the front door. A dark store-room opens out of it, and that is a place to be run past at night; for I don't know what may be among those tubs and jars and old tea-chests, when there is nobody in there with a dimly-burning light, letting a mouldy air come out at the door, in which there is the smell of soap, pickles, pepper, candles, and coffee, all at one whiff. Then there are the two parlours; the parlour in which we sit of an evening, my mother and I and Peggotty—for Peggotty is quite our companion, when her work is done and we are alone—and the best parlour where we sit on a Sunday; grandly, but not so comfortably. There is something of a doleful air about that room to me, for Peggotty has told me—I don't know when, but apparently ages ago —about my father's funeral, and the company having their black cloaks put on. One Sunday night my mother reads to Peggotty and me in there, how Lazarus was raised up from the dead. And I am so frightened that they are afterwards obliged to take me out of bed, and show me the quiet churchyard out of the bedroom window, with the dead all lying in their graves at rest, below the solemn moon.

There is nothing half so green that I know anywhere, as the grass of that churchyard; nothing half so shady as its trees; nothing half so quiet as its tombstones.

The sheep are feeding there, when I kneel up, early in the morning, in my little bed in a closet within my mother's room, to look out at it; and I see the red light shining on the sun-dial, and think within myself, 'Is the sun-dial glad,* I wonder, that it can tell the time again?'

Here is our pew in the church. What a high-backed pew! With a window near it, out of which our house can be seen, and *is* seen many times during the morning's service, by Peggotty, who likes to make herself as sure as she can that it's not being robbed, or is not in flames. But though Peggotty's eye wanders, she is much offended if mine does, and frowns to me, as I stand upon the seat, that I am to look at the clergyman. But I can't always look at him—I know him without that white thing on, and I am afraid of his wondering why I stare so, and perhaps stopping the service to inquire —and what am I to do? It's a dreadful thing to gape, but I must do something. I look at my mother, but *she* pretends not to see me. I look at a boy in the aisle, and *he* makes faces at me. I look at the sunlight coming through the open door in the porch, and there I see a stray sheep—I don't mean a sinner, but mutton—half making up his mind to come into the church, I feel that if I looked at him any longer, I might be tempted to say something out loud; and what would become of me then! I look up at the monumental tablets on the wall, and try to think of Mr. Bodgers late of this parish, and what the feelings of Mrs. Bodgers must have been, when affliction sore long time Mr. Bodgers bore, and physicians were in vain. I wonder whether they called in Mr. Chillip, and he was in vain; and if so, how he likes to be reminded of it once a week. I look from Mr. Chillip, in his Sunday neckcloth, to the pulpit; and think what a good place it would be to play in, and what a castle it would make, with another boy coming up the stairs to attack it, and having the velvet cushion with the tassels thrown down on his head. In time my eyes gradually shut up; and, from seeming to hear the clergyman singing a drowsy song in the heat, I hear nothing, until I fall off the seat with a crash, and am taken out, more dead than alive, by Peggotty.

Wilkie Collins

From THE MOONSTONE

From PREFACE TO A NEW EDITION

While this work was still in course of periodical publication in England and in the United States, and when not more than one-third of it was completed, the bitterest affliction of my life and the severest illness from which I have ever suffered fell on me together. At the time when my mother lay dying in her little cottage in the country, I was struck prostrate, in London—crippled in every limb, by the torture of rheumatic gout. Under the weight of this double calamity, I had my duty to the public still to bear in mind. My good readers in England and in America, whom I had never yet disappointed, were expecting their regular weekly instalments of the new story. I held to the story—for my own sake as well as for theirs. In the intervals of grief, in the occasional remissions of pain, I dictated from my bed that portion of *The Moonstone* which has since proved most successful in amusing the public—the 'Narrative of Miss Clack'. Of the physical sacrifice which the effort cost me I shall say nothing. I only look back now at the blessed relief which my occupation (forced as it was) brought to my mind. The Art which had been always the pride and the pleasure of my life became now more than ever 'its own exceeding great reward'. I doubt if I should have lived to write another book, if the responsibility of the weekly publication of this story had not forced me to rally my sinking energies of body and mind—to dry my useless tears, and to conquer my merciless pains.

The novel completed, I awaited its reception by the public with an eagerness of anxiety which I have never felt before or since for the fate of any other writings of mine. If *The Moonstone* had failed, my mortification would have been bitter indeed. As it was, the welcome accorded to the story in England, in America, and on the Continent of Europe was instantly and universally favourable. Never have I had better reason than this work has given me to feel gratefully to novel-readers of all nations. Everywhere my characters made friends, and my story aroused interest. Everywhere the public favour looked over my faults—and repaid me a hundredfold for the hard toil which these pages cost me in the dark time of sickness and grief.

Wilkie Collins

From THE MOONSTONE

MR. BLAKE UNDER OPIUM

At this time, no unpractised eyes would have detected any change in him. But, as the minutes of the new morning wore away, the swiftly subtle progress of the influence began to show itself more plainly. The sublime intoxication of opium gleamed in his eyes; the dew of a stealthy perspiration began to glisten on his face. In five minutes more the talk which he still kept up with me failed in coherence. He held steadily to the subject of the Diamond; but he ceased to complete his sentences. A little later, the sentences dropped to single words. Then there was an interval of silence. Then he sat up in bed. Then, still busy with the subject of the Diamond, he began to talk again—not to me, but to himself. That change told me that the first stage in the experiment was reached. The stimulant influence of the opium had got him.

The time, now, was twenty-three minutes past twelve. The next half-hour, at most, would decide the question of whether he would, or would not, get up from his bed, and leave the room.

In the breathless interest of watching him—in the unutterable triumph of seeing the first result of the experiment declare itself in the manner, and nearly at the time, which I had anticipated—I had utterly forgotten the two companions of my night vigil. Looking towards them now, I saw the Law (as represented by Mr. Bruff's papers) lying unheeded on the floor. Mr. Bruff himself was looking eagerly through a crevice left in the imperfectly drawn curtains of the bed. And Betteredge, oblivious of all respect for social distinctions, was peeping over Mr. Bruff's shoulder.

They both started back on finding that I was looking at them, like two boys caught out by their schoolmaster in a fault. I signed to them to take off their boots quietly, as I was taking off mine. If Mr. Blake gave us the chance of following him, it was vitally necessary to follow him without noise.

Ten minutes passed—and nothing happened. Then he suddenly threw the bedclothes off him. He put one leg out of bed. He waited.

278

'I wish I had never taken it out of the bank,' he said to himself. 'It was safe in the bank.'

My heart throbbed fast; the pulses at my temples beat furiously. The doubt about the safety of the Diamond was once more the dominant impression in his brain! On that one pivot the whole success of the experiment turned. The prospect thus suddenly opened before me was too much for my shattered nerves. I was obliged to look away from him—or I should have lost my self-control.

There was another interval of silence.

When I could trust myself to look back at him, he was out of his bed, standing erect at the side of it. The pupils of his eyes were now contracted; his eyeballs gleamed in the light of the candle as he moved his head slowly to and fro. He was thinking; he was doubting—he spoke again.

'How do I know?' he said. 'The Indians may be hidden in the house.'

He stopped, and walked slowly to the other end of the room. He turned—waited—came back to the bed.

'It's not even locked up,' he went on. 'It's in the drawer of her cabinet. And the drawer doesn't lock.'

He sat down on the side of the bed. 'Anybody might take it,' he said.

He rose again restlessly, and reiterated his first words.

'How do I know? The Indians may be hidden in the house.'

He waited again. I drew back behind the half curtain of the bed. He looked about the room, with a vacant glitter in his eyes. It was a breathless moment. There was a pause of some sort. A pause in the action of the opium? a pause in the action of the brain? Who could tell? Everything depended, now, on what he did next.

He laid himself down again on the bed!

A horrible doubt crossed my mind. Was it possible that the sedative action of the opium was making itself felt already? It was not in my experience that it should do this. But what is experience where opium is concerned? There are probably no two men in existence on whom the drug acts in exactly the same manner. Was some constitutional peculiarity in him feeling the influence in some new way? Were we to fail on the very brink of success?

No! He got up again abruptly. 'How the devil am I to sleep,' he said, 'with *this* on my mind?'

He looked at the light burning on the table at the head of his bed. After a moment, he took the candle in his hand.

I blew out the second candle burning behind the closed curtains. I drew back, with Mr. Bruff and Betteredge, into the farthest corner by the bed. I signed to them to be silent, as if their lives had depended on it.

We waited—seeing and hearing nothing. We waited, hidden from him by the curtains.

The light which he was holding on the other side of us moved suddenly. The next moment he passed us, swift and noiseless, with the candle in his hand.

He opened the bedroom door, and went out.

We followed him along the corridor. We followed him down the stairs. We followed him along the second corridor. He never looked back; he never hesitated.

He opened the sitting-room door, and went in, leaving it open behind him.

THE SMALLEST THEATRE IN THE WORLD

Life of Charles Dickens	John Forster
Dickens (Great Writers)	F. T. Marzials
Dickens (English Men of Letters)	A. W. Ward
Dickens as a Social Reformer	W. W. Crotch
Dickens as I Knew Him	G. Dolby
Dickens: The Story of His Life	W. Dexter
Charles Dickens, Letters of	Ed. by M. Dickens and Georgina Hogarth

Chapter Twelve

SUNSET—AND SUNRISE

[1880—and the '60's]

It was Summer, but too early in the season for dust and heat to have become a menace; London was neither uninhabited nor uninhabitable.

England had been Victorian for forty-three years, and was so to remain for another generation. With the Sovereign herself Time had dealt not too kindly. The once-piquant little face had become flabby and lined, the slender figure unromantically stout. Other changes were perhaps less obvious. But implacable in her antagonisms as she was firm in her friendships, she was still teaching her ministers that whatever they might or might not concede to her sex, the one thing never to be forgotten was that, by the Grace of God, they were dealing with Victoria, *Regina et Imperatrix.* Her vehement and indignant pen leapt to paper whenever the prerogative of the British Empire or the British Crown was questioned. For the rest, she still mourned the Prince Consort, though it might be surmised that after nearly twenty years that mourning had become a trifle habitual, and still scolded her middle-aged Heir Apparent as if he were a fourth-form boy who had been caught smoking in his dormitory, and kept him ignorant of any state affairs which involved a greater intellectual strain than the laying of a foundation-stone or the opening of a city hall.

Regarding the world in general, it may be recorded that Mr. Gladstone had again become Prime Minister, that Anthony Trollope, most laborious of novelists, was being laboriously parodied in *Punch* as 'Anthony Dollop', and that feminine jerseys were fashionable, while for evening wear bands of black ribbon took the place of sleeves. *The Warehouseman and Drapers' Trade Journal* announced to its startled readers that shop-assistants in certain Edinburgh establishments had actually been provided with seats; while a passenger was killed at Camden Town while descending the steps of his second-class compartment, and the railway was blamed for refusing to build carriages with continuous footboards. The newspapers—incredibly stolid affairs, un-paragraphed, un-illustrated, and when full open about the size of a small bed-spread—announced a mysterious murder in Ireland and another in Harley Street. A crowded and passionate meeting was held in Exeter Hall to protest against the Marquis of Ripon's appointment as Viceroy of India, on the ground that His Lordship was a Roman Catholic. Elsewhere, Sarah Bernhardt was fined £4,000 for breach of contract, the French Government committed the double futility of expelling the Jesuits from their establishments and annexing Tahiti; the King of Greece visited the Guild-hall, and the Kelly gang of bushrangers was ambushed and exterminated in Australia.

All of which was sufficiently thrilling—if you lived in the eighteen-eighties.

But the less tangible world of literature had also its

excursions and alarms. Even to-day, viewing it with
the superior detachment afforded by the lapse of half
a century, one realizes how interesting a world it was.
Living links with the eighteenth century still existed.
Carlyle, born before George the Third lost his wits and
a sturdy student of fifteen when he died, might still be
seen taking his morning walks in Chelsea; Lord
Nelson's daughter Horatia drove abroad in her carriage; Trelawney, friend of Byron and Shelley, held
romantic and querulous court at Worthing. Mr.
Tennyson was still exhibiting in his poems the art
which almost conceals art; Lord Beaconsfield, who
would have rewarded him with a baronetcy—he
offered Carlyle one at the same time, and had both
offers turned down—was still exhibiting in his novels
the art which concealed nothing. Mrs. Browning,
though no longer living, was far from forgotten; her
husband, obscure only so far as his poetry was concerned, was very much alive. Mr. Harrison Ainsworth
was still writing historical novels by the naphtha-flare
of his own imagination. Mr. John Ruskin was writing
about Art, and particularly Turner's Art, in stained-
glass English.

These were the old-timers, the traditionalists, the
practised hands. But there were others. A young man
Wilde, for example, of Trinity College, Dublin, and of
Oxford, was exciting the London dinner-parties with
his epigrams; his rival in wit, an American-born artist
named Whistler, was defying all the canons of the
Royal Academy; an incomparable writer of light verse

was collaborating with an incomparable master of melody in the Gilbert and Sullivan operas. There was also an eccentric and consumptive young Scotsman named Stevenson who looked like developing into something more than a writer of rather charming essays and fantastic adventure-stories. . . . The rising generation, in short, with the rising generation's contempt for their elders.

Between them and the old-timers were others who had shocked and startled in their day, but were now accepted with scarcely a shrug.

.   .   .   .

A little, prim man, with a mane of hair which had once been red but was now turning grey, a high forehead, and a chin whose weakness was emphasized by a slight beard, hurried along the crowded pavements of Holborn. He was neatly dressed, but somehow the neatness seemed incongruous, as though a supervising personality was responsible for it. Two other points were noticeable—a certain strained alertness which goes with defective hearing, and a childish apprehension. He might have been a small boy who had played truant, and raided his money-box to buy an unauthorized ticket to London.

The little man found himself opposite a turning. He dodged the traffic successfully, and considerably flushed, and with the air of guilt still more obvious, entered Chancery Lane. There was a restaurant close at hand where, in the days of his freedom—no, that

285

were rank disloyalty—the days before every hour of his existence was so splendidly regulated—he had been in the habit of dropping in for lunch or dinner. Would Thomas, the head-waiter, still be there, or being there, remember him?

Thomas, in his familiar black-and-white, like a welcoming magpie, came forward to greet him, raising his magnificent voice as a concession to the deafness. Various customers glanced up. A stout American gentleman, wearing one of the weird little bowler hats which were fashionable in those days, nudged a thin American lady in a boater.

'Guess that's the one and only,' he murmured.

'What's the little looney *done*, anyway?' snapped the lady.

The stout American gentleman enlightened her, and then, becoming ashamed of his enthusiasm, abruptly and noisily resumed his meal.

'I trust I see you well, Sir?' said Thomas to the little man. 'You certainly are looking in better health than when the London Restaurant last had the pleasure of serving you.'

'I *am* healthier,' admitted the little man.

'Stouter, if one may be permitted to say so.'

'Er—perhaps.'

'Are you still residing at Guilford Street?'

'No. I have left London.' He glanced nervously over his shoulder. 'I am sharing a house with a friend in Putney—Number Two, the Pines.'

Thomas, curiously enough, had an aunt by marriage

who lived in Putney. A sweetly pretty spot, but growing suburban.

'I am growing to *like* Suburbia,' said the little man, and then, with sudden eagerness, 'Have you any asparagus?'

The waiter had, the finest of the season. He hurried away to bring supplies. When they came, the little man ate slowly, vacantly, and with that air of distinguished remoteness which seemed to go with his high-pitched voice and flickering gestures. The distant clatter of the buses and drays—Chancery Lane itself was too narrow for many vehicles beside hansom-cabs—came in a subdued murmur. Thomas reappeared presently to ask what else he might have the pleasure of supplying. The little man felt in his pocket, and discovered that he had only half-a-crown.

'Coffee, if you please,' he said.

The coffee came. He stirred it, sipped and, leaning back in his seat, half closed his eyes and drifted into a reverie.

. . . .

Four young men were living together in a house in Chelsea. They were all exceptionally gifted young men, as none knew better than themselves. If the Thames which flowed so placidly a few yards from their windows had possessed any inflammatory possibilities whatever, it is quite certain that, individually or collectively, they would have set it ablaze.

The nominal tenant of the house was known as Dante

Gabriel Rossetti. (He had long ago discarded his second and more commonplace Christian name of Charles. The number of distinguished persons who have hastened to shorten their signatures by getting rid of the names given them before coherent protest was possible must run into scores!) His father was wholly Italian; his mother half Italian, half English. He himself, though he never in his life visited Italy, has been not inaccurately described as a Florentine of the Florentines. His dreaming eyes, and mocking mouth with its hint of sensuality suggest a personality not merely un-English, but Mediæval.

Rossetti had been among the lucky ones when the fairies' gifts were distributed. One might, indeed, say that his luck was unique. Art is a jealous mistress, Poetry not less jealous and he who would woo either with success must forswear all other loves. This is inevitable; a human lifetime is not long enough for devotion to more than one. But every rule produces its exceptions, and Rossetti was the exception. Poets and artists have never yet been in agreement concerning his real status. He began by writing, became intrigued by painting, and applied to Ford Madox Brown for lessons. Brown, though only seven years Rossetti's senior, was already an artist with an unchallenged reputation for faithful and sensitive work. Doubting his pupil's single-mindedness, he gave him jam-jars to decorate. Before long the jam-jars were forgotten; Rossetti the Poet had submerged himself in Rossetti the Artist, and he and Brown had become close friends.

288

Nor did the generosity of the gods end there. John Ruskin saw and admired his work, and with the paternal fortune behind him—Ruskin senior had been a well-to-do wine-merchant—could afford to dabble in practical philanthropy. He undertook to buy a sufficient number of Rossetti's paintings to free the artist from all future financial troubles.

But financial only. Into his life came the inevitable woman, the consumptive, exquisitely lovely Elizabeth Siddal. She had been, and was, a model; he painted her so many times that his pictures might almost be termed a series of portraits of her. They married, her health notwithstanding; went to Paris, and came back to live in his house near Blackfriars Bridge.

Their idyll ended on the evening when he discovered her dead from an overdose of laudanum, taken, it was charitably stated, to relieve neuralgia.

In an ecstasy of grief he buried with her body a book of poems he had written and never published. Soon afterwards he left the scene of intolerable memories and moved to Chelsea. The Gods had repented of their generosity.

His brother William, who later married a daughter of Ford Madox Brown, joined him there. Of the two remaining tenants, one, named George Meredith, was the son of a naval outfitter who had been destined for a lawyer's office, but who found the attraction of journalism too strong to be resisted. He had begun his career with a not particularly inspired poem on the recently-fought Battle of Chillianwallah. The poem had appeared in a monthly magazine, and since then he had widened his outlook by editing a provincial weekly and writing occasional articles for the London dailies. Still in the early thirties, one would have credited him with being industrious and versatile, and perhaps laughed a little at his exuberant energy and passion for physical exercise.

The last of the four was a poet with limitations, but within those limitations brilliantly gifted. If his genius had advanced with advancing years, the laurels of the Poet Laureate himself might have been in danger. It did not so advance, but halted, desiccated in a Sahara of respectability. The youthful master of metre, the magician in whose hands the very syllables seemed to acquire hypnotic qualities, could give the world no songs with a richer note, no deeper message, in his old age. If it be true that Hell is Heaven that has come too late, it may also be Heaven that has come too soon.

The name of the poet was Algernon Charles Swinburne.

An odd quartette, with odd friends. London, stolid, respectable London, to whom Art was represented by 'Shoeing the Bay Mare' and Poetry by 'The Queen of the May', sneered at them. But a little uneasily. One didn't want to judge too harshly—especially if one wasn't quite sure how much was eccentricity and how much genius beyond one's immediate comprehension. Or alternatively, how soon the queer pictures painted by these Pre-Raphaelites (for so they called themselves, to indicate a reversion to the ancient simplicities of art) and the queer poems they wrote, were going to become fashionable.

.   .   .   .

The little man dreaming over his coffee startled the restaurant by a sudden gurgle of reminiscent laughter. Since those far-away Chelsea days the Pre-Raphaelites had become very definitely fashionable.

Those Chelsea days! Life then, though it had its tragic and bitter moments—and only the artistic temperament knew how bitter and tragic they were—had its lighter moments too. For example, the affair of the zebu, a sacred Brahmin cow which Dante Rossetti had somehow or other discovered in London and set his heart on buying. The owner had demanded twenty pounds for it. Rossetti, whom all the art-patrons in Europe could never have made a rich man, had raised five pounds, borrowed the other fifteen from his brother, and brought home the zebu in triumph. The animal's tastes, however, were not Pre-Raphaelite. Suddenly attacking its new owner, it chased him round and round the garden, and finally drove him to seek refuge in a tree. It was re-sold on the first opportunity, and artistic Chelsea stopped chuckling.

There had been domestic problems, too, which had a distinctly humorous side. The hours for food, sleep, work and recreation were beyond mutual adjustment. Meredith was a habitual early-riser, Dante Rossetti did not ever begin work until the afternoon, Swinburne's comings and goings were so erratic that no

291

reliance could be placed on them at all. William Rossetti was the most normal of the four—and mattered least.

They had many friends, as young and enthusiastic as themselves, and as confident of some day making a Philistine world perceive that, as poor John Keats had long ago insisted, Truth and Beauty were one, the only trouble being that Pre-Raphaelite eyesight was needed to see it.

William Morris, known with irreverent familiarity as 'Topsy', was one of the friends. Of him, whatever the final verdict, it should at least be written that he worshipped loveliness of form and colour, and dedicated the whole of his strenuous life to the service of Art. He saw about him buildings, dress, furniture, pictures, books and pottery which were laboriously and smugly hideous, and whose makers revolted his soul by their mid-Victorian ignorance of the first elements of purity of design. And seeing at the same time that the most blazing indignation and bitterest denunciation would by themselves change nothing and lead nowhere, he modelled, carved, printed and painted from his own designs and by his own hands as well. A mediæval craftsman, his sympathies were wide enough to make him the champion of classes who knew nothing and cared nothing for the spirit of beauty that meant so much to him: a dreamer of dreams who at the same time translated his dreams into action, eager to carry out 'things I have thought of for bettering the world as far as lies in me'. Something of this one may read from the unforgettable portrait painted by Watts, from the massive head, and the sensitive mouth, a little over-weighted by the broad, frank brows. It has been shrewdly said that he was not merely a typical English-man, but a typical Londoner of the middle class, and that Chaucer, among all the figures in English litera-ture, was perhaps his nearest parallel.

He had built, decorated and furnished a lovely dwell-ing-place of his own—the Red House, Upton—where his greatest project came into being. It was nothing less than the formation of a chosen company of crafts-men whose ideals were as high as his own. Mural decoration, carving, stained glass, metal-work, jewel-lery and decorated furniture, including embroidery and stamped leather—such were to be among their activities. The new firm came into being. Rossetti was one member of it, Madox Brown another, Burne-Jones, a fellow Pre-Raphaelite, another, Falkner, an Oxford tutor with an artistic bias, another, with Morris him-self as chief inspiration. (That the company should ultimately break up was probably as inevitable as the breaking up of the household at Chelsea, and due to the same causes. There were too many warring per-sonalities to make for sustained co-operation. And Morris himself possessed a volcanic temper which he did not always take the trouble to control.)

· · · · · · · · ·

Christina Rossetti, sister of the artist and a writer of delicate and wistful verse, was an occasional visitor.

293

So also was Coventry Patmore, a poet whom Destiny had converted into an assistant in the British Museum and temperament into a Roman Catholic; whose best-known work, 'The Angel in the House', was a tribute to his wife, but whose most perfect poem was inspired by his little son. William Allingham, another civil servant, who married a water-colour artist and wrote gracefully, and George Frederick Watts, the artist, were others. A jolly company, still meeting occasionally but not with the same spirit. Youth is beyond recapture.

To-day, he who had been one of them worked and played and ate and slept in a household as punctiliously organized as a high-class girls' school;—ten o'clock breakfast, a walk from eleven till one, luncheon one-thirty, rest in his bedroom from two-thirty until four-thirty, two hours more work, an hour's reading aloud, dinner at eight, more work from nine till midnight, bed. He had his own intimate possessions—his books, his engravings, his brass candlesticks, his statuette of Victor Hugo, his print of Jonson, his writing-table. A statue in the little garden overlooked by his window had been brought from Cheyne Walk to remind him, not too insistently, of the vanished past, vanished friends.

.   .   .   .

The Americans finished their meal, and rose to leave. As they passed the little man, the woman murmured, 'He *is* looney, like I told you!' 'Sh-h-h!' reproved her companion. But the 'looney' had not heard her. And the coffee on the table beside him had grown cold. He was still immersed in his dreams.

The swing door opened and a middle-aged man entered. A quietly competent man, with a will of iron successfully hidden by a natural courtesy. Part family doctor, part family solicitor, with, perhaps, a broad-minded if rather superficial interest in modern literature—so the casual observer might have classified him. But it would be an erroneous classification. Mr. Walter Theodore Watts (later, the addition of his mother's surname converted that homely monosyllable into the more imposing 'Watts-Dunton'), was a cultured writer, with definite ideas of his own concerning poetry and a far from feeble pen when it came to expressing them. He was exactly the type which a century earlier would have accompanied and firmly but tactfully controlled a sprig of the aristocracy who was rounding off his education by undertaking the Grand Tour.

He glanced penetratingly towards the little man, and the other turned guiltily.

'Aha!' said Mr. Walter Theodore Watts. 'Somehow I thought I might find you here. . . . We have been uneasy, very uneasy. If you had mentioned that you were running up to Town' . . . He raised his voice. 'We will return to the Pines together.'

'As you please,' said Algernon Charles Swinburne. He sighed, rose from his seat, brushed a crumb from his spruce suit, and followed his genial gaoler back into captivity.

A. C. Swinburne

From THE TRIUMPH OF TIME

There lived a singer in France of old
    By the tideless dolorous midland sea.
In a land of sand and ruin and gold
    There shone one woman, and none but she.
And finding life for her lover's sake fail,
Being fain to see her, he bade set sail,
Touched land, and saw her as life grew cold,
    And praised God, seeing; and so died he.

Died, praising God for his gift and grace:
    For she bowed down to him weeping, and said
'Live'; and her tears were shed on his face
    Or ever the life in his face was shed.
The sharp years fell through her hair, and stung
Once, and her close lips touched him and clung
Once, and grew one with his lips for a space;
    And so drew back, and the man was dead.

O brother, the gods were good to you,
    Sleep, and be glad while the world endures.
Be well content as the years wear through;
    Give thanks for life, and the loves and lures;
Give thanks for life, O brother, and death,
For the sweet last sound of her feet, her breath,
For gifts she gave you, gracious and few,
    Tears and kisses, that lady of yours.

Rest, and be glad of the gods; but I,
    How shall I praise them or how take rest?
There is not room under all the sky
    For me that know not of worst or best,

Dream or desire of the days before,
Sweet things or bitterness, any more,
Love will not come to me now though I die,
    As love came close to you, breast to breast.

I shall never be friends again with roses;
    I shall loathe sweet tunes, where a note grown
        strong
Relents and recoils, and climbs and closes,
    As a wave of the sea turned back by song.
There are sounds where the soul's delight takes fire,
Face to face with its own desire;
A delight that rebels, a desire that reposes;
    I shall hate sweet music my whole life long.

The pulse of war and passion of wonder,
    The heavens that murmur, the sounds that
        shine,
The stars that sing and the loves that thunder,
    The music burning at heart like wine,
An armed archangel whose hands raise up
All senses mixed in the spirit's cup
Till flesh and blood are molten in sunder—
    These things are over, and no more mine.

A. C. Swinburne

A FORSAKEN GARDEN

In a coign of the cliff between lowland and highland,
    At the sea-down's edge between windward and lee,
Walled round with rocks as an inland island,
    The ghost of a garden fronts the sea.
A girdle of brushwood and thorn encloses
    The steep square slope of the blossomless bed

297

Where the weeds that grew green from the graves of its
  roses
      Now lie dead.

The fields fall southward, abrupt and broken,
    To the low last edge of the long lone land,
If a step should sound or a word be spoken,
    Would a ghost not rise at the strange guest's hand?
So long have the grey bare walks lain guestless,
    Through branches and briars if a man make way,
He shall find no life but the sea-wind's, restless
      Night and day.

The dense hard passage is blind and stifled,
    That crawls by a track none turn to climb
To the strait waste place that the years have rifled
    Of all but the thorns that are touched not of time.
The thorns he spares when the rose is taken;
    The rocks are left when he wastes the plain.
The wind that wanders, the weeds wind-shaken,
      These remain.

Not a flower to be pressed of the foot that falls not;
    As the heart of a dead man the seed-plots are dry;
From the thicket of thorns whence the nightingale calls
  not,
    Could she call, there were never a rose to reply.
Over the meadows that blossom and wither,
    Rings but the note of a sea-bird's song;
Only the sun and the rain come hither
      All year long.

The sun burns sere and the rain dishevels
    One gaunt bleak blossom of scentless breath.

Only the wind here hovers and revels
    In a round where life seems barren as death.
Here there was laughing of old, there was weeping,
    Haply, of lovers none ever will know,
Whose eyes went seaward a hundred sleeping
        Years ago.

Heart handfast in hand as they stood, 'Look thither',
    Did he whisper? 'look forth from the flowers to the
        sea;
For the foam-flower endure when the rose-blossoms
    wither,
    And men that love lightly may die—but we?'
And the same wind sang and the same waves whitened,
    And or ever the garden's last petals were shed,
In the lips that had whispered, the eyes that had
    lightened,
        Love was dead.

Or they loved their life through, and then went
    whither?
    And were one to the end—but what end who
        knows?
Love deep as the sea as a rose must wither,
    As the rose-red seaweed that mocks the rose.
Shall the dead take thought for the dead to love them
    What love was ever as deep as a grave?
They are loveless now as the grass above them
        Or the wave.

All are at one now, roses and lovers,
    Not known of the cliffs and the fields and the sea,
Not a breath of the time that has been hovers
    In the air now soft with a summer to be.

Not a breath shall there sweeten the seasons hereafter
    Of the flowers or the lovers that laugh now or weep
When as they that are free now of weeping and
        laughter,
            We shall sleep.

Here death may deal not again for ever:
    Here change may come not till all change end.
From the graves they have made they shall rise up
        never,
    Who have left nought living to ravage and rend.
Earth, stones, and thorns of the wild ground growing,
    While the sun and rain live, these shall be:
Till a last wind's breath upon all these blowing
            Roll the sea.

Till the slow sea rise and the sheer cliff crumble,
    Till terrace and meadow the deep gulfs drink,
Till the strength of the waves of the high tides humble
    The fields that lessen, the rocks that shrink,
Here now in his triumph where all things falter,
    Stretched out on the spoils that his own hand
        spread,
As a god self-slain on his own strange altar,
            Death lies dead.

Dante Gabriel Rossetti

From MY SISTER'S SLEEP

She fell asleep on Christmas Eve.
    At length the long-ungranted shade
    Of weary eyelids overweigh'd
The pain nought else might yet relieve.

.   .   .   .

With anxious softly-stepping haste
    Our mother went where Margaret lay,
    Fearing the sounds o'erhead—should they
Have broken her long watched-for rest!

She stopped an instant, calm, and turned;
    But suddenly turned back again;
    And all her features seemed in pain
With woe, and her eyes gazed and yearned.

For my part, I but hid my face,
    And held my breath, and spoke no word:
    There was none spoken; but I heard
The silence for a little space.

Our mother bowed herself and wept:
    And both my arms fell, and I said,
    'God knows I knew that she was dead.'
And there, all white, my sister slept.

Then kneeling, upon Christmas morn
    A little after twelve o'clock,
    We said, ere the first quarter struck,
'Christ's blessing on the newly born!'

Dante Gabriel Rossetti

LOVE SIGHT

When do I see thee most, beloved one?
    When in the light the spirits of mine eyes
    Before thy face, their altar, solemnize
The worship of that Love through thee made known?

Or when, in the dusk hours (we two alone),
   Close-kiss'd and eloquent of still replies
    Thy twilight-hidden glimmering visage lies,
And my soul only sees thy soul its own?

O love, my love! if I no more should see
Thyself, nor on the earth the shadow of thee,
   Nor image of thine eyes in any spring,—
How then should sound upon Life's darkening slope
The ground-whirl of the perish'd leaves of Hope,
    The wind of Death's imperishable wing?

Christina Rossetti

REMEMBER

Remember me when I am gone away,
Gone far away into the silent land;
When you can no more hold me by the hand,
Nor I half turn to go, yet, turning, stay.
Remember me when no more day by day
You tell me of our future that you planned:
Only remember me; you understand
It will be late to counsel then or pray.
Yet if you should forget me for a while,
And afterwards remember, do not grieve:
For if the darkness and corruption leave
A vestige of the thoughts that once I had,
Better by far you should forget and smile,
Than that you should remember and be sad.

John Ruskin

FROM SESAME AND LILIES

I hope it will not be long before royal or national libraries will be founded in every considerable city, with a royal series of books in them; the same series in every one of them, chosen books, the best in every kind, prepared for that national series in the most perfect way possible; their text printed all on leaves of equal size, broad of margin, and divided into pleasant volumes, light in the hand, beautiful, and strong, and thorough as examples of binders' work; and that these great libraries will be accessible to all clean and orderly persons at all times of the day and evening; strict law being enforced for this cleanliness and quietness.

George Meredith

From MODERN LOVE

We saw the swallows gathering in the sky,
And in the osier-isle we heard them noise.
We had not to look back on summer joys,
Or forward to a summer of bright dye;
But in the largeness of the evening earth
Our spirits grew as we went side by side.
The hour became her husband and my bride.
Love that had robbed us so, thus blessed our
    dearth!
The pilgrims of the year waxed very loud
In multitudinous chatterings, as the flood
Full brown came from the West, and like pale
    blood
Expanded to the upper crimson cloud.
Love that had robbed us of immortal things,
This little moment mercifully gave,
Where I have seen across the twilight wave
The swan sail with her young beneath her wings.

George Meredith

SHY AS THE SQUIRREL

Shy as the squirrel and wayward as the swallow,
 Swift as the swallow along the river's light
Circleting the surface to meet his mirror'd winglets,
 Fleeter she seems in her stay than in her flight.
Shy as the squirrel that leaps among the pine-tops,
 Wayward as the swallow overhead at set of sun,
She whom I love is hard to catch and conquer,
 Hard, but O the glory of the winning were she
  won! . . .

All the girls are out with their baskets for the primrose;
 Up lanes, woods through, they troop in joyful
  bands,
My sweet leads: she knows not why, but now she loiters,
 Eyes the bent anemones, and hangs her hands.
Such a look will tell that the violets are peeping,
 Coming the rose: and unaware a cry
Springs in her bosom for odours and for colour,
 Covert and the nightingale; she knows not why.

  . . . .

Cool was the woodside; cool as her white dairy
 Keeping sweet the cream-pan; and there the boys
  from school,
Cricketing below, rush'd brown and red with sunshine;
 O the dark translucence of the deep-eyed cool!
Spying from the farm, herself she fetch'd a pitcher
 Full of milk, and tilted for each in turn the beak.
Then a little fellow, mouth up and on tiptoe
 Said, 'I will kiss you'; she laugh'd and lean'd her
  cheek.

304

William Morris

From .The Earthly Paradise

JULY

Fair was the morn to-day, the blossom's scent
Floated across the fresh grass, and the bees
With low vexed song from rose to lily went,
A gentle wind was in the heavy trees,
And thine eyes shone with joyous memories;
Fair was the early morn, and fair wert thou,
And I was happy—Ah, be happy now!

Peace and content without us, love within
That hour there was, now thunder and wild rain,
Have wrapped the cowering world, and foolish sin,
And nameless pride, have made us wise in vain;
Ah, love! Although the morn shall come again,
And on new rose-buds the new sun shall smile,
Can we regain what we have lost meanwhile?

E'en now the west grows clear of storm and threat,
But midst the lightning did the fair sun die—
Ah, he shall rise again for ages yet,
He cannot waste his life—but thou and I—
Who knows if next morn this felicity
My lips may feel, or if thou still shalt live
This seal of love renewed once more to give?

William Morris

From NEWS FROM NOWHERE

EDUCATION—A VISION OF THE FUTURE

'I can assure you (said my guide) our children learn, whether they go through a "system of teaching" or not. Why, you will not find one of these children about here, boy or girl, who cannot swim, and every one of them has been used to tumbling about the little forest ponies—there's one of them now! They all of them know how to cook; the bigger lads can mow; many can thatch and do odd jobs at carpentering; or they know how to keep shop. I can tell you they know plenty of things.'

'Yes, but their mental education, the teaching of their minds,' said I, kindly translating my phrase.

'Guest,' said he, 'perhaps you have not learned to do these things I have been speaking about; and if that's the case, don't you run away with the idea that it doesn't take some skill to do them, and doesn't give plenty of work for one's mind; you would change your opinion if you saw a Dorsetshire lad thatching, for instance. But, however, I understand you to be speaking of book-learning; and as to that, it is a simple affair. Most children, seeing books lying about, manage to read by the time they are four years old; though I am told it has not always been so. As to writing, we do not encourage them to scrawl too early (though scrawl a little they will), because it gets them into a habit of ugly writing; and what's the use of a lot of ugly writing being done, when rough printing can be done so easily. You understand that handsome writing we like, and

306

many people will write their books out when they make them, or get them written; I mean books of which only a few copies are needed—poems, and such like, you know. However, I am wandering from my lambs; but you must excuse me, for I am interested in this matter of writing, being myself a fair writer.'

'Well,' said I, 'about the children; when they know how to read and write, don't they learn something else —languages, for instance?'

'Of course,' he said; 'sometimes even before they can read, they can talk French, which is the nearest language talked on the other side of the water; and they soon get to know German also, which is talked by a huge number of communes and colleges on the mainland. These are the principal languages we speak in these islands, along with English or Welsh, or Irish, which is another form of Welsh; and children pick them up very quickly, because their elders all know them; and besides our guests from oversea often bring their children with them, and the little ones get together, and rub their speech into one another.'

'And the older languages?' said I.

'O yes,' said he, 'they mostly learn Latin and Greek along with the modern ones, when they do anything more than merely pick up the latter.'

'And history?' said I; 'how do you teach history?'

'Well,' said he, 'when a person can read, of course he reads what he likes to; and he can easily get someone to tell him what are the best books to read on such or such a subject; or to explain what he doesn't understand in the books when he is reading them.'

'Well,' said I, 'what else do they learn? I suppose they don't all learn history?'

'No, no,' said he; 'some don't care about it; in fact, I don't think many do. I have heard my great-grand-

307

father say that it is mostly in periods of turmoil and strife and confusion that people care much about history; and you know,' said my friend, with an amiable smile, 'we are not like that now. No; many people study facts about the make of things and the matters of cause and effect, so that knowledge increases on us, if that be good; and some, as you heard about friend Bob yonder, will spend time over mathematics. 'Tis no use forcing people's tastes.'

Said I: 'But you don't mean that children learn all these things?'

Said he: 'That depends on what you mean by children; and also you must remember how much they differ. As a rule, they don't do much reading, except for a few story-books, till they are about fifteen years old; we don't encourage early bookishness; though you will find some children who *will* take to books very early; which perhaps is not good for them; but it's no use thwarting them; and very often it doesn't last long with them, and they find their level before they are twenty years old. You see, children are mostly given to imitating their elders, and when they see people about them engaged in genuinely amusing work, like house-building and street-paving, and gardening, and the like, that is what they want to be doing; so I don't think we need fear having too many book-learned men.'

Coventry Patmore

THE TOYS

My little Son, who look'd from thoughtful eyes
And moved and spoke in quiet grown-up wise,

Having my law the seventh time disobey'd,
I struck him, and dismiss'd
With hard words and unkiss'd,
—His Mother, who was patient, being dead,
Then, fearing lest his grief should hinder sleep,
I visited his bed,
But found him slumbering deep,
With darken'd eyelids, and their lashes yet
From his late sobbing wet.
And I, with moan,
Kissing away his tears, left others of my own;
For, on a table drawn beside his head,
He had put, within his reach,
A box of counters and a red-vein'd stone,
A piece of glass abraded by the beach,
And six or seven shells,
A bottle with bluebells,
And two French copper coins, ranged there with
    careful art,
To comfort his sad heart.
So when that night I pray'd
To God, I wept, and said:
Ah, when at last we lie with tranced breath,
Not vexing Thee in death,
And Thou rememberest of what toys
We made our joys,
How weakly understood
Thy great commanded good,
Then, fatherly not less
Than I whom Thou hast moulded from the clay,
Thou'lt leave Thy wrath, and say,
'I will be sorry for their childishness.'

Coventry Patmore

THE KISS

'I saw you take his kiss!' ''Tis true.'
'O modesty!' ''Twas strictly kept:
He thought me asleep: at least, I knew
He thought I thought he thought I slept.'

William Allingham

FOUR DUCKS ON A POND

Four ducks on a pond,
And a green bank beyond,
A blue sky of spring,
White clouds on the wing;
What a little thing
　　To remember for years,
　　To remember with tears.

Theodore Watts-Dunton

From THE SILENT VOICES

Beyond the sun, beyond the furthest star,
Shines still the land which poets still may win,
Whose poems are their lives—whose souls within
Hold naught in dread save Art's high conscience bar—
Who have for muse a maiden free from scar—
　　Who know how beauty dies at touch of sin—
　　Who love mankind, yet, having gods for kin,
Breathe zephyrs, in the street, from climes afar.

310

Heedless of phantom Fame—heedless of all
    Save pity and love to light the life of Man—
    True poets work, winning a sunnier span
For Nature's martyr—Night's ancestral thrall;
True poets work, yet listen for the call
Bidding them join their country and their clan.

SUNSET—AND SUNRISE

311

EXTRACTS

313

317